The Fall
of the
Asante Empire

THE HUNDRED-YEAR WAR
FOR AFRICA'S GOLD COAST

Robert B. Edgerton

THE FREE PRESS

New York   London   Toronto   Sydney   Tokyo   Singapore

THE FREE PRESS
A Division of Simon & Schuster
1230 Avenue of the Americas
New York, NY 10020

THE FREE PRESS and colophon are trademarks
of Simon & Schuster Inc.

Text design by Carla Bolte

Manufactured in the United States of America

10 9 8 7 6 5 4 3 2 1

Library of Congress Cataloging-In-Publication Data

Edgerton, Robert B.
         The fall of the Asante Empire: the hundred-year war for Africa's
Gold Coast / Robert B. Edgerton.
         p.   cm.
    Includes bibliographical references and index.
    ISBN: 0-7432-3638-6
    1. Ashanti (Kingdom)—History.   2. Ashanti (African People)—
History.   3. Ghana—History.   I. Title.
DT507.E34   1998
966.7'018—dc20   94-36626
                                      CIP

For information regarding special discounts for bulk purchases, please contact Simon &
Schuster Special Sales at 1-800-456-6798 or business@simonandschuster.com

Contents

Preface

When during the past century Westerners thought about Africa, it is unlikely that they paid much attention to the military prowess of the African societies that were reportedly being conquered with little difficulty by one European force or another. There was one notable exception. The dramatic 1879 war between the Zulus and the British immediately captured the imagination of people throughout the West. In the first great battle of their six-month-long war, the Zulus very nearly annihilated a large British force, killing 52 officers, 806 soldiers, and about 500 of their African allies. More than a century later, the pageantry of red-coated Britons wielding bayonets against the short stabbing spears of flamboyantly costumed, impossibly brave Zulu warriors continues to be celebrated in books, on television, and in epic motion pictures such as *Zulu* and *Zulu Dawn*. The extraordinary bravery and the military success of the Zulus earned them the respect of the British who fought against them and fascinated generations of Europeans and Americans, who have read about their resistance or seen it depicted in films. But for most people in Europe and America, recognition of the valor of African fighting men begins and ends with the Zulus. It has gone very largely unnoticed that both before and after the Anglo-Zulu war, African soldiers fought against invading European armies whose modern rifles, machine guns, and artillery killed them in terrible numbers. The men, and sometimes women, in these African armies were often gallant, and sometimes they won battles despite their inferior arms. But most of the battles these African soldiers fought made little impact on European consciousness at the time, and they have since faded into almost complete obscurity.

Some of the longest and most effective military resistance to European conquest took place in West Africa; by far the longest was the century-long struggle of the Asante of Ghana against the British. From 1807 to 1900, Asante armies fought numerous small and large battles against the British. In several of these they were the clear victors, the only West African army to defeat a European army in more than one major engagement. In the final conflict of 1900, despite the British use of machine guns and powerful 75-mm artillery, the Asante several times forced British columns to retreat. One of the British invasions of the Asante kingdom was led by Sir Garnet Wolseley, Britain's best-known general at the time and the man who later commanded British troops during the Zulu war. Wolseley had fought and been wounded in several previous wars, but he called his campaign against the Asante the "most horrible war" he had ever fought in. And he very nearly did not win it.

The Asante and the British fought more than one horrible battle. They fought bravely and cruelly as they struggled with disease and starvation as well as bullets and bayonets. Most of all they struggled with their colossal incomprehension of one another's values, religious beliefs, diplomacy, sense of honor, and national purpose. Much of this misunderstanding was the inevitable consequence of the British insistence on their racial and cultural supremacy, but the Asante too could be arrogant and self-righteous. The roots of conflict lay in the differing cultural heritages and economic interests of the two peoples. Although the most fundamental cause of the conflict was economic, the Asante practices of human sacrifice and slavery also played a part, as did British ignorance about the significance of the Golden Stool. Not only did the two nations misunderstand one another, they consistently underestimated one another's military strength.

What follows will describe the conflict between these two proud peoples, especially their military campaigns and something of the men who fought in them. The emphasis will be on the military resistance of the Asante, but that can only be understood by examining the actions of the British, not least because most of the first-hand accounts of these wars were written by them. Over the course of the nineteenth century, the Asante and British troops fought dozens of battles. Some were small-scale affairs fought more or less by mistake. Others were well-planned campaigns that involved many thousands of men. The Asante fought with such bravery that from the first battle to the last the British sang their praises. Despite an inferiority in weapons that grew as the years passed, the Asante willingness to face death in battle never wavered. How they fought and why they did so is the subject of this book.

Acknowledgments

THIS BOOK DESCRIBES THE MILITARY CONFLICT BETWEEN THE Asante and British that filled the nineteenth century. In the mid-1980s, when my long-standing interest in this subject was piqued enough to start this project, all of those people who had firsthand knowledge of the events had passed on, and although searches of the Public Record Office in London, the Balme Library at the University of Ghana, the Basel Missionary Archives, the British Museum, and many other libraries and archives yielded much, I discovered nothing of major significance that previous scholars had missed.

Instead of continuing my frustrated search for something original, I found myself relying heavily on the published work of scholars, missionaries, soldiers, travelers, and newspaper correspondents. To modern-day scholars who find themselves cited in the bibliography, I extend my thanks for their marvelous work, as I do to all of those earlier merchants, missionaries, soldiers, colonial officers, and newsmen who braved inclement weather, deadly diseases, and bullets to record their experiences of that tumultuous century.

This book, like my two earlier books for The Free Press on African resistance to colonial rule—*Like Lions They Fought* and *Mau Mau*—is meant mainly for the general reading public rather than scholars. To make the book as accessible as possible to these readers I have avoided the use of technical anthropological terms for various aspects of Asante society and culture, and I have held the use of Asante terms to an absolute minimum. For example, I have referred to the Asante monarch as "king" rather than *Asantehene*, the Asante term, which is routinely used by most scholars when referring to the holder of this office. I have also tried to reduce the number of place-names for villages, rivers, districts, and the like as well as the personal names of men and women whose roles were not central to the events being described. For this I apologize to the Asante people, but I hope that they will understand that my purpose is to make their history more easily understood to outsiders.

I would like to thank John McLeod of the British Museum for helping me to get started long ago, Merrick Posnansky for good advice about sources, various people at the University of London for helping me track down fugitive unpublished materials, and many of my students in the Department of Anthropology at the University of California, Los Angeles (UCLA), for critically reviewing earlier versions of the manuscript. Doran Ross, Associate Director of the Fowler Museum at UCLA, has my gratitude for so generously helping me locate illustrations. I thank John Olmsted for skillfully and good-naturedly making the manuscript ready for the light of day, and Sharon Belkin for drawing the maps. I am especially grateful to my editor, Adam Bellow, for giving me his continuing support and for his enduring interest in the African experience.

My greatest debt is to my wife, Karen Ito, for her astute anthropological criticism of the manuscript and, even more, for making everything worthwhile.

1

A Cause Worth Dying For

AT THE START OF THE NINETEENTH CENTURY, WHEN ASANTE AND British interests first collided, the Asante Empire was at its height. Incomparably the most powerful state in West Africa, it ruled over more than three million people throughout what is now Ghana (then called the Gold Coast). This was more than half as many people as there were in the United States at that time and more than one quarter as many as the population of Britain, which was only eleven million in 1801. In area the empire was larger than England, Wales, and Scotland combined or, from an American perspective, the state of Wyoming. From south to north it stretched for over four hundred miles, and it dominated nearly five hundred miles of coastline.

If one could have flown over this large area at that time, the dominant impression would have been a seemingly endless expanse of dense tropical forest, only occasionally broken by clearings for a few large towns, smaller villages, and widely scattered plantations. One would see little to suggest the presence of the complex civilization that the Asante leaders had developed over the preceding two hundred years by military conquests that gave them dominion over defeated peoples, many of whom were forced into slavery. During the first half of the eighteenth century, the Asante armies

1

fought and won over twenty major battles that extended their empire to include all of present-day Ghana. These were anything but bloodless victories, and this remarkable success could not have been achieved unless a very large number of Asante men and women believed that their empire was worth dying for.

Great states had existed in West Africa for centuries before the Asante Empire—or Greater Asante, as historians now prefer to call it—came into being. Far to the east of modern Ghana, the ancient kingdom of Ghana flourished for about a thousand years before it collapsed and disappeared in the middle of the thirteenth century. Its capital city of Kumbi Saleh, some one hundred miles north of modern Bamako, was the largest yet seen in West Africa, having about fifteen thousand people. Ghana owed its greatness to its army of two hundred thousand men, whose iron-tipped spears allowed them to exact tribute and collect taxes from smaller states and chiefs over much of the western Sudan. Ghana also maintained trade routes north to the Arab world, and it began West Africa's flourishing trade in gold. Arab visitors raved about the wealth and elegance of the court, mentioning such extravagances as royal guard dogs wearing gold and silver collars and a thousand royal horses with silken halters that slept on carpets attended by three men for each horse.[1]

Ghana was succeeded by many other states in the western Sudan, the greatest being Mali, which remained powerful until sometime after 1400 A.D. Farther to the east the Songhay Empire arose, and directly to the north of the Asante were the Mossi states. All of these states emerged in the savanna zone north of the great forest belt that covered the land closer to the sea. Free of the tsetse fly of the forest area, horses thrived there and trade flourished. Contact with the Arab world of merchants and scholars enriched these African states as well. The kingdoms of the southern forests were smaller in size and less opulent, but when the earliest Portuguese traders came to the Gold Coast in the 1470s, they found surprisingly regal men ready to trade with them shrewdly and with dignity. For example, at their new trading post of Elmina, they met a king whose jewels, brocaded jacket, and elegant manners, combined with his shrewdness, fairness, and good judgment, made a highly favorable impression.

Along the coast and just inland from Elmina lay numerous kingdoms of Akan- or Twi-speaking peoples, whose land contained many of the richest gold deposits in the world. This gold and Akan proximity to the European traders' guns and gunpowder would soon give them a powerful advantage over the older and previously more powerful states to the north, which lacked ready access to firearms. These Akan people shared similar religious beliefs and governmental practices and were excellent farmers and skilled cattlemen despite the great heat and humidity. They manufactured many tradable goods, from cotton cloth to spears and fishhooks, and were highly accomplished gold miners. They also kept slaves, most of whom came to them from the north in return for gold. The abundance of these two sources of wealth—slaves and gold—would bring more and more Europeans to the area until the British achieved a monopoly on trade and finally conquered the Asante.

The tropical forest zone of the Gold Coast has two distinct rainy seasons, May–June and September–October, when torrents of rain flood the rivers and create almost impassable mud. The temperature often reaches 90°F, with humidity reaching 90 percent. In addition to several large rivers—the Tano, Pra, and Volta—the entire area is cut by innumerable streams. The Asante homeland is wet, luxuriant forest, so dark in many places that there is not enough light to read by. The only dry period is December–January when dry winds blow south from the Sahara and nighttime temperatures fall into the sixties. When the rains begin again in February and March, hail the size of musket balls is not uncommon.

The heartland of the Asante people was a forested area centered some one hundred fifty miles from the coast. At the end of the seventeenth century, there were two great powers in the forest, the kingdom of Akwamu to the southeast of the Asante and the kingdom of Denkyira to the southwest. Denkyira possessed the richest veins of gold in the region, dominated the coastal trade, and held the Asante as a tributary state until 1701, when, shortly after they first came to the attention of the Portuguese, the Asante defeated the Denkyira in battle. The leader of the Asante at that time was Osei Tutu, who had brought a number of smaller chiefdoms together by conquest and had attracted other immigrants through the appeal of his governance. The Asante, like other Akan groups, made stools the symbols of political authority. Now each chief was made to bury his personal stool while Osei Tutu and his legendary priest, Anokye, gave the kingdom new unity by conjuring down from the sky, as Asante tradition has it, a Golden Stool said to contain the soul or spirit of the entire nation. Whatever legerdemain may have been involved, the idea was a brilliant success. The stool remains a powerful symbol of Asante unity to this day.

Armed with a new sense of national unity, the Asante were ready to break their economic dependence on the Denkyira with newly acquired guns supplied by the Dutch who believed that the Denkyira were thwarting their trade with tribes farther north. Aware that the Asante were restive, the Denkyira king attempted to force them into a premature attack by raping one of Osei Tutu's favorite wives, who was paying a courtesy visit to the Denkyira court. Incensed by this calculatedly public insult, Osei Tutu sent his forces to battle in 1698, but it was not until 1701, when other kingdoms tributary to the Denkyira turned against them, that the Asante finally won, beginning the series of conquests that gave them preeminence over the Gold Coast.[2]

The origins of the Asante people are unknown. The Asante themselves say that they "came forth from the ground very long ago" somewhere in the southern part of the rain forest.[3] Their culture probably developed from small bands of hunters, gatherers, and farmers, who have left fragments of stone axes and pottery throughout the forest zone. Sometime during the first millennium A.D., iron working was introduced to the area from the north. Many other influences were to follow. Before the Asante emerged as a kingdom under Osei Tutu, groups of related people must have migrated through the forest zone for hundreds of years. Lineages expanded and broke up as people quarreled or needed more land. Larger chiefdoms fled from their enemies, and new people migrated into the area. Early in the nineteenth century an English visitor to the Asante capital was surprised to learn that the Asante believed the British were so quarrelsome that they chose to live in wheeled houses in order to escape from their angry neighbors.[4] This Asante perception mirrored their own past.

From 1300 to 1500 A.D., a prolonged drought in the savanna of the West Sudan drove many thousands of people to the well-watered forest zone where they mingled with the Akan speakers already there. Archeological finds show that they lived in thatch-roofed, mud-walled houses, each with its own cistern, built around central courtyards. They farmed, raised cattle, sheep, and goats, and hunted game, especially antelope. In addition to antelope, elephants, leopards, and lions, all of which had value to the Asante for meat, ivory, and hides, the nearby forests were home to innumerable baboons and other monkeys, hyenas, civet cats, anteaters, sloths, wild boar, and porcupine. Tsetse fly–borne disease must have been less of a problem than it became later, because the Asante had horses in earlier times. In addition to having brass foundries and iron smelters, some of the larger towns manufactured textiles using the same spindle whorls used in Ghana today. They left behind many beads, ivory carvings, tobacco pipes, and stone or ceramic weights, presumably for weighing gold dust.[5]

With the Asante conquest of the Denkyira, the dynamics of the Gold Coast changed radically. The Asante now had access to the European traders at the coast, and with the rich Denkyira gold deposits they could purchase more slaves to work in their mines, cultivate their fields, and serve in their armies. Their gold also allowed them to purchase the guns they needed to defeat other kingdoms, and this they did with remarkable success. By 1750 they had defeated and largely incorporated into their empire nearly twenty kingdoms, including the Gonja and Dagomba of the savanna lands well to the north of metropolitan Asante. Welding these subject peoples into a relatively peaceful and subservient empire required great statesmanship, but the Asante also used force against conquered people when that was thought necessary.

Most of these conquests were directed by Osei Tutu's successor, Opoku Ware, after his death in 1719. Opoku Ware's thirty-year rule led to a remarkable expansion of the Asante Empire, more extensive than that brought about by any previous or succeeding king. In 1766 John Hippisley, the governor of the British trading company at Cape Coast, wrote that Opoku Ware was the wisest and most valiant man of his time in West Africa.[6] When he died in 1750, a Gonja obituary notice recalled him this way:

In that year, Opoku, king of the Asante, died, may Allah curse him and place his soul in hell. It was he who injured the people of Gonja, oppressing them and robbing them of their property at will. He ruled violently, as a tyrant, delighting in his authority. People of all the horizons feared him greatly.[7]

Asante traditions glorify their military victories, and there can be no doubt that war was the engine that drove them to prominence. But their far-flung subject people could not have been held together, much less made to contribute to the prosperity of the empire, without skillful governance. Beginning with Opoku Ware's successor, Osei Kwadwo, far-reaching steps were taken to permit the Asante government in the capital city of Kumase to rule effectively. Unlike the Romans, who stationed professional soldiers—the legions—in conquered territories to maintain order, Asante kings had no full-time soldiers. All their fighting men, whether free or slave, were only part-time soldiers who returned to their ordinary economic pursuits after each campaign ended. Lacking the military resources to police all of their newly conquered territories, Osei Kwadwo instituted effective practices of returning to loyal chiefs and kings of these subject territories much of the tribute they delivered to Kumase, often augmented by generous gifts from the royal treasury. The new Asante king also augmented the established system of spies who reported to him, an always important source of information, but his most valuable contribution was to begin the development of a skilled bureaucracy to oversee every aspect of government.[8] During the second half of the eighteenth century, Asante leaders tried to keep the empire together with shrewd diplomacy balanced with force. Though there would be fighting, none changed the course of empire until 1807, when the Asante came into conflict with the British. The first battle was fought largely by accident, but soon after, the British began to seek the destruction of the Asante Empire, and generations of Asante men and women fought and often died to defend it.

The Warrior Tradition in Africa

In most of Africa south of the Sahara, warfare and the warrior tradition were so inextricably tied to everything of importance—honor, wealth, religion, politics, even art and sexuality—that it is no exaggeration to say that most men's reputations, fortunes, and futures depended on their martial valor. To be sure, some small societies had no tradition of warfare and tried to avoid fighting by fleeing into dense forests, remote mountains, or barren deserts. Others only now and then engaged in warfare that led to great loss of life or property; for the most part, these societies fought only to capture women or animals or to prove their courage, not to slaughter their enemies. But a large number of African societies used their huge armies to kill, enslave, and conquer their neighbors in wars that continued seemingly without end.

Prior to the large-scale introduction of firearms from Europe, African armies shared a similar set of weapons. Except in the savannas and deserts of western and central Africa, where men rode horses and camels, African soldiers fought on foot. Frequently protected by tough cowhide shields, they threw spears or stabbed with them, used bows and sometimes poisoned arrows, and carried swords, clubs, and knives. While their weapons were similar, their tactics varied greatly. Some relied on stealth to surprise their enemies, some specialized in ambushes; others favored massive two-pronged enveloping attacks, and still others built formidable fortresses. Although some societies maintained peaceful relations with their neighbors or made alliances that protected their interests, warfare was an ever-present fact of life over much of Africa.

In addition to fighting among themselves, Africans fought against foreigners who came in search of ivory, gold, hides, and slaves. Chinese, Malay, and Indian traders were usually content to carry out peaceful trade from anchorages along the coast, as were those Arabs who crossed the Sahara to trade with the great African states of West Africa. However, the great Arab caravans, containing as many as a thousand men armed with muskets who marched a thousand miles or more into the interior of East Africa in search of slaves and ivory, sometimes met with resistance.

The Portuguese were the first Europeans to reach Africa, and at times they too relied on peaceful trade; but as early as 1575 a Portuguese priest in Angola wrote to his superiors that the Africans would have to be conquered by force because "the conversion of these barbarians will not be attained by love".[9] Angolans resisted Portuguese demands for slaves and for conversion to Christianity

BOUNDARY OF THE ASANTE EMPIRE

Boundary of Modern Ghana

GONJA

DAGOMBA

GYAMAN

Mampong

Edwesu   •Dwaben
        •KUMASE
        •Kokofu
        •Bekwai

Ofin R.

Ordah R.

Pra R.

AKWAPIM

Adanse

AKYEM

DENKYIRA

ASSIN

WASSA

Pra River

FANTE
STATES

ACCRA

Winneba

NZIMA

Cape Coast Castle

Elmina

Sekondi

THE ASANTE EMPIRE
Early in the 19th Century

0   20 40 60 80 100
miles

so fiercely that they fought them every year from the mid-1500s to 1680, when the Portuguese troops finally established their rule. Their profits were immense, especially from the slave trade. (The Portuguese eventually shipped millions of slaves to Brazil, most of them from Angola.) However, in West Africa, where the Portuguese had sought gold and slaves since their arrival in the late fifteenth century, force was not an option, since most fifteenth century West African kingdoms could mobilize armies of twenty or thirty thousand men. Given the thickly forested terrain, the endemic diseases, the heat and rain, neither the Portuguese nor the other European powers who followed them to West Africa chose to try a contest of arms with a West African power until the nineteenth century. Eighteenth-century European writers left vivid accounts of West African armies now largely armed with muskets but still sometimes using bows and arrows or crossbows. The soldiers' ability to march long distances carrying heavy loads impressed most observers, and so did their discipline in battle. To protect themselves against such armies, several kingdoms surrounded their cities with thick walls and deep ditches filled with sharpened stakes. The city of Kano, in northern Nigeria, was surrounded by a fifty-foot-high, forty-foot thick wall and by two rings of ditches. The enclosed area was half the size of Manhattan.[10]

Some of the earliest fighting took place in southern Africa, where British troops fought seven wars against the Xhosa people—"Kaffirs," as they were disparagingly called—in the nineteenth century. In one of these, even though the British eventually managed to win, the Xhosa held off the invaders for over a year, inflicting heavy casualties on some of the most famous battalions in the British army.[11] A few years later in Natal, to the north, Zulu bravery earned the undying respect of the British. Later in the century British troops usually required little more than punitive expeditions—"nigger hunts" they called them—to pacify and "civilize" restive tribes. Sometimes, though, a particular tribal group like the Kikuyu fought so hard to protect their land that more extreme measures were required. One officer wrote, "There is only one way of improving the Wakikuyu [and] that is to wipe them out; I should be only too delighted to do so, but we have to depend on them for food."[12] The Kikuyu were not renowned as warriors, but these small, naked men with their spears, swords, and bows and poisoned arrows, resisted the British for so long that in 1904 three large British columns were sent against them "to put them in the right frame of mind." Armed with repeating rifles and machine guns, the British burned homesteads, destroyed crops, rounded up cattle, sheep, and goats, and killed about one thousand five hundred people, a number so large that they were unwilling to reveal the truth to London.[13] After 1890 European armies were equipped with Maxim machine guns, but even with these weapons it took British forces in Uganda ten years to defeat and capture Kabarega, the king of the Nyoro.

The Germans were not to be outdone by the British. Their attempts to conquer the large country of Tanganyika (now Tanzania) began with Imperial German Marines going ashore and more or less literally shooting everyone they saw, as one contemporary observer put it.[14] Later they sent large expeditions inland to conquer societies that were slow to submit. In 1891 a powerful German column, well-armed with machine guns and artillery, was routed with many casualties by Hehe tribesmen armed only with spears. It would be seven more years before the Hehe were finally subdued. The subsequent administration of Tanganyika by the Germans was so draconian that in 1905 several tribes rose against them. Three years later between 250,000 and 300,000 Africans were dead, most from starvation, but many from machine-gun bullets. When the Herero of Southwest Africa rebelled against the brutality of the German settlers (brutality that included punishing men and women alike by sadistically flogging them, not on their backs, but on their stomachs and genitals), the kaiser sent twenty thousand first-line troops of the Imperial German Army, equipped with the most modern weapons, to put down the rebellion. After over two years of almost unimaginably brutal fighting, the Herero were nearly annihilated. German losses were about one thousand four hundred dead and another one thousand or so wounded, not a small price to pay for a victory over eighty thousand poorly armed cattle herders in the barren lands of Southwest Africa. When the war finally became a rout, untold numbers of women and children were shot, bayoneted, and even burned alive. The Hereros had fought brutally, too, but the Germans easily outdid them.[15]

The German suppression of the Herero rebellion, though brutal by any standard, was hardly unique. At the same time that the Herero rebelled, the Shona and Ndebele of Southern Rhodesia (Zambia) and Mozambique rose against their British and Portuguese colonizers. It is not known how many were killed, but ten thousand is probably conservative. Nor did rebellion end in the early twentieth century. The well-known Mau Mau uprising in post–World War II Kenya led to the deaths of some eleven thousand Africans. Over one thousand were hanged as criminals and many others died of torture in British detention camps.[16] Three years earlier the French army joined French settlers on Madagascar in putting down another rebellion. When French torture chambers closed and the shooting ended, it is estimated that at least 50,000 and perhaps as many as 120,000 Malagasy tribesmen had been killed.[17]

Throughout West Africa even badly-armed African armies found causes worth dying for as they resisted British, French, and German forces. Most of the serious fighting took place after 1885, when the Berlin Conference divided Africa into various spheres of European interest, although some particularly fierce combat took place in 1857 between the French and the Tokolar Empire. France took the lion's share of West Africa, fighting mostly in the open grasslands north of the forest zone, where their troops were occasionally bested and were often made to respect the bravery and skill of their African opponents, but the French were ultimately victorious. A few African leaders, like the famous Samori, gave French troops trouble for years, but most of these battles were relatively small ones that ended in French control of yet another part of West Africa— Senegal, Mauritania, Guinea, the Ivory Coast, Mali, Upper Volta, Niger, Togo, Benin, Chad, Congo, Cameroun, Gabon, and the Central African Republic; an empire of four million square miles.

Some of the French fighting was done in the forest zone; for example, the series of battles between French legionnaires and the army of Dahomey, led by its women warriors—Amazons, as a credulous European press decided to call them. These Dahomean women attacked so fiercely that the French called them suicidal, and the hand-to-hand fighting that followed (during which some legionnaires had their noses bitten off) was demoralizing to the French, who nevertheless went on to defeat the Dahomean forces in a series of small-scale battles.[18]

Many West African armies resisted European invaders with great bravery and martial skill, but no army fought more courageously or well than the Asante, and none fought over such a long period of time. The Asante Empire that its armies defended so valiantly had no huge cities or monumental architecture to set it apart from its neighbors. Its works of art were beautiful, but that was true of the art of most West African peoples. By local standards it was a new empire with only a little over a hundred years of ascendancy, and not until its first contact with the British in 1807 would it become known to Europeans as a major West African power.

Probably the most remarkable aspect of the Asante state was the success of its political structure, which balanced the powers of its king and its oligarchy in controlling the endless competition for wealth and power by members of its privileged upper class, the threats of rebellion by its subject kingdoms, and most perplexing, its enormous and sometimes restive slave population. Its success had much to do with religion and ritual, but it was also a product of a large and growing government bureaucracy that oversaw the affairs of state. The empire had a military government at the time of Osei Tutu, but in 1807 it was rapidly evolving into a rational, civilian-led, bureaucratic state.[19] The single most impressive accomplishment of the Asante rulers lay in creating a national identity and deep patriotism that survived the worst dislocations that military defeat could bring. The odds against such an achievement were enormous because the Asante Empire was a recent congeries of defeated states, in most of which hostility to Asante rule was plain to see. It was also dependent on the labor and military service of slaves, many of whom were ill-treated and rebellious. Its privileged ruling class was bitterly divided on many issues, including when to have recourse to war.

Over the course of the nineteenth century, this hodgepodge of people would split apart in many ways, but there was always a surprisingly large core that was willing to fight and die for the Asante union. One measure of a society is its ability to instill in its people a willingness to die—for their king, their country, their gods, their honor. This the Asante did, and it is no small achievement that its people were so steadfast for so long.

2

The Empire of Gold

THE CAPITAL CITY OF DWABEN DISTRICT WAS BOTH LARGER AND than Kumase, having perhaps forty thousand residents, but the Asante kingdom was centered in Kumase, a city built on the side of a rocky hill. In the early nineteenth century it ordinarily held some twenty-five thousand people, but it was large enough to accommodate a hundred thousand on important ceremonial occasions. In addition to the Kumase division or district, which contained several other sizable villages, the districts of Bekwai, Dwaben, Kokofu, Mampon, and Nsuta made up metropolitan Asante, where probably just under one million Akan-speaking people lived in the four thousand-square-mile core of the kingdom. To put these populations in perspective, in 1801 Glasgow had only seventy-seven thousand inhabitants and Manchester ninety thousand, while New York and Philadelphia, America's largest cities, each had fewer than forty-five thousand inhabitants.[1]

The Asante government in Kumase exacted tribute primarily in slaves and gold from the forty neighboring kingdoms that Asante armies had defeated in battle or intimidated into submission. So dominant was the Asante state in the early nineteenth century that all the European powers maintaining forts along the coast paid rent to the Asante king,[2] and whenever an Asante envoy visited the Dutch trading center at Elmina on the coast, he was honored by a seven-gun salute—European traders were not usually given to such deferential behavior.[3] Much of the credit for the ascendancy of the Asante Empire must go to the wise and inspirational leadership of generations of kings, councillors, and priests, especially King Osei Tutu, who was instrumental in founding the Asante state. But it is unlikely that even the wisest of leaders could have achieved such political dominance if they had not possessed the enormous wealth in gold that allowed them to acquire European firearms, that gave their large and highly organized army a decisive advantage over its neighbors.

As early as 800 A.D. the ancient state of Ghana to the northwest was known to Arabs as "the land of gold," even though its deposits were far less rich than those of the Asante.[4] In 1471, the Portuguese, newly arrived on the coast at Elmina, south of the Asante kingdom, were so impressed by the flecks of gold that sparkled in the streams as they emptied into the sea that they called the area the Gold Coast. The name stuck.[5] The sixteenth-century West African gold production has been estimated at nine tons a year, and the total amount mined from early times to 1900 was at least seven thousand tons.[6] Many millions of dollars' worth of gold dust were maintained in the Asante treasury in Kumase, but private individuals also held huge sums. One government official who died in 1814 left an estimated $500,000 in gold dust, and another a few years later left over $300,000.[7] Gold dust had long been the official medium of exchange throughout the region, and the weighing and appraising (and adulterating) of gold was a major industry. In Kumase alone, one hundred men worked as full-time specialists converting gold ingots into gold dust.[8]

The European traders who sailed to West Africa from the Netherlands, Sweden, Denmark, Portugal, Spain, and Brandenburg (as Prussia was then known) in search of gold, ivory, and slaves built trade forts, or "castles," along the coast, but they did not bring enough armed men to permit them to establish their power beyond the walls of their forts. They were able to carry on trade on the coast of West Africa only because the Africans found them useful, not because they were feared or even terribly much respected. One of these trading enterprises was known as the African

Company of Merchants; it had replaced the original British Royal African Company in 1750. This trading company was chartered by Parliament, which paid it an annual allowance to maintain its principal fort at Cape Coast. At the start of the nineteenth century, this British company shared the Gold Coast trade with a comparable Dutch company located farther west at Elmina and a Danish one to the east at Accra.

The existence of the Asante kingdom was apparently not known to Portuguese traders until 1698, when its war with the Denkyira began, but its prosperity and power became generally known to Europeans soon after. Arab traders and dignitaries also knew of Asante by this time and some had almost certainly visited Kumase, but the first person to leave a written record of such a visit was the director-general of the Dutch trading company, J. P. T. Huydecoper, in 1816. Huydecoper, the son of a Dutch trader and an African mother, was able to speak Asante well enough to have intricate political conversations with the king, Osei Bonsu, and he wrote about these talks in some detail. He did not, however, have an eye for Asante life and seldom recorded anything of interest about what he saw in the capital, despite spending an entire year there. He was followed to Kumase the next year by four Britons, one of whom, a twenty-six-year-old named Thomas Edward Bowdich, wrote a fascinating and largely accurate account of his five-month residence in the Asante capital.[9]

Bowdich traveled to Kumase because John Hope Smith, the new British governor of the African Company of Merchants at Cape Coast, decided to send a mission to the Asante to negotiate a treaty and to establish a resident merchant among them before Britain's Dutch competitors could fully capitalize on Huydecoper's visit. Smith gave command of the mission to Frederick James, a veteran officer of the company, who would be accompanied by Bowdich (who happened to be Smith's nephew) as its scientific observer, William Hutchinson, who would become the British resident in the Asante capital, and Henry Tedlie, a young physician.[10] In addition to three interpreters, Smith also sent an African carpenter, bricklayer, and cooper to build Hutchinson a house that would serve as the company's embassy and over one hundred Africans to carry the mission's supplies. Governor Smith instructed his men to learn everything possible about the Asante kingdom, its power, trade relationships, and anything else that might be useful to the British merchants.

The Bowdich expedition left Cape Coast in late April 1817 to begin the 140-mile journey to Kumase. It was an unfortunate time for such a trip because the spring rains were due in May, and once they struck, the travelers would have hard going with slippery mud and flooded rivers. The best route followed a war-ravaged path through the seemingly impenetrable jungle that lay between the pounding surf of the coast and the Asante capital. White men, who were usually unable to walk any great distance in the West African heat and humidity, were typically transported in large, canopied, hammocklike contraptions carried by four Africans. It would take the British caravan almost a month to reach Kumase, an average progression of only five miles per day.

Near the coast the going was relatively easy as the single-file column pressed its way along a pulverized quartz path; but soon the sea breezes of the coast were left behind, and the heavily laden carriers entered the tropical rain forest that would envelop them for the next month. Although the forest's lofty canopy of trees, some of which soared to over two hundred feet, created a relatively cool shade, the midday temperature still reached 90°F, and at night it did not drop below the mid-seventies. Much of the way was through mangrove swamps, where putrefying vegetation and dark stagnant water gave off a suffocatingly vile odor. There were few flowers to brighten the way at that time of year, but large butterflies and dainty hummingbirds darted around the men, and there were flocks of larger birds such as hornbills, crown birds, parrots, toucans, warblers, and cranes, not to mention numerous crows, hawks, and vultures. At night leopards could be heard coughing, lions roaring, and beetles chirping loudly like crickets, but nothing made as much noise as the little rabbit-sized pothos, a kind of lemur that sometimes screeched so piercingly that sleep was impossible. The tropical rain forest was inhabited by all manner of animals, including miniature zebra and full-sized elephants, with large numbers of civet cats, wild hogs, anteaters, antelope, sloths, monkeys, and even chimpanzees, but the dense unbroken underbrush of vines, ferns, and creepers usually kept man and animals apart from one another. Snakes—including a fourteen-foot-long python—and scorpions came into closer contact, as did voracious ants that would attack sleeping humans. Mosquito bites also annoyed the men, although no one then realized that the result could be a deadly bout of malaria. In 1817 and for the remainder of the century, it was believed that "fever," as it was known, was caused by poisonous air, particularly the decaying and malodorous effluvia of swamps. In fact, the word *malaria* was a contraction of the Italian words for bad air, "mal aria."

At first the Europeans were impressed by the magnificence of the rain forest's immense trees, but soon they felt depressed by the solid walls and ceiling of dark green, which seemed to entrap and suffocate them. For most of the journey they could not see more than a few feet on either side of the path. Increasingly claustrophobic, they longed for clearings or rises that would permit them to escape from the jungle even for a short while. Eventually they came to a few open places where the land had once been cultivated, and there were occasional ridges, one of which rose to one thousand five hundred feet. When it was possible for the Britons to look out over the forest beneath them, all agreed that the spectacle was truly magnificent. After passing through a dark, trackless stretch of jungle near the border between the coastal Fante people, bitter enemies of their Asante overlords, and metropolitan Asante, they encountered abandoned villages where the ground was littered with human skulls, relics of an earlier Asante invasion of the south. When the column soon after reached a small clearing, Bowdich, undaunted by the earlier grisly sight, wrote that

> Nothing could be more beautiful than its scenery . . . light and shade were most happily blended . . . trees towering in the shrubbery, waved to the most gentle air a rich foliage of dark green . . . the tamarind and smaller mimosas heightening its effect by their livelier tint . . . the cotton trees overtopped the whole, enwreathed in convolvuli, and several elegant little trees, unknown to me, rose in the background, intermixed with palms, and made the *coup d'oeil* enchanting.[11]

As the British mission crossed the Pra River and entered metropolitan Asante, it began to encounter inhabited villages. Some of them were small, with their thatched-roof mud houses somewhat the worse for wear, but even these places had one wide main street, and most villages struck the visitors as being surprisingly clean. Coastal villages had never made this impression. The members of the mission also commented favorably on the lush fields that lay outside the villages. The Asante inhabitants of these towns, whom Bowdich described as clean and cheerful, were also friendly and respectful, a sharp contrast to the sullen Fante the column had previously endured.

On the nineteenth of May, the column came to a halt one mile south of Kumase. Messengers were sent to announce the arrival to the Asante king, who sent word to the British mission to wait in a nearby village until he finished his bathing (high-ranking Asante bathed at least once a day, using imported Portuguese soap, and none among them was more fastidious than King Osei Bonsu). At two o'clock the expedition was invited to enter Kumase. The first thing the men saw was an offering of a dead sheep wrapped in red silk, suspended over their pathway by two tall poles. Before they had time to speculate about the possible meaning of this sacrifice, they were greeted—or, more accurately, engulfed—by more than five thousand people, most of them warriors, firing their muskets in the air so often that it soon became difficult for the English visitors to see their welcomers through the smoke. But they could not fail to hear the deafening cacophony of the drums, elephant-tusk horns, reed flutes, wooden rattles, and iron gongs played with what Bowdich called "a zeal bordering on phrensy."[12] When the air cleared enough for the white men to see, Bowdich and his comrades found themselves encircled by warriors and their officers who bounded about passionately waving Danish, Dutch, and British flags, some of which had been set on fire by discharges from their muskets.

For half an hour the throng continued its welcoming dance, led by military officers whose dress excited the wonder of the white men. Each officer wore an immense cap topped by three-foot-long plumes of eagle feathers, with gilded ram's horns thrusting out to the front. On their chests they wore red cloth vests covered with amulets of gold and silver, as well as various small brass bells, shells, and knives that jangled as they moved. Three or four animals' tails hung down from each arm, and long leopards' tails dangled down their backs, covering a small bow. A quiver of poisoned arrows hung from their right wrists, and each man brandished a small spear covered with red cloth and silk tassels in his left hand. They wore loose cotton trousers that were stuffed into soft, red leather boots reaching to mid-thigh, where they were attached by small chains to cartridge belts worn around the waist. Finally, each man held between his teeth a two-foot-long iron chain that had a scrap of paper covered with Arabic writing attached to the end. Although the British officers were dressed in imposing scarlet and white uniforms and carried swords, they must have felt underdressed.

When the welcoming ceased, the British-led column moved on to deposit their supplies and gifts in a large house that had been assigned to them. As they did, they were serenaded by various bands that this time melodiously played drums, horns, and flutes in concert. The visitors were soon ordered to walk toward the king's palace while much of the population of Kumase gathered around to stare at the white men. As they made their way through the throng, they were exposed to the spectacle of a man being led along to his execution. He was made to walk with his hands tied behind his back, a knife passed through his cheeks to prevent him from uttering a curse that could endanger the king. One ear had been cut off and was carried by a man who walked ahead; the other ear hung by a small strip of skin. His bare back was gashed and bleeding, and small knives had been thrust up under each shoulder blade. The wretched man was being led along by a cord that had been passed through his nose. It is likely that he was paraded before the British visitors as an object warning of what would happen to malefactors.

After this unfortunate man had been led away, the four Englishman and their interpreters were led down a very broad street toward the marketplace, where they were stunned by the "magnificence and novelty" of the next scene that "burst" upon them, as Bowdich put it.[13] As they entered the market area, which Bowdich estimated to be a mile in circumference, they were confronted by an enormous throng of people, and they had to avert their eyes to escape the blinding glare produced by the sun reflecting off masses of gold ornaments worn and carried by the king, his court, various attendants, and thousands of soldiers. As the British visitors were staring in frank amazement at the display of gold, no fewer than one hundred bands began to play, alternating between drum and horn motifs and softer, more melodic tunes featuring long flutes and instruments that resembled bagpipes. As the music continued, scores of huge silk umbrellas, each large enough to provide shade for thirty people, sprung open, adding bright splashes of scarlet and yellow to the scene.

The Britons were invited to come forward to take the hand of each military officer, chief, noble, and important figure in the king's entourage. Most of these men wore heavy silks thrown over the left shoulder like a Roman toga, and they displayed so much gold and silver that the British visitors continued to be dazzled. Some wore ornamental lumps of gold attached to their wrists that were so heavy they had to be supported by boy attendants. Others had solid gold, life-size wolves' or rams' heads suspended from their gold-handled swords. Bowdich noted that these swords were apparently not reserved for ceremonies: their blades were rusted in blood. Large numbers of young officers bedecked in leopard skins, equipped with elephant-hide cartridge boxes encrusted with gold, silver, blue agate, and shells, and carrying gold-handled swords and long Danish muskets, also ornamented with gold, sat on the ground. Next, the Britons were startled to find themselves facing seventeen men of apparently superior rank who were dressed as Arabs. As the Englishmen passed by, these men, whom the British interpreters called Moors, glared at them with undisguised hostility. As the visitors passed by the master of the bands, the keeper of the royal burial ground, the gold horn blower, and many other dignitaries, there was a prolonged clamor of horns and drums announcing the presence of King Osei Bonsu.

Before they could approach the king, the white visitors met the royal executioner, a huge, heavily muscled man wearing a gold breastplate and holding before him the execution stool, which was clotted in blood and nearly covered by a thick deposit of human fat. He shook the stool in a clear warning of what awaited anyone who violated Asante law.[14] Four of the king's spokesmen came next, then finally the keeper of the treasury, who ostentatiously displayed the boxes, scales, and weights of his office, all made of solid gold. Finally, the white men reached the king, who courteously extended his hand. About forty to forty-five years old, the heavyset Osei Bonsu was every inch a monarch. His dress was magnificent but restrained. He wore a rich green silk toga, and his golden ornaments were of the finest workmanship. Even his white leather sandals were delicately ornamented with gold and silver. There were gold castanets on his finger and thumb, which he clapped to enforce silence. His head was shaved except for a quarter-sized tuft of hair on his temple, and he had a three-inch-long beard.[15] All the European visitors characterized him as handsome, friendly, and dignified. When another English visitor was introduced to him four years later, he was too drunk to carry on a dignified conversation, but he was nevertheless courteous and his bearing was regal.

After the king greeted the Englishmen, they were passed on to meet beautiful female attendants, small boys holding elephant tails whose job it was to clean up the king's spit, and obese eunuchs who oversaw his hundreds of wives. Prominently displayed under a protective umbrella was a stool, entirely encased in gold, whose significance the Englishmen did not understand. This was the Golden Stool, the most powerful and sacred symbol in Asante culture. The Asante believed it had been conjured down from the skies during the reign of Osei Tutu, over one hundred years earlier. The stool not only symbolized the king's authority to rule, but it was thought to contain the soul of the Asante people and to assure their well-being. As the English visitors moved farther from the king and his retinue, they were greeted by numerous older men of high rank who were carried by their slaves, as well as the children of chiefs and nobleman who were so weighed down by their golden jewelry that they too had to be carried. Finally, as the white men were escorted to their quarters, they were entertained by royal dancers, dwarfs, mimics, and buffoons.

At eight that evening, his way lighted by hundreds of torches, the king paid a visit to the Englishmen, asked their names for a second time, and wished them a good night. Bowdich and his colleagues could not agree on how many people they had seen in Kumase, but they all estimated the number of soldiers alone at thirty thousand. When Huydecoper visited a year earlier, he estimated that he had been greeted by fifty thousand people and had been introduced to sixty generals in a single day. Still astonished by the power and pomp of the Asante court but exhausted by the excitement of the day, the four Britons slept for the first time in Kumase.

In the ensuing days the visitors exchanged gifts and pleasantries with the king, to whom they had been instructed to give pledges of harmony, friendship, and goodwill. Surrounded by his councilors, interpreters and large retinue, Osei Bonsu met his visitors in any one of the many round rooms that made up a five-acre palace complex dominated by a large European-style two-story building made of stone. Despite the intimidating ambience Bowdich did his best to convince the Asante King that British motives were wholly altruistic, consisting of nothing more than a desire to share the benefits of British civilization with the Asante. King Osei Bonsu readily acknowledged the superiority of British technology, but wryly observing that one of the northern provinces that the Asante had conquered was as inferior to the Asante as the Asante were to the British, he assured Bowdich that there was not a single person in his kingdom who would go there solely to share Asante art and technology. This being so, the king pointedly asked, "Now, how do you wish to persuade me that it is only for so flimsy a motive that you have left this fine and happy England . . .?" The next day an Asante prince asked Bowdich why, if Britain were so selfless, it had behaved so differently in India.[16] Bowdich was astonished that the Asante had heard anything about India and was at a loss for words. Events would soon confirm the Asante suspicion that altruism was not Governor Smith's motive for sending his representatives to Kumase.

As the days passed, the British visitors continued to be impressed by the size of Kumase, the complexity of its court and government, and the novelty of Asante life, but initially they were severely limited in their ability to learn much about the Asante state because, unless they were summoned to meet the king, they were usually restricted to their residences. Even so, there were memorable experiences. When they were invited to dine with the king and members of his court, they were first served what they referred to as a "relish . . . sufficient for an army" consisting of soups, stews, plantains, yams, rice, wine, spirits, oranges, and "every fruit." Next, dinner was served on a large table under four scarlet umbrellas. The plates were gold, the knives, forks, and spoons were silver. The table held an entire roast pig, roasted ducks, chickens, stews, vegetables, and fruit, accompanied by port and Madeira wine, gin, and Dutch cordials served in glasses. Bowdich was an educated Englishman from the port city of Bristol who read Latin, Greek and French, but he wrote that "we never saw a dinner more handsomely served, and never ate a better."[17] Two decades later, when another English visitor was received in Kumase, he was served an equally impressive dinner while being serenaded by a Dutch-trained brass band wearing blue dress uniforms trimmed in red.[18] Osei Bonsu sometimes wore European clothing to dinners like these, a custom that some of his successors continued.

Bowdich was much impressed by Osei Bonsu's good nature and by his shrewd, inquiring mind. Huydecoper wrote that though he could "argue like a lawyer" and had a quick temper, he usually was in good humor and fond of joking.[19] Bowdich was also quite taken by the Asante upper classes, or, as he referred to them, the "higher orders." They were not only wealthy—some owned vast estates and thousands of slaves and lent huge sums to the government from time to time—they were courteous, well-mannered, digni-fied, and proud of their honor to such an extent that a social dis-grace, including something as unintended as public flatulence, could drive a man to commit suicide. While Bowdich was in Ku-mase, the king publicly reproved one of his many sons for minor misconduct. The ten-year-old boy's pride was so wounded that he promptly killed himself by putting a blunderbuss in his mouth and firing it with his foot.[20]

Bowdich was struck by the physical stature of men among the "higher orders." Many were over six feet tall and powerfully built. He was also taken by the beauty of the women of this class, whom he described as having the "finest figures," elaborately shaved heads (with a single tuft of hair surrounded by several concentric circles on the left side), and beautiful clothes. A British visitor four years later also commented on their beauty and gentility.[21] Other ob-servers attributed the size, strength, and physical beauty of the upper classes (known as *sikapo*, "people of wealth") to the ability of wealthy Asante men to choose only the most beautiful women as wives.[22] Although he did not say so directly, Bowdich seemed disappointed that these elegant women were so aloof to the English visitors. When Bowdich described the social freedoms enjoyed by Englishwomen of his class, the Asante women were delighted, but the husbands of these higher-order women were so horrified that they ordered their wives away. He also wrote approvingly of the grace of upper-class Asante men and women as they danced, not wildly as "primitive" Africans were expected to do, but in a stately, even staid, fashion that resembled a waltz. More than two decades later another British visitor made almost identical observations about the beauty, elegance, and grace of the king's wives, whom he was allowed to watch parade past, a sight no Asante man except the king could witness.[23]

The king's wives were even more remote than women of the higher orders. In fact, no one other than the king and his harem eunuchs was permitted to see the six or so wives who lived in the vast royal palace at any given time. His two or three hundred other wives lived in seclusion away from the palace. Bowdich did report that there were many prostitutes in Kumase, that many lower-ranking Asante women made open sexual advances toward the British visitors, and that several nobles offered them women as well. He did not, as one might expect of an Englishman of that era, indicate whether any of these offers were accepted. Huydecoper was much more open in his journal. Although his Christian wife and children were waiting in Elmina, when an Asante general offered him a "very young girl for my wife," he accepted with the "greatest pleasure."[24]

Men and women of the higher orders bathed every morning with soap and warm water, wore scrupulously clean clothes, and ornamented themselves profusely. They cleaned their teeth several times every day with a brushing stick (chewed on the end until it was furred) and shaved their armpits to reduce body odor, which they found repellent. They also regarded belching and flatulence as disgusting.[25] The lower orders (known as *ahiato*), on the other hand, were said to be small in stature, filthy, ungrateful, insolent, and licentious, an opinion strongly expressed by Osei Bonsu. Bowdich had little contact with these poorer members of Asante society, and he did not fully understand that, while some poor people were free, most were slaves, of which there were at least five different categories.[26]

In the 1840s Asante king Kwaku Dua described slaves to a British visitor as "stupid and little better than beasts."[27] He was no doubt referring to newly captured people from northern tribes who circumcised their men, cicatrized marks on the faces and bodies of both men and women, spoke non-Akan languages, and came from less complex social systems. Over time some became incorporated into Asante society as freemen and even achieved wealth and high social rank. Slaves were usually reasonably well treated, but escape from a cruel master was permitted if the slave swore a powerful oath that bound him to another man. Slaves could also achieve sanctuary from a tyrannical master by claiming sanctuary at a temple.[28] Even so, most slaves could be sent away as human sacrifices by their masters at any time, and many were compelled to perform onerous labor clearing fields or mining gold, while others were forced into military service. When slaves died, all but a few were thought unworthy of burial. Instead they were thrown into a nearby river where their bodies were eaten by large fish.[29] In addition to slaves there were "pawns," free men and women sold into servitude as collateral for a loan. When the loan was paid off, they were freed. The impact of class and slave distinctions in Asante was mitigated somewhat by an law that forbade anyone to discuss another's social origins, and this proscription was taken so seriously that Akan-speaking slaves easily became valued members of Asante families.

The Asante could not mine their gold, cultivate their fields, or man their army without the slaves (and some poor free men), who made up the lower orders, but the presence of large numbers of foreign-born slaves in Asante posed a difficult problem for the government. In 1841 King Kwaku Dua told a British visitor that military detachments often had to be sent throughout the empire to bring these people under control.[30] The British decision in 1807 to terminate the maritime slave trade had made it difficult for the Asante to dispose of surplus slaves, and the Asante government was well aware of the threat these unruly people posed to public order.[31] Bowdich and his companions learned about this threat at first hand when they were assaulted by a crowd of people in Kumase and had to use their swords to escape serious injury. The sharp division between upper and lower classes that was so noticeable in the early nineteenth century diminished somewhat over time as fewer new slaves were brought into metropolitan Asante and previously enslaved people became more fully incorporated into Asante society.

The English visitors were favorably impressed by Kumase. Built on open land, it was relatively large—over four miles in circumference—was divided into seventy-seven wards, and had twenty-seven main streets, one of which was one hundred yards wide. The banyan tree–shaded streets were swept every day, and the city was remarkably clean. Trash too was collected and burned every day. While many houses were small, single-story huts (often used for military prisoners), many others, especially those near the king's two-story stone palace, were large, neat, two-story buildings that were scrupulously clean, nicely decorated with polished-clay red bas-relief designs, and well-maintained. Bowdich was surprised to discover that most of these major structures had indoor toilets that were flushed by pouring gallons of boiling water down them. Several hundred buildings near the king's palace were open to the street in front. Elevated above the street by several feet, they were accessible by polished clay steps that led into a large room with a similarly polished floor and glistening whitewashed walls that extended to a bamboo roof, neatly thatched with palm leaves. These rooms were the offices of the many government officials who conducted the business of the state. Behind these public rooms another thirty to forty rooms served as living quarters for the bureaucrats' many relatives.

The work of Kumase's potters, goldsmiths, weavers, painters, and craftsman also pleased Bowdich. He admired their tasteful treatment of gold, iron, leather, shells, feathers, and cloth. These craftsmen lived in the suburbs of Kumase, but their work was to be seen everywhere, especially in the markets, several of which were open every day from eight A.M. to sunset, crowded with people from hundreds of miles distant, speaking dozens of dialects and languages. Items typically available for sale included beef, mutton, wild hog, antelope, monkey's flesh, chickens, ducks, yams, plantains, maize, sugarcane, rice, various vegetables and fruit, huge smoked land snails, salted fish from the coast, and eggs. There were also supplies of tobacco, smoking pipes (many of which were three feet long), beads, looking glasses, sandals, beads, silk and cotton cloth, pillows, thread, calabashes, and gunpowder.[32] Beer, palm wine, rum, and gin were readily available, too.[33] Many a small English or American city of that time was less well provisioned.

The complexity of court life justifiably intrigued the European visitor. In addition to the "Moors" who served the King, other Arab visitors came from as far away as Baghdad. There may have been as many as one thousand Muslim men, their wives, and children in Kumase, and some men had considerable religious influence. But despite determined efforts they were never able to achieve a major voice in Asante politics.[34] There were also government officials of all ranks, and an ongoing parade of chiefs, military officers, nobles, and members of the royal clan from outlying districts. The titles of these people confused European visitors, who tried, mostly inappropriately, to apply familiar terms to them. They were known by many titles in Asante, but generically they were referred to as *amradofo*, "those responsible for maintaining the law."[35]

Even an outsider like Bowdich could easily appreciate the unceasing and dangerous intrigues that swirled around the palace. Kumase was the center of Asante power; everyone there talked about politics as they vied for favor and position, but one's words had to be carefully measured. An Asante proverb said that "words are like vomit, they cannot be taken back."[36] Men of talent could rise quickly in Kumase, but they could fall even faster. Someone who had overplayed his hand was liable to arrest and possible execution. Despite the danger some people took great risks in the political rough and tumble, and men and women alike risked their lives in forbidden sexual liaisons. Only a few people were largely above the law. Several noble families were exempt from capital punishment, and the king's sisters were free to pursue open sexual liaisons with any ranking man of their fancy.

Daily life in the royal palace was fascinating. State business was a serious and continuous feature of court life, often lasting well into the night under torchlight, but there were lighter moments, too. The king retained a troop of small boys, who performed as "royal pickpockets" by purloining sundry valuables from people at the market. If the victim was able to catch one of these nimble thieves, he could beat him as severely as he wished, short of inflicting a mortal blow; but this rarely happened, and most boys escaped to the palace to enjoy their spoils. The king was also surrounded by gifted mimics, able to repeat, for example, a long English sentence with perfect accent, even though they did not know a word of the language. Often their mimicry was at the considerable expense of some unlucky visitor to the court. And as at European courts, there was the inevitable buffoon, whose antics were said to be hilarious. A good deal less amusing were some one hundred sullen albinos, whose function in the court was obscure. Finally, the king lavished his personal affection on dozens of pet cats that imperiously had the run of the palace, including the king's lap, which several typically sat upon.

In early September Bowdich witnessed the annual yam festival (*odwira*), which dramatized the power of the state and reinforced bonds of loyalty and patriotism. When the yams were ready for harvest, all the district chiefs and military leaders of the empire, including all the many tributary districts, were required to attend the festival with their retainers. Bowdich found the "number, splendor and variety" of the arrivals "as astonishing as entertaining," but he was distressed to discover that as each of these important men arrived, one of his slaves was sacrificed at each quarter of Kumase. As the arrivals paraded by King Osei Bonsu, two parties of executioners, each one hundred strong, slowly danced past, displaying the skulls of all the kings and chiefs who had been conquered by Asante armies or executed for subsequent treachery or rebellion. They drummed on the skulls with their knives, conveying an unmistakable message of menace to the arriving notables, some of whom would in fact be executed for past offenses before the festival ended. Even though their crimes, usually some form of treason, might have been committed in the previous year, these men were not executed until this dramatic annual festival took place. Usually taken by surprise, the accused was seized, tried publicly, and if found guilty, executed as an object lesson to all. Those notables who had been loyal would be presented with honors and valuable gifts by the king.

Group after group of great men passed by, each preceded by its band of men playing drums and horns, followed by retainers, who repeatedly fired their muskets into the air. Darkness fell, but the

procession continued, now illuminated by hundreds of huge torches. As they approached the king, they passed by Moors, royal servants, and messengers of all sorts, court criers, military
commanders with their gold swords, ostrich fans, and huge gold
ornaments, girls bearing silver bowls filled with palm wine, children of the nobility, and various other dignitaries. Finally, as each
great man reached the king, he raised his sword and swore an oath
of allegiance. The festivities, accompanied by a growing display of
sexual license, continued until 4 A.M.

> The next morning the King ordered a large quantity of rum to be
> poured into brass pans, in various parts of the town; the crowd press-
> ing around, and drinking like hogs; freemen and slaves, women and
> children, shrieking, kicking, and trampling each other under foot,
> pushed head foremost into the pans, and spilling much more than
> they drank. In less than an hour, excepting the principal men, not a
> sober person was to be seen, parties of four reeling and rolling under
> the weight of another, whom they affected to be carrying home;
> strings of women covered in red paint, hand in hand, falling down
> like rows of cards; the commonest mechanics and slaves declaiming
> on state palavers (formal discussions); the most discordant music, the
> most obscene songs, children of both sexes prostrate in insensibility.
> All wore their handsomest cloths, which they trailed after them to a
> great length, in a drunken emulation of extravagance and dirtiness.[37]

Perhaps one hundred criminals were executed during the festival
that Bowdich witnessed, and a large number of slaves were sacrificed so that their blood, poured into the holes left when the yams
were dug up, would create continued fertility. However, the climax
to the festival was not human sacrifice, but the spectacle of melting
down the royal gold ornaments while the populace and the visiting
tributary chiefs looked on, presumably suitably impressed. Soon the
gold would be reworked into wonderfully new and novel creations.

The tributary states in the Asante Empire were controlled by
their own chiefs or kings, backed by the threat and the actuality of
Asante punitive expeditions. But in metropolitan Asante, especially
in Kumase, order was maintained by various police forces. The
highly visible executioners were constant reminders that Asante
law must be obeyed, and anyone tempted to break a law knew that

a police spy, or simply an indignant Asante, would be likely to turn them in for punishment. As a result, Asante justice could be remarkably efficient. When a British visitor lost a valuable gold seal in 1820, he informed the king, who matter-of-factly assured him that it would promptly be found and returned. A gong was sounded, and the resulting search turned up the gold within an hour.[38] There were also uniformed police in Kumase who maintained order and made certain that no one entered or left the city without the permission of the government. These men, distinguished by their long hair, carried whips, knives, and muskets. There were also highway police stationed at various points up and down the highway system of metropolitan Asante. Sometimes as many as six hundred police would man checkpoints on the Asante frontier, where they interrogated all travelers about their business, inspected their goods for contraband, enforced trade embargoes, and collected toll fees. Smugglers or escaped criminals were arrested. No one passed these police posts without careful scrutiny; indeed, there was an Asante saying about their notorious efficiency: "If you leave a crime behind you on a journey, you will meet it ahead of you."[39] At a time when England was plagued by riots, metropolitan Asante was remarkably orderly.

Nothing impressed European visitors more than public executions. Huydecoper was made aware of many executions during his stay. He wrote that he had "certain knowledge" of the deaths of eighty Fante. He also reported that a rebellious chief was tortured for some time before he was put to death. After pepper had been rubbed into innumerable cuts on his body, the man's ears, nose, and arms were cut off before he was finally decapitated. Huydecoper wrote that when he witnessed the execution of a young man in the company of Osei Bonsu, "The King asked me if I was not afraid. I said I was not, but that the sight distressed me. 'Oh,' said the King, 'This is nothing. It happens here quite frequently.'|"[40] European visitors, especially missionaries, tended to exaggerate the frequency of human executions, but there can be little doubt that the king spoke the truth. Two decades later, one of many executioners in Kumase, a young man who appeared to be not yet eighteen, told a European visitor that he had personally executed eighty people.[41]

Like Huydecoper and other Europeans who would visit Kumase in the ensuing years, Bowdich was appalled by the human executions. They were impossible to ignore. On various occasions when large crowds were assembled in Kumase and could be suitably impressed, criminals were executed. After being convicted by a court, these men (like the man Bowdich saw when he first arrived in Kumase) were usually marched to their execution with large knives driven through their cheeks so that they could not utter magically dangerous curses against their accusers or the king. Bowdich was surprised that their expressions were so apathetic. On one occasion Bowdich saw thirteen victims surrounded by their executioners, who were dressed in shaggy black vests and hats that made them resemble bears. Men and women, chanting in a dirgelike fashion, encircled the condemned. Rum and palm wine was poured copiously while horns played and muskets were fired into the air. Finally, an executioner cut off a condemned man's hand with his sword, then threw the man on the ground before he patiently hacked his head off in a sawing motion with a small knife that was intentionally not very sharp.

Bowdich and the other Britons could not bear to witness any more executions, but they were told that all thirteen men died in a similar way and that numerous people, including women, had later been sacrificed for religious reasons. Hutchinson wrote that he had once come upon the headless bodies of two women lying in the market as vultures pecked at them. Vultures were sacred birds that could not be killed, and a woman who accidentally caught one in her basket was executed.[42] Hutchinson also wrote about another execution scene that the king personally witnessed. Osei Bonsu sat drinking palm wine from a silver goblet while the executions proceeded. As each head was severed, the king, still seated, imitated a dancing motion, which apparently signified his pleasure.[43] The Asante practice of execution, whether of criminals or for religious purposes, would plague the British conscience for the remainder of the century.

Bowdich was a gifted and reliable observer, but there was much about Asante culture that he could neither see nor readily comprehend.[44] For one thing, he thought that King Osei Bonsu was an autocrat, a natural conclusion for someone who only saw the king on public occasions, when his role as absolute monarch was acted out to the fullest. It was true that many lesser officeholders displeased the king at their peril. One provincial administrator, who lived in Kumase in great luxury, traveled in such pomp that whenever he went anywhere, even a short distance, he insisted on being carried in his taffeta hammock, protected by a huge silk umbrella and accompanied by a troop of sycophants who constantly praised him. Some actually swept the ground he would walk on before he stepped out of his hammock. Yet when he overstepped his orders in trying to settle a provincial dispute, the king stripped him of all his property, leaving him a beggar.[45]

The king was the government's chief executive, the commander in chief of its army, and the judge of its highest court. According to the Asante constitution, only he could order executions. In actuality, however, the king's powers were greatly circumscribed, as some European visitors understood as early as 1819.[46] Osei Bonsu was at pains to act as if his whim were law when in public, but where matters of significant import for the Asante state were at issue, he shared power with a national assembly of some two hundred men, representing all regions of the empire, that regularly managed the affairs of government and decided all disputes as a supreme tribunal. Its members were the senior chiefs of the traditional districts of the state. In addition, the king was advised—and sometimes dominated—by an inner council of eighteen nobles: powerful military commanders, some princes, major government officials such as the treasurer, some ceremonial officers, two of the king's chamberlains, the head physician, a senior priest, and often most influential of all, the queen mother. The council—known as the *Asante Kotoko*, meaning the Asante porcupine ("no one dares touch them")—ordinarily met every day with considerable pomp, attended by servants, court criers, soldiers, and the seemingly ever-present executioners. Frequently their deliberations continued under torchlight until late at night. Like the British privy council, the inner council was both a court of law and a legislature. In addition to the public deliberations of this body, these and other powerful people often had access to the king's ear, and no prudent king would wisely offend the wealthiest and most powerful people in his realm. For example, the king once apologized to Joseph

Dupuis, who visited Kumase in 1820, for a decision he had made, saying, "Don't be angry . . . I must do what the old men say; I cannot help it."[47] In every sense the king served at the pleasure of his most influential subjects and could be removed for misconduct, as would happen later in the century.

An Asante king owed his throne—his stool—to the political faction that put him in power. He had to retain their favor to survive, while doing as little as possible not to offend other powerful factions, some of which were led by aristocrats and members of the royal family.[48] Four noble families wielded great power. Until recently they had not been subject to capital punishment, and one of these men ruled over the government when the king was out of Kumase. A wise king would go to extraordinary lengths to avoid offending these nobles. For example, when one of Osei Bonsu's wives was accused of having sexual relations with another man, the king ordered her executed as Asante law permitted him to do. However, when he was informed that this particular wife was the daughter of a powerful noble and military commander, he quickly spared her and even offered her a gift of gold if she were to remarry.[49]

Despite these limitations on their power, Asante kings lived majestically. The palace staff was elaborate, and it did much to create an aura of majesty. Among the more than a score of separate departments established to serve the king were spokesmen, stool carriers, drummers, umbrella carriers, bathroom attendants, elephant-tail switchers, fan bearers, cooks, heralds, sword bearers, gun bearers, ministers, eunuchs, and the ubiquitous executioners.[50] At several points around the city, particularly the great market, there were six- to eight-foot-high circular platforms of polished clay painted red, where the king sat under his great umbrella, greeting his subjects and sipping palm wine, which he ceremoniously allowed to drip through his beard to the ground. Palm wine was to be quaffed in a single gulp, and etiquette called for much of it to run down through a man's beard.

Some fifty to one hundred of his attendants sat below him on steps cut into the platform. The chief of each district also occupied a stool and was supported by a similarly large and diverse staff of officials and retainers. This panoply of power served the king and his loyal chiefs well, but the actual governance of the nation was carried out by hundreds of bureaucrats concerned with such essentials as diplomacy, trade, and taxation. For example, because a central concern of the government was the prevention of the emergence of a powerful merchant class that might challenge royal power, laws were established restricting the accumulation of gold and slaves, the principal forms of wealth. Hundreds of government tax collectors belonging to the treasury department enforced a harsh estate tax by quickly descending on the house of anyone of substance who died. A very small percentage of his wealth was awarded to his heir, but the greater portion was confiscated and became the property of the king.[51]

Even though these taxes prevented the inheritance of wealth, nothing was more important to most Asante than its accumulation during their lifetime. A famous Asante proverb said that "one becomes famous not by being noble born but by being wealthy."[52] Another said, "If power is for sale, sell your mother to obtain it. Once you have the power there are several ways of getting her back." For a people who so revered their parents, this was the ultimate sacrifice.[53] Wealth was not only its own reward, it brought great social prestige and formal honors.

Some men, and a few women as well, became sufficiently wealthy through entrepreneurial activities that they were honored by the king as belonging to a kind of nobility, which was symbolized by the right to be preceded in public by troops of well-born boys, known as *asikofo*, who carried elephants' tails. Such honor was done to such a distinguished person (the king, after all, would inherit his wealth) that the king would delegate some of his own sons to serve him and to carry the elephants' tails.[54] This honor was so coveted that at least one man was tempted to claim it fraudulently. During the reign of Osei Yaw (1824–1833), this man claimed to possess a great fortune that he willed to the King. Duly honored as a result, the man enjoyed the benefits of nobility, but when his large pots of gold were opened after his funeral, they were found to contain worthless brass filings. His disinterred corpse was tried, found guilty, and beheaded, depriving his soul of everlasting life.[55]

Given this national fascination with wealth, it is not surprising that there was a government department of the treasury that was greatly concerned with maintaining accurate weights and measures for gold and for assessing its purity. Assuring the safety and purity of the state's gold called for many locked chests and gimlet-eyed guardians, and locks and keys were both necessary and a mark of personal prestige. There was also a need for careful accountants who were, needless to say, closely watched. Although some literate persons were recruited to Kumase to enhance Asante diplomatic relations and some written records were kept, Asante was essentially a preliterate state. As a consequence, the Asante treasury featured overlapping responsibilities and many cross-checks against dishonesty.[56] In 1819, desiring even tighter control over the treasury, Osei Bonsu eagerly sought to have his children receive a British education. British Resident Hutchinson was happy to oblige, and arrangements were well under way for some of his sons to go to Cape Coast and, perhaps, later to England. However, the "Aristocracy and Great Chiefs" opposed this innovation, and the king was forced to abandon the idea. The head of the exchequer, Opoku Frere, the second most powerful man in Asante, later confided to Hutchinson that the opposition arose because he and other wealthy men were accustomed to cheating the king "a little," and they feared that they would be unable to continue this practice if the king's relatives acquired a European education.[57]

Another source of power in the state was religion. The British referred to all Asante religious objects and activities as "fetish," borrowing a Portuguese term that was used disparagingly to reduce them to a superstitious idolatry or a magical dread of certain objects. In reality the Asante had a complicated religion that recognized a supreme creator as well as numerous lesser gods, who took a more active interest in human affairs. The most powerful of these was the river god, Tano. Most houses contained a shrine to a particular god, who was propitiated in various ways. There were many religious ceremonies, too, along with beliefs in divination, evil spirits, magic, and witchcraft. It is not altogether clear how much power Asante priests (many of whom were women) had, but they did play a vital role in helping people deal with misfortune, sickness, and death. It is clear though that at times they opposed the king on certain issues and that there was an inherent tension between the priests and the monarch.[58] Priests derived much of their power from the supernatural assistance of *mmoatia*, forest dwarfs who resembled small human beings except that they communicated only by whistling and their feet pointed backwards. Human sacrifice and small objects thought to have supernatural power were a part of Asante religious life, but they were hardly the totality of it.

Asante religion was centered around the belief that every person had an immortal soul. After death the soul became a spirit for a time, and if the person died prematurely or at the hands of another, that spirit could bring harm to the living. Most ancestral spirits, however, went quietly to the underworld, where life was lived much as it had been on earth. (This was one of the reasons why slaves were sacrificed to serve their masters and why a wife sometimes demanded to be sacrificed after her husband's death.) These ancestors were thought to join with other supernatural forces to reward people who adhered to Asante values and laws and to punish offenders, keeping all on their best behavior. Sometimes these spirits took corporeal form as, for example, a huge bird with great talons that would swoop down on offenders at night. There were also red-haired albinos with flowing beards and very tall women with enormously pendulous breasts that could frighten wrongdoers to death.[59] It was thought that eventually a person's soul would be reborn through a woman of its own lineage.

One of Bowdich's misconceptions that would be shared by almost all British political and military leaders who followed him to the Gold Coast was that the Asante "lived for war." It is true that their army was a formidable instrument of power that must receive the credit for the success of the Asante expansion and nineteenth-century dominance over such a large area. It is also true that many senior Asante military commanders were, like British army officers, men who longed for the military action that could bring them glory, wealth, and power. Yet there had long been powerful proponents of peace in Asante who favored diplomacy and trade relationships over military conquest. Indeed, the Asante invested an inordinate amount of money and energy in the development of diplomacy. The government stressed the training of diplomats, who were instructed in the arts of negotiation and taught to respect the sanctity of treaties, a view that British officials often did not reciprocate in their treaty negotiations with the Asante.[60] They made regular use of envoys and diplomatic missions in the search for peace. The highest-ranking diplomatic officers carried gold-hilted swords and a golden axe on their missions to symbolize their willingness to cut through any difficulty to achieve their purpose.[61] The British misunderstanding of these symbols—that is, as threatening martial action—led them to dismiss several important Asante missions, and they would never understand the subtlety and allusiveness of the Asante negotiating style nor the fact that for many powerful Asante the greatest good was not war but peace, open roads, and trade.[62] As a result, they consistently miscalculated Asante intentions—not surprising, given their contempt for Asante culture and their belief that the Asante sought only war.

War, indeed, had built the Asante Empire, but peace was necessary to maintain it because the Asante depended on tribute and trade. Except for the six districts that made up metropolitan Asante, all of the conquered districts paid an annual tribute. A relatively poor northern district that lacked gold might pay only five hundred slaves, two hundred cattle, four hundred sheep, and several hundred cotton and silk cloths to Kumase, but richer districts were assessed two thousand slaves as well as gold and other valuables.[63] Tribute also included skilled labor such as doctors, potters, smiths, and leather workers and goods such as sandals, leather pouches, elephant tails, fly whisks, and musical instruments.[64] Because the amount and kind of tribute a district could reasonably pay was subject to changing circumstances, a special court was established in Kumase to adjudicate such matters. The need to pay annual tribute was softened somewhat for tributary chiefs because the Asante king usually returned a portion of it as gifts.

In addition to tribute the Asante relied on trade, sending gold, ivory, and slaves south to the coast for firearms, gunpowder, and other European goods. To do so, they had to pass through the territory of sometimes hostile tributary people, such as the Fante, or use them as middlemen. Without a modicum of peace, the Asante could not obtain the weapons and gunpowder needed to maintain their army and control their subject states. They also required peace to continue their profitable trade to the north. In return for sea salt obtained at the coast and kola nuts that helped to suppress thirst in these arid lands, the Asante received the slaves they needed both to trade to the Europeans at the coast and to fuel their own economy. Salt was so valuable that a handful of it would often bring as many as two slaves in return. The trade in gold, ivory, and slaves was monopolized by the wealthy, but the commoners participated widely in the salt and kola nut exchange.[65] Trade to the west and east was less important but it also took place.

To maintain these trade relationships, the Asante built and maintained a system of roads. At least five roads led north toward their tributary states, and an equal number fanned out to the south. Only two roads, both relatively unimportant, ran to the west or the east. Even when located in the relatively more open territory of the north, these roads required enormous manpower to build and more to maintain. Cutting roads through the dense tropical rain forest to the south required herculean efforts, as British military engineers discovered during their invasion of 1873/74. And preventing millions of rapidly growing roots, vines, and creepers from growing back called for continuous labor by thousands of men and women, most of whom were slaves. It also called for numerous detachments of highway police to assure the safe passage of goods up and down these roadways. The Asante government took great care to maintain a network of police and military depots to assure that trade would proceed peaceably and that taxes and tribute would flow to Kumase.

The Asante possessed more gold and used more of it as ornaments and symbols of rank than any other West African people. Much of the gold lay within metropolitan Asante, but many more rich deposits lay in districts that were tributary to them. The Portuguese were so impressed by the quantity of gold the Asante brought to the coast that they named their principal trading fort Elmina—"the mine." Some gold was obtained by panning in streams—work almost entirely done by women and children—but much of the region was dotted with small mine pits dug a few yards into the earth. There were deep shafts as well, several dug one hundred feet deep before sending out tunnels several hundred feet in length. One mine had a timber-shored tunnel three hundred yards long with numerous large galleries where the gold was worked.[66] To reach a vein of gold, miners had to chop their way through hard rock such as feldspar or granite, work that could only be done by men, and in some mines gunpowder was used to blast the rock away. The diggers gave the chunks of ore to women who carried it to crushing areas where men put it on granite slabs and pounded it to bits with hammers before women milled it to powder and washed it to separate the gold. The work was usually done by slaves supervised by the family they belonged to, but sometimes thousands of men, women, and children worked together to mine a rich reef of gold.[67] In peak years as many as forty thousand mines were being worked.[68]

In law all gold belonged to the king, and some mines were directly managed by the treasury, but others were under local control. When a nugget was found, it was supposed to be taken to the local chief, who sent it on to the king, who in return sent the chief some gold dust as his commission. There were tight controls, and the chiefs' spies were willing to report misconduct in anticipation of sharing a reward. Still there *was* cheating, especially after the gold had been reduced to dust when it could be adulterated with silver, copper, or coral.[69] Gold may originally have been mined by the Asante themselves, but at least by the seventeenth century, slave labor was used almost exclusively, perhaps because shafts collapsed by heavy rains and rising groundwater made mining such a dangerous activity. Much gold was extracted by having a slave dig into the soil above a known reef, then handing the earth up for panning until he hit the water table. Slaves slept and ate in these pits, being fed by the freemen who panned the gold on the surface.[70] So great was the Asante demand for slaves in these times that the Portuguese actually imported slaves to the Asante from as far away as Angola![71]

Well before Bowdich's visit slaves were also essential for Asante food production. Originally, Asante farmers practiced shifting cultivation to exploit the fertile but shallow, easily exhausted forest soil. Fields were cleared by chopping and burning the undergrowth, leaving a layer of ash as fertilizer. Yams and plantains were probably the main crop until the sixteenth century, when along with iron hoes many new crops were introduced by Europeans. Cassava, peanuts, maize, oranges, avocados, tomatoes, and pineapples thrived, and productivity grew.[72] As villages and towns multiplied, the need for more food led to the development of large plantations to supply the urban dwellers. The labor needed to clear the forest and cultivate the fields of these plantations was increasingly provided by slaves.

Confined to Kumase, the earlier European visitors were able to learn little about country life. In addition to Kumase and Dwaben there were several towns of five thousand to seven thousand people. Salaga, a market town to the north, was twice as large as Kumase, but the great majority of the people in metropolitan Asante lived in villages of a few hundred to a thousand people. The key to Asante village life was the relationship between a mother and her children. In addition to natural ties of affection, the role of the mother was central because the Asante reckoned both descent and inheritance through the female line. A mother's brother was the legal guardian of her children; her husband had few legal responsibilities for them, except the obligations to see that they were well cared for and well behaved and to find and pay for a suitable wife for his son.[73] A husband had some legal rights over his wife, including the right to cut off her nose for adultery, her lips for betraying a secret, or her ears for listening to his private conversation. Women mutilated in these ways were not an uncommon sight, especially in Kumase.[74] However, women had relative equality with men in many ways, including the right to initiate divorce. Every Asante belonged to a group of people related through women, and it was this group—the *ntoro*, or "lineage" in English—that gave them legitimacy in the world of living Asante and ties to their ancestors, to whom animal and human sacrifices had to be made on special occasions. These various lineages belonged to one of eight clans, one of which was the royal Okoyo clan. Lineage ties were so strong that wherever a man might live, the village where his lineage was centered was his home, and it was there that he would want to be buried to be close to his ancestors.[75]

Veneration of ancestors and respect for authority were combined in the office of chief. Each lineage had its head, who occupied a stool and served as a councillor to the village chief. Each village had a formally acknowledged leader, or chief, chosen by a council of elders representing the various lineages and clans in the village. The chief had the power to resolve minor disputes and to collect taxes, but like the king he was bound by a sworn oath to consult the elders on all matters of importance and to follow their advice. Although the Asante system has been likened to English feudalism, the Asante chiefs ruled not because of a contractual relationship with their people, or vassals, but because various kin groups chose them to lead—elected them in fact—and because religious authority cemented their power. Only the chief had the authority to serve as an intermediary between the people and the ancestors. Each chief had a stool, as the king did, that represented the soul of his people while linking them to ancestors whose blessings on the living were essential to their well-being. Approximately every three weeks the chief was responsible for directing a religious ceremony—the *Adae*—during which the ancestors were praised, their great deeds recounted, and their favors beseeched. Assured that all was well with their world, everyone joined in drinking palm wine and joyously dancing to the rhythm of dozens of drums.[76]

Unlike the excitement and danger of life in Kumase, life in these rural villages was usually routine and tranquil. There were some specialized village settlements of artisans, religious specialists, goldsmiths, and slaves, but most villages consisted of families, free and slave, that lived by cultivation. A village usually had only one street, but like those in Kumase, it too was wide, often over fifty yards, and it was swept clean every day. The rectangular houses with high-pitched thatched roofs were small and simple, as were their furnishings, but they were uniformly clean. Because dirt, trash, and refuse were thought to be dangerous, women and children had the daily chore of gathering up all trash and depositing it in a midden outside the village. Because menstruation was dangerous, too, women were secluded in huts during their menses, and a woman who touched her husband at this time could be killed. Latrines were situated far away from the houses of the village, which were built on both sides of the single long wide road that also served as the village meeting place. The village was surrounded by its fields and domestic animals—mostly chickens, ducks, geese, sheep, and dogs. Shaded by huge trees, people promenaded along this street and sat in the shade, chatting or playing a complicated board game called *ware* that resembled pachisi.

The king and wealthy people wore elegant sandals decorated with gold, but common people went barefooted, except during the rainy season when they wore wooden clogs to keep their feet out of the mud. Prominent people often wore silk, but ordinary Asante wore cotton, and slaves dressed in barkcloth. Garments signaled the wearer's rank, and their color expressed various meanings. Lighter colors could express innocence or rejoicing. White was worn by chiefs after making a sacrifice or by ordinary people after winning a court case. Dark colors were worn for funerals or mourning. Usually worn like a toga thrown over the shoulder but also worn tied around the waist, most clothes bore intricate designs that carried various meanings.[77] Some women wore *kente*-cloth dresses made by stitching together numerous handwoven strips of cotton or silk. Silk threads were laboriously pulled out of imported silk cloth before being rewoven into an Asante design. Many *kente*-cloth designs are so beautiful that they are displayed in museums throughout the world. There were also sumptuary laws that restricted certain *kente* designs to various great men and women as exclusive symbols of their prestige. Many cotton or silk patterns were designed expressly for the king and could only be worn with his permission.

Each day of the week had special significance for the Asante, who like other Akan-speaking people named their children after the day of the week on which they were born ("Wednesday's child," etc.). Warfare should be avoided on Sunday, although certain Sundays called for joyous celebration, and no one throughout the kingdom was permitted to work the fields on Thursday, thought to be a day of great danger because a powerful earthquake once struck on that day.[78] With the day of the week always in mind, village life revolved around the agricultural cycle, as villagers weeded, planted, harvested, and carried their crops to market. Men cut down trees and prepared the land for cultivation, but women did most of the daily work. Men also traded, fished, and hunted, while women collected the huge snails that played a major part in Asante cuisine. Children worked in the fields, cared for domestic animals, and watched over their younger siblings. They also found time to play, to listen to storytellers, and to overhear adults gossiping, a favorite pastime in most Asante communities. Most families ate only two meals, a large breakfast in late morning, followed by rest, then dinner late in the afternoon. The intense political intrigue of the capital was largely absent, but people were always concerned about taxes, military call-ups, the coming and going of traders, and of course the weather. They were also concerned with the health of their animals and supernatural threats to their well-being. For all but the most intrepid, the forest world outside the village was dangerous, even evil. Safety lay in the village world and its fields where, for the most part, Asante people had the same joys and sorrows as rural villagers in most parts of the world. Economic chores varied depending on the season and on ceremonial occasions, but ordinarily, everyone was in bed by 9 P.M. and up the next morning before dawn broke at 6 A.M.

For all the complexity of Asante life, nothing was more fundamental for the people than their reverence for the land. This message was sent to the spirit of the earth on the morning of each *Adae* ceremony:

> *Spirit of the Earth, sorrow is yours,*
> *Spirit of the Earth, woe is yours,*
> *Earth with its dust.*
> *Earth, if I am about to die,*
> *It is upon you that I depend;*
> *Earth, while I am yet alive,*
> *It is upon you that I put my trust:*
> *Earth, who receives my body.*
> *We are addressing you and you will understand.*
> *We are addressing you and you will understand.*[79]

As a rule, village life was placid and predictable without the pageantry, thrill, or menace of Kumase, but now and then life could be disrupted by heavy rains, epidemics, or crop failure and sometimes by mobilization for war, and each village chief had to decide which men were to answer the call of mobilization. The British were wrong in thinking that the Asante lived only for war. For much of the nineteenth century they were able to live in peace. But despite Asante desires to maintain peace with the British, they found themselves at war with British forces on several occasions during the century. The first clash was in 1807. The last and climactic battles were fought in 1900.

✵

3

"A Bravery Not to Be Exceeded"

THE ASANTE ARMY, WHOSE SIZE AND MARTIAL ZEAL SO IMPRESSED
the early English visitors when they first entered Kumase, had every
reason to be triumphant. Fourteen years earlier, in 1803, an Asante
army of perhaps fifty thousand men had driven their northern enemies into open ground, where they were defeated with huge losses
by a decisive charge ordered by the Asante general Amankwatia III.
Asante muskets proved much superior to the spears and arrows of
the northerners, and thousands were killed. Another district then
rebelled, and its army, too, was crushed. By now thoroughly intimidated, neighboring districts hurriedly sent delegations bearing gifts
and pledges of peaceful relations to the new Asante king, Osei
Bonsu, who had been elected to the stool in 1800.

To the north the Asante were now at the pinnacle of their
power, but some of the coastal districts were still rebellious, and
others had never been conquered. In order to reach the various fortified trading posts that the white men had built along the coast,
Asante traders had to travel through the territory of various groups
of coastal people who, though nominally tributary, were far
enough away from Kumase to flaunt their independence. Unlike
armies that quartered troops in their conquered territory, the As-

ante army marched away after a victory, confident that indirect rule could be maintained without the need to station troops in every conquered state.

One of the largest coastal societies was the Fante, an Akan-speaking people, who were perhaps 400,000 in number. They were implacably hostile to the Asante. Unless an Asante army was near-by to threaten them, they blocked Asante access to the British trading center at Cape Coast, due south of Kumase. The Fante as middlemen were greedy and insolent not only to the Asante but equally so to the British, whom they cheated at every opportunity. Soon after King Osei Bonsu came to power, the Fante government declared it unlawful for the white men to trade guns, gunpowder, lead, or iron to the Asante. To meet their growing need for firearms and to dispose of their surplus slaves, the Asante were compelled to trade with the Danes farther to the east at Accra or with the Dutch to the west at Elmina. Dutch traders, who respect-ed Asante power and wanted to curry their favor, did their best to circumvent the Fante and to accommodate the Asante trading needs; but the British, who by the start of the nineteenth century had become the dominant trading power on the Gold Coast, op-posed Asante trade, fearing that it would only benefit their Dutch competitors. Also, the British officers of the African Company had chosen to make an alliance with the Fante, who surrounded them at Cape Coast. Their London superiors urged them to be more re-ceptive to Asante interests, but the British merchants in the Gold Coast ignored their advice and continued to support the Fante, whose actions towards Asante traders not surprisingly became even more insolent and obstructive.[1]

Soon after, a seemingly minor event brought the Asante into conflict with the British for the first time. It began in 1806, one year after Lord Nelson won the battle of Trafalgar, among three Assin chiefdoms to the south of metropolitan Asante. They had been conquered by the Asante and were tributary to Kumase. A rel-ative of an Assin chief named Aputai rifled the grave of a promi-nent man in another district, stealing many valuables including gold. The offended chief could not receive satisfaction on his own, so he judiciously appealed to the Asante king to adjudicate the dis-pute according to Asante law. After due deliberation King Osei

Bonsu ordered Aputai to pay restitution, since his relative had despoiled the grave. Not only did Chief Aputai refuse to do so, he ordered his armed men to attack the aggrieved chief. Alarmed by such an outrageous breach of the law, King Osei Bonsu dispatched two envoys, who bore the golden regalia that assured the diplomats' personal inviolability wherever they traveled, to demand that Aputai cease hostilities and pay restitution. In an unthinkable affront Aputai killed the emissaries and suspended their mutilated bodies from trees on the Asante frontier. By Asante law this was an act of war, and King Osei Bonsu promptly marched against Aputai with a large army, routing his forces after killing large numbers of them. Together with another rebellious Assin chief, Aputai now fled farther to the south, where he sought sanctuary with the Fante.

Although the Asante king's army was quite capable of crushing the numerous but militarily inept Fante, Osei Bonsu again exercised extraordinary restraint, sending more royal diplomats to the offending Fante chief to demand the surrender of the fugitive chiefs and a pledge of good wishes toward Kumase. He even sent a handsome gift of gold, a glorious state silk umbrella, and fifteen slaves. Before the Fante chief could decide what to do, Aputai and his fellow fugitive fled even farther south into Fante territory. Osei Bonsu again sent royal messengers with gifts, and as before, they were killed and decapitated. Their heads, the mouths stuffed with feces, were placed on the path the Asante troops would have to take to invade Fante land. It was an insult of unimaginable magnitude.

By now thoroughly outraged, King Osei Bonsu ordered his army forward. As the Fante melted away, the fugitives fled to Cape Coast, where they next asked the British governor, one Colonel Torrane, for asylum. Magnanimously, Colonel Torrane (whose rank was an honorary title, not a military one) promised to protect the men, even against what he called "force of arms"; but when he learned that a large Asante army was on the march, he became decidedly less sure of himself and sent a flag of truce to the Asante king. Although the British fort at Cape Castle was old, having been built in 1652 by Swedes, it was strongly constructed, with twelve cannon mounted behind high stone walls. Torrane, however, had only a score of white men to defend it and no confidence that the notoriously feckless Fante could defend themselves, much less help him. Despite their military weakness, Torrane's Fante allies arrogantly refused to allow Torrane's flag of truce to go forward, and the Asante attacked, scattering the Fante soldiers, who, according to a British observer, "fled like sheep."[2] Two thousand Fante refugees, many of them terrified women and children from nearby villages, were allowed into the fort, but thousands of others were overtaken by the Asantes and slaughtered on the beach. Many others huddled against the walls, hoping that the Asante soldiers would not dare to approach the fort's deadly cannon and musket fire. They did dare, and although British fire killed them by the hundreds, the Asante slaughtered these refugees, too.

Furious that the white men were firing on his troops, the Asante commander ordered that the fort be taken. Twice the Asante charged to the fort's main gate but were unable to batter it open. Despite horrific casualties (the British fired so often that the white men's shoulders were painfully bruised), the Asante charged again, this time led by a man who carried a huge flaming torch. Near the gate he was shot dead. He fell on the torch, extinguishing it, and the attack failed.

When the Asante withdrew at sunset, they had fought against the British guns for six bloody hours. Several of the British defenders had fired their muskets three hundred times, and at such close range, it was almost impossible to miss. For fully one mile the beach was littered with thousands of Fante and Asante bodies, and the sand above the high-tide line was stained red. The Asante had attacked in such dense formations that every charge of grapeshot from British cannons had killed twenty or thirty men. King Osei Bonsu said that he lost three thousand men.[3] Later, a shaken Colonel Torrane wrote that the Asante had "fought with a bravery not to be exceeded."[4]

Following a brief truce, during which the Asante generously allowed the British to reinforce the fort by sea, Torrane sent soldiers to the Asante king under a flag of truce. Osei Bonsu received them courteously and sent them back to the fort along with messengers of his own. The king insisted that nothing could be settled until Torrane met him face-to-face. The Asante king further demanded that Torrane come to him, and Torrane meekly agreed. In order to impress the Asante king, Governor Torrane took it upon himself to seize the two Assin fugitive chiefs whom he had promised his protection and deliver them to Osei Bonsu. Somehow the remarkable Aputai managed to escape, but the other chief, named Chibu, was delivered to the Asante.

Dressed in their sweat-stained scarlet uniforms, Torrane and the handful of British officers who accompanied him to King Osei Bonsu's camp were cowed by the size and grandeur of the Asante delegation. In a scene reminiscent of Bowdich's reception in Kumase, Torrane was received by many guards, elegantly dressed in silk and ornamented with gold, who were seated under large umbrellas and attended by hundreds of servants. One of these men was a tall, athletic Arab officer from somewhere to the north of Timbuktu. His men fought with bows and arrows as well as muskets, and several of their arrows with barbed iron heads were found in the fort.[5] Why he and his men were fighting beside the Asante is not known.

Although most of the British officers felt dishonored by Torrane's treachery in handing over a man to whom he had promised sanctuary, Osei Bonsu was pleased, later saying to a British visitor, "From the hour Torrane delivered up Cheboo (Chibu), . . . I took the English for my friends, because I saw their object was trade only and they did not care for the people. Torrane was a man of sense, and he pleased me much."[6] As if to prove the king's point, when Osei Bonsu demanded that all two thousand Fante refugees in the fort be handed over to him as slaves, Torrane did not refuse, as might have been expected of an Englishman whose country would ban the international trade in slaves only a few months later. Instead, Torrane bargained to be allowed to keep one thousand of these refugees for himself. The king agreed, and to the amazement and horror of the other British officers, Torrane did not protect these people. Instead, Torrane, who was in debt, sold them to a slave dealer, who shipped them to America. When John Swanzy, a member of the garrison that had fought so valiantly against the Asante, heard about this outrage, he angrily pulled himself out of a serious attack of malaria and sailed by canoe from Fort James at Accra (some one hundred kilometers away), where he had just become commander, to Cape Coast in an attempt to help the refugees. He arrived too late to do anything but save a handful of people whose ship had not yet sailed and express his contempt for Torrane. Exhausted, Swanzy died a few days later.

Torrane's actions were seen by the coastal people and the Asante alike as a British admission of Asante military supremacy. The British later learned that just before the truce was agreed upon, the Asante commander had issued orders for several thousand men to maintain musket fire on the fort's defenders while several thousand more brought forward enough gunpowder to breach the fort's gate. Had this attack been carried out, it almost certainly would have succeeded, something both the Asante and the British understood quite well.[7] Nothing happened between 1807, the time of this battle, and 1817, when Bowdich arrived in Kumase, to alter the Asante conviction that they were the supreme military power in the Gold Coast.

Hoping that the British would now encourage the Fante to allow Asante traders to pass peacefully through their territory to the coast, Osei Bonsu withdrew his army from the coast. It had been a long campaign, there had been many casualties (especially those inflicted by British guns at Cape Coast), and many of the surviving soldiers were suffering from smallpox and dysentery. As soon as the Asante army was gone, the Fante once again denied Asante traders free access to the coast, and once again the British did not intervene to protect them. Four years later, in 1811, the king sent another army to the coast to punish the Fante, and after the by now predictably overwhelming victory, the Asante army withdrew. But the Fante restricted trade again and again the British stood by. In 1814 an even larger Asante army dealt the Fante an even more decisive defeat, scattering their army, destroying many villages, and leaving large areas depopulated. Even then the British traders took no steps to restrain their Fante allies or to provide the Asante with the friendship and trade they asked for. In neither of these campaigns did the Asante make any hostile gesture toward the British.

Late in 1816 Captain Sir James Yeo, the senior Royal Navy officer assigned to West Africa and a veteran of the War of 1812 against the United States, expressed his view of the situation in a report that the Admiralty took seriously enough to forward to the Colonial Office:

The people of the coast called Fantees have done everything in their power to prevent the Ashantees, natives of the interior, from having any communication with it [the coast]; as by excluding them from the trade, they act as brokers between the Ashantees and the European merchants. They are a vile, abandoned set of people who rob both one and the other; and what is more extraordinary, we have countenanced them in it, although it is both unjust to the Ashantees and in direct opposition to our commercial interests, as a free trade with the natives of the interior would be of great national importance, and which the King of the Ashantees is most anxious to establish.[8]

What Captain Yeo and others saw so clearly, the merchants of the African Company were now reluctantly forced to acknowledge as well. They knew that the Asante were preparing another invasion of the coast to devastate the Fante yet again, and perpetual war was decidedly bad for business. Ten years earlier, King Osei Bonsu had suggested to the merchants that they send one of their officers to the Asante capital as their resident representative. Not until ten years had passed and the British fear of a Dutch trade monopoly with the Asante had grown did the Bowdich mission to Kumase in 1817 set forth.

The Asante Army

The Asante army that devastated the Fante and could have taken the British fort at Cape Coast was large by any standard and was far larger than any of its West African opponents. Bowdich estimated its strength in full mobilization at 200,000, and this may not have been an overestimate.[9] But even if its actual size were only half this, it was still larger than that of its most formidable foe, the kingdom of Dahomey to the east, whose women warriors—the so-called Amazons—would later so capture the fancy of European visitors, including Sir Richard Burton. The large size of the Asante army was only one reason for its military prowess, however, and not the most important one. Its great successes against other African armies came in part from its advantage in firearms, but more important was its remarkable organization and the exceptional discipline and bravery of its officers and men.

Because the availability of Asante gold enabled them to acquire large numbers of muskets before their northern neighbors could (they were farther from the coastal trading routes), the Asante were able to defeat them and make them tributary states. Part of this tribute would be paid in able-bodied male slaves to serve in the Asante army, helping to increase its size even further. In fact, although all officers in the army were metropolitan Asantes and the high-ranking commanders were usually aristocrats, the great majority of the common soldiers were slaves.[10] Slaves not needed for the army or the Asante economy were traded to the coast for more muskets and gunpowder. Success in battle also heightened Asante esprit and confirmed the belief that bravery would bring victories, not to mention the spoils of war. Success bred arrogance, an attitude the Asante were well known for.

Much like the president of the United States, the Asante king was the commander in chief of the army, and it was for him to appoint its field commanders. But the decision to go to war lay with the inner council and the national assembly, much as it does with the U.S. Congress. The field commander and all of his high-ranking officers were much like feudatory lords in Europe. Most were aristocrats or royal leaders of large districts during peacetime but took prescribed roles in the national army in times of war. Though these leaders were referred to as chiefs by the British, the title understates their role and power. They were, more accurately, "priest-chiefs" (*Obene Okomofo*), whose stool gave them powers that were established equally by Asante law and religion. In many respects they closely resembled the lord lieutenants of an English county in their ability to retain the loyalty of men in their district, as well as the legal right to call them to war when needed. Unlike many African armies, the Asante did not call up men in regiments based on age or the date on which they were circumcised. In fact, the Asante did not practice circumcision at all, believing that the body should be kept intact, a belief that put them very much at odds with their Islamicized northern neighbors, many of whom would fight against them later in the century. The foundation of the Asante army was territorial: men from the same district owed allegiance to their leader.

Beginning early in the nineteenth century, the king maintained a small force of several hundred regular soldiers to serve as a kind of royal guards unit. Later in the century, other full-time guards units were established, and there was also a full-time medical corps, a drum company, and about one thousand regular war messengers, or couriers, whose ability rapidly to communicate information over a considerable distance in battle was vital.[11] Like British bugle calls, Asante "talking drums" could convey certain kinds of standardized information over considerable distances. So too could traditional melodies played on elephant-tusk horns, but for complicated messages to be conveyed in the noise and confusion of battle, messengers were vital. The remainder of the army, and by far its largest part, consisted of slaves, retainers, or freemen owing obedience to their chief or district king, who had the right to summon them to war. These chiefs were given quotas to fill depending on the extent of the mobilization and the seasonal needs for agricultural labor or other activities. The largest of these quotas were given to the kings of Dwaben or Bekwai, either of which could easily mobilize over ten thousand men. These part-time soldiers were expected to own their own muskets and other weapons; the king was required to provide them with gunpowder and shot. Sometimes these locally raised armies marched directly to battle after assembling in their own districts and being joined by senior Asante commanders, but on those occasions when a major campaign had been ordered, they marched to Kumase where the entire army came together to prepare for war.

Chiefs or district kings who failed to respond to the Asante king's request for soldiers risked royal displeasure that could easily take the extreme form of a punitive expedition against them. But it was not only fear that led to cooperation. A successful campaign could lead to great amounts of booty in the form of gold, guns, gunpowder, captives, and land. In principle all war booty belonged to the king, but he usually returned at least two thirds of it to his commanders, who in turn shared it with those loyal to them. For many powerful men war was the royal road to glory and riches. The victorious General Amankwatia III, for example, who had triumphed in 1803, was given the town of Sreso, seven miles from Kumase, with nearly all of its eight thousand inhabitants as his personal soldiers, slaves, or retainers. When he visited the court in Kumase, the flourish his horn players loudly trumpeted meant "no one dares trouble me."[12] Other generals had equally boastful airs. These men might fall out of favor and lose their wealth or be killed in battle, but there were always others eager to lead an army to glory and riches.

The organization and tactics of the Asante army on the march were highly standardized. Originally modeled after ants, who march in several columns before joining at the crucial moment, the army in a traditional fully-mobilized campaign was led by two or three thousand scouts (*akwansrafo*) who marched well in advance of the regular troops, often at night to avoid detection. Most of these scouts were professional hunters who, when detected, used their skill as marksmen to snipe at their enemy's advanced forces, often from a perch high in a tree. To draw the enemy's fire and force them to reveal their positions in the jungle foliage, they carried long wooden sticks with hooks on the end to shake trees as if someone were in them. Because it was considered unlucky for a scout to be killed, these men were not expected to become involved in any prolonged fighting. After exchanging a few shots with the enemy, the scouts typically withdrew through the next wave of troops, the advance guard (*twafo*).

When the forest was open enough to permit maneuvers, a condition common in the north of Kumase but rare in the south, this guard advanced in two or three long lines. After the men in the first line fired their muskets, the next line advanced through them while they reloaded. Then the rear line advanced, and the entire process was repeated or the advance was halted. No one was permitted to retreat. To assure that no one did, the advance guard was backed up by a line of trusted metropolitan Asante freemen known as sword bearers (*afonasoato*). Armed with hippopotamus-hide whips and heavy swords, these men flogged or slashed anyone who attempted to flee. The same practice, though not often publicized, was common in European armies during the nineteenth century and on both sides during the American Civil War. Behind the brave Confederate soldiers who charged to their deaths at Gettysburg were others with bayonets (they were called "file closers") to make certain they did not change their minds. All of these armies understood the importance of making it as dangerous for its troops to retreat as it was for them to advance. Asante soldiers were taught to repeat this saying: "If I go forward, I die; if I flee, I die; better to go forward and die in the mouth of battle."[13]

Behind these sword bearers would come the main body (*adonten*), which could consist of twenty thousand men or more. An equally large force marched on each flank with orders to surround the enemy. The commander of the army followed the main body, surrounded by his retainers and bodyguard. In each of these large forces, there were hundreds of men who were armed only with knives to dispatch the enemy's wounded. Behind the main body marched many thousands of slaves who carried supplies on their heads and all manner of camp followers, including many women.[14] Finally, there was a smaller rear guard (*kyidom*) that always faced the rear during an engagement in case the enemy attempted to encircle the army.[15] Each of the flank units as well as the rear guard had its own senior commanders in addition to many lower-ranking officers. Men from the various Asante districts had traditional places in the flank units, the rear guard, or the main body that marched forward in every campaign. They understood the tactics necessary for them to succeed in battle. Of course, some battles did not develop as planned, and these formations became jumbled together.

Before marching toward battle, the fully mobilized army assembled in Kumase, where gunpowder and shot from the king's apparently huge armory (no European is known actually to have seen it), located three miles outside of the city, were distributed to the men. Much of the gunpowder was of inferior quality, having been adulterated by European traders or damaged in transit, and their ammunition was inferior, too. Unlike contemporaneous European armies, whose men usually fired lead bullets that more or less fitted the bore of their muskets, the Asante typically fired an assortment of nails or slugs cut from the lead or iron bars that European traders sold to them. Their guns were six-foot-long muskets known as "Long Danes," after the Danish traders who introduced them to the region. These heavy, flintlock weapons were often shoddily manufactured (many of them in Birmingham, England), but they could be deadly at short range. Difficult and time-consuming to reload (it took seven distinct movements and up to a minute to do so), rifles as long and heavy (nearly twenty pounds) as these were hardly ideal for jungle warfare.[16] Yet they were the only firearms then available on the Gold Coast, and they were well cared for and lavishly decorated, often with patterns of red shells attached to the stocks. Very early in the nineteenth century some soldiers carried poisoned arrows and javelins, while officers and sword bearers carried heavy swords, but after 1807 these weapons were not used against the British. Horses were known to have survived in Kumase, but because they could not survive in the tsetse fly–infested forest zone to the south, there was no cavalry. Although high-ranking officers sometimes rode horses in Kumase with all the hauteur of a European guards officer, they did not ride to battle. Instead, they were carried in ornate hammocks.

On ceremonial occasions both officers and common soldiers were elaborately uniformed. In addition to the officers described by Bowdich (see chapter 1), these same British visitors to Kumase came upon hundreds of what appeared to be junior officers wearing leopard-skin tunics covered with cockleshells. Several small blue-handled knives in silver and gold sheaths were fastened to the front of their tunics, and similarly ornamented elephant-hide cartridge belts were worn around their waists. Each man carried a gold-handled sword in a scabbard behind his left shoulder, and half a dozen brightly colored silk scarves and white horse's tails streamed from their arms, which cradled their long Danish muskets, richly ornamented with gold and red shells. When Bowdich and his companions passed by these men, they then came upon thousands of soldiers who sat so closely together that the British visitors could not pass through them without stepping on their feet, "to which they were perfectly indifferent," Bowdich wrote.[17] Each man wore a cap made of anteater and leopard skin, carried a cluster of small knives on his shoulders and hips, and wore cartridge pouches embossed with red shells and brass bells. The stocks of their muskets were covered with leopard skin. Their faces and arms were painted with long white stripes. A few wore iron chain collars that signified their exceptional bravery in past battles. Bowdich wrote that they were prouder of these collars "than of gold."[18]

Once the army was on the march, they simplified their uniforms. The ordinary troops went barefoot; most wore only a cotton cloth tied around the waist like a girdle and carried gourds of gunpowder and pouches of shot as well as their weapons. Many officers and soldiers wore cotton shirts covered with Muslim amulets intended to ward off harm. Most of these men carried maize flour, dried beans, cassava, ground nuts, and other provisions in a large skin bag slung over the shoulder, but some had food carried for them by their younger brothers or unarmed slaves. When close to their enemy, they ate only maize meal mixed with water and ground nuts in order not to reveal their position by lighting fires. Consistent with their high social rank, officers were accompanied by slaves who carried their food; some of their wives accompanied them, too. High-ranking officers were carried in palanquins under vast umbrellas. Officers and men alike let their beards grow on the march, and soldiers let their hair grow as well, often tying it up in a dozen or so foot-long spikes. Specialists joined the march as well: priests with shrines to various gods, physicians, Muslim religious advisers, diplomats, and councillors. Of special importance were medical orderlies, who treated the wounded on the field or carried them to the rear and also carried away the dead. It was important to the Asante that their dead not fall into enemy hands where they would be decapitated, leaving their souls defiled. Throughout their wars of the entire nineteenth century, the British were amazed by the ability of the Asante to remove their dead despite being under devastating fire.

At an imposing ceremony conducted before an assemblage of as many of the men of the army as could congregate in Kumase's marketplace, the king appointed a general to the command of the army by three times tapping him lightly on the head with a gold-handled sword, then handing it to him. As thousands watched, the general swore to return it encrusted with the blood of the king's enemies.[19] All Asante soldiers had already taken a sacred oath to the chief of their district pledging their obedience to him, and when the army was assembled in Kumase, these commanders in turn swore their obedience to the king. As members of the court and inner council looked on, each commander approached the king and in a solemn ceremony removed his golden sandals before he unsheathed a ceremonial sword, raised its point to the sky, then lowered it to the earth, and prostrated himself. The king placed his left foot on the commander's head and declared, "If you ever become my enemy, may the gods slay you." Rising and gesticulating with his sword, the commander then repeated the following oath: "I speak the forbidden name of Thursday, I mention the great forbidden name that if I do not help you to rule this nation; that if I ever bear false witness against you; that if I ever make war upon you; that if you summon me by night, if you summon me by day, and I do not come, then I have incurred the penalty of speaking the great forbidden word and of speaking the forbidden name of Thursday."[20] The penalty for breaking this oath was death. The king now thanked the general and shook his hand. Next, sandal bearers returned the golden sandals to the commander, who would no longer be required to walk barefoot like a slave, and there was joyous cheering, drumming and horn blowing.

One of these newly sworn commanders was a man named Apokoo, a descendant of one of the four original noble families that founded the state. Apokoo was so charming, courteous, and humorous that Bowdich was thoroughly taken by him during his visit to Kumase in 1817. His jokes were apparently as funny as they were frequent, because Bowdich commented on his excellent sense of humor. He owned many books in English, French, and Dutch, wanted to learn how to read and write, and even wanted Bowdich to teach him to box and play tennis, something the British visitors apparently spoke about in Kumase. Apokoo was fascinated by British history, especially military campaigns, and could never hear Bowdich's tales of the victorious British campaign in Spain often enough. He visited Bowdich almost daily and often invited him to dinner, occasions that the sensitive Englishman enjoyed. Yet Apokoo was first and foremost a general who had won many great victories, and he had reputation for ferocity in battle along with a taste for cruelty. His trademark was to order his prisoners' arms cut off before telling them they were free to go. (Another general was famous for cutting off his prisoners' legs before leaving them to die, and a third senior general killed his prisoners outright by crushing their skulls with rocks.)[21]

Very much like the British army they would so often confront, this was an army led by men of high social class and, often, of great wealth. The high-ranking commanders who led the Asante went to war with their stools—the embodiment of their honor, their entitlement to rule, the souls of their family and their ancestors—and these they publicly swore to defend with their lives. They were every bit as serious about this vow as their British adversaries were about swearing to die rather than allow their regimental or queen's battle flags (colours, as they were called) to fall to their enemies. British annals of war attest to the sacrifices of many officers and men who gave up their lives to save these battle flags. The Asante felt every bit as strongly about their stools, and many commanders chose to die when their stools were imperiled.

Before finally leaving for battle, Asante officers repeated an oath that they would choose death over dishonor, and after several losing battles Asante officers *did* kill themselves rather than live in shame after suffering defeat by the British. Others killed themselves rather than surrender. The common soldiers were usually astonishingly brave, but the Asante army sometimes suffered such severe reverses that these men broke from their disciplined formations despite the sword-wielding "military police" who tried to stop them. But Asante officers almost never fled. They stood by their stools and fought to the death or sometimes swallowed the poison they carried in small pouches or blew themselves up with gunpowder when defeat was unavoidable. One defeated officer tied heavy gold ornaments around his neck and dived into a river.[22] Despite the common soldiers' great bravery, it was the Asante officers who were the driving force behind the army. They were known as "pushers" (*dompiato*), because they literally drove their men from behind, exhorting their junior officers to push the slave soldiers forward to victory. The penalty for cowardice in battle was usually death, quickly inflicted by sword. Occasionally, a coward's life might be spared in return for a large monetary payment, but such a man would be forced to wear women's waist beads, his eyebrows were shaved off, his hair cut to signify cowardice, and his wife became legally available for seduction by anyone, without her disgraced husband having any right to claim damages.[23]

The most senior of the Asante officers usually remained well back from the actual combat though the battle sometimes engulfed them, and it was not unheard of for senior commanders to be killed. Usually, however, the commander sat serenely under his huge umbrella, surrounded by his retinue of priests, wives, and bodyguards. While his personal band provided lighthearted music, the commander played a board game with one dignitary or another to display his utter indifference to danger and his confidence in victory. As the battle progressed, the heads of slain enemies were brought to him to serve as footrests. The hearts of high-ranking enemies were cut out by priests and eaten by the king (if he accompanied the army, as he often did on major campaigns) or by senior officers in order to partake of the bravery the enemy had shown. After a victorious battle, the fingers, bones, and teeth of distinguished enemies would be worn as symbols of conquest.[24]

As brave and loyal as most Asante generals were, there were occasional exceptions. Several high-ranking officers were tried and executed for cowardice, and others were found guilty of stealing from the king.[25] In 1817, for example, two generals were accused by other officers of selling prisoners as slaves for their private profit as well as stealing gold that also rightfully belonged to the king. One of these men, a senior commander, was dethroned from his stool, and all his gold, land, and slaves were confiscated along with twenty-nine of his thirty wives. He was publicly humiliated by having his legs shackled to a large log for three days.[26]

Before the army could march out of Kumase on a major campaign, every religious precaution was taken to assure its invincibility. At least twelve days of ritual preparation were needed before the army could be declared ready for war. Men were provided with new talismans, especially bits of paper inscribed with Koranic verses, or strips of cured flesh taken from brave enemies. Some of their weapons were loaded with potent magical materials thought capable of weakening their enemies, and numerous dramatic protective rituals were carried out. On the eve of one great battle, the king had the bones of his recently deceased mother and sister disinterred from the royal tomb of Bantama. After they were carefully washed in a mixture of rum and water, numerous executions were carried out, including those of some prominent men, to obtain the blood needed to wash these bones and assure victory in the coming war. After the bones had been immersed in human blood, they were cleaned and wrapped in silk, strings of gold, and other valuable cloths before being reburied.[27]

Most important of all, priests were required to determine the most propitious day for the army to march. The Asante calendar was marked by perhaps as many as two hundred "evil" days during the year when no serious government business could be undertaken and the army could not march or engage in combat unless attacked.[28] Sunday was a particularly unlucky day for battle, but as events unfolded, several crucial British attacks against the Asante came on that day. September was the most favorable month for war, but few battles against the British took place during this month because it was the rainy season and the Europeans usually avoided battle during the rains.[29]

As the army made its preparations to march, women throughout metropolitan Asante stripped themselves naked, decorated their bodies with white clay, and marched through the streets beating drums. If they came upon a man who had failed to join the army, they beat him as well. They also sang songs of ridicule so wounding that war shirkers might be driven to suicide.[30] While the army was away, these women, brandishing wooden swords and guns, danced war pantomimes in the main streets of their villages to assure the safety and success of the absent men. A European witness called these women "ferocious."[31] Some wives even followed their husbands to war, where they cooked for them and, during battle, provided them with water and reserves of powder. They also encouraged them by singing songs of heroism.

The army was also accompanied by carpenters to build shelters, blacksmiths to repair weapons, and sutlers to sell food and drink. There were even moneylenders who would lend men gold dust at high interest rates so that they could make purchases from the sutlers.[32] There were also many thousands of slaves who carried supplies of all sorts from gin to gunpowder, with the value of the former being nearly as great as the latter. During battle these men waited behind the firing line, making a sound like the whistling of bullets by tapping the straw porter's pillows they wore on their heads with their fingers. These sounds were so realistic that when some European captives passed by them in 1873, they ducked their heads in fear.[33]

When the ritual preparations had been completed and a propitious day was finally identified, the army left Kumase in narrow columns of men who slowly wound their way out of the city. The size of a fully mobilized Asante army is difficult to exaggerate, and its impression on onlookers must have been profound. The one that marched out of Kumase early in 1874 to meet the invading British troops began to march by the palace at 8 A.M. The last troops did not clear the city until eleven hours later, shortly after dark at 7 P.M. (This army was more than twice as large as the Confederate army Robert E. Lee had led north from Virginia to fight at Gettysburg ten years before. An even larger army had marched to the coast in 1806.) Once the army left Kumase, it typically split into several divisions that took different routes in order to deceive the enemy about its true destination and to avoid exhausting its food supplies.

As the army marched, bands played, their horns trumpeting the power and menace of one great man after another, and "talking" drums batted out standardized messages such as one that meant, "Tomorrow we shall kill you, very, very early in the morning."[34] The horns also played well-known flourishes. One went like this:

The hero loves a fight,
The hero loves a fight,
You love a good fight, a good fight,
Fighting is good, yes . . .
Fighting is good, yes . . .[35]

In addition to these martial airs, there was good-natured bantering among the men, but discipline was ordinarily nearly as strict as it was in the tightly controlled British army. The army usually marched slowly with many halts. Some halts were made as a show of force in a tributary state, some because the rains were too heavy, and many because the day was not thought to be propitious for travel. When a large river had to be crossed, and there were many, canoes had to be found or bridges constructed by pounding four large forked tree trunks into the stream bed, placing beams along these forked pillars, then positioning cross-beams that were finally covered with four to six inches of dirt.[36] Although the army seldom chose to move rapidly, it could move at great speed when called on to do so. European prisoners who marched with an Asante army unit in 1873 wrote that they were "able to march day after day at a quick, steady pace, with short intervals of rest, and a modicum of food. They lie down to sound sleep at night, after a light supper of corn, waking refreshed and strengthened to resume their way at sunrise."[37]

Highway police maintained order along the line of march, cooking fires were prohibited when the enemy was nearby, and officers' orders were obeyed at all times, even in the heat of battle. For example, during a battle in 1824, a British officer was wounded and lost consciousness. He suddenly regained consciousness when an Asante soldier began to cut his head off. Too weak to resist, he expected to die and was amazed when an Asante officer, whom he recognized as a man he had once done a small kindness while the man was on a trading mission to the coast, ordered the soldier to stop. Despite the heat of the moment, the man immediately obeyed the order. This was only one example of Asante discipline. In battle after battle, Asante troops marched in perfect order, their guns carried at exactly the same angle, before they turned toward the enemy and fired volleys on command, the only African army that was known to do so. A European army could hardly have been better drilled, as several British officers who saw them in action observed.

Sometimes weeks at a time were spent in huge encampments where the men slept on latticelike beds with backrests and carried out camp duties such as preparing food and maintaining their weapons with great care.[38] One notable and puzzling failing was the lack of sanitation. The Asante were meticulous about disposing of human waste in their towns and villages, but the army on campaign did not dig latrines, and when it was camped in one area for any length of time, diseases such as dysentery and smallpox regularly took a huge toll of lives. Another problem was sexuality. The army might remain in a camp for weeks and even months at a time. Many officers and other men of high social rank had their wives with them, as did some of lesser rank, and they did not abstain from sexual relations at night, but most men had no women of their own, and most women in neighboring villages had either fled or were carefully guarded. Any female captives belonged to the king, who would later give them to deserving commanders, and ordinary soldiers were kept away from them on pain of death. As campaigns dragged on, tensions grew. The sounds of officers having sexual relations in their huts were not music to the ears of their sexually deprived soldiers.

As an Asante army neared its enemy, omens became especially important. If necessary, the Asante would spend days hidden in forest camps while they awaited more information, avoided "evil" days, or heeded the omens sent by dreams, flights of birds or beetles, and the advice offered by the Muslim and Asante diviners and prophets who always accompanied the army on campaign. Long before an Asante army neared its enemy, spies had usually provided its commanders with precise information about everything of military importance. These spies were sometimes in place so long that it was said that the Asante "cooked their wars" for years before they attacked the enemy.[39] For example, well in advance of a planned campaign, some Asante traders who visited a potentially hostile kingdom would publicly criticize their king and complain about Asante life to the enemy, hoping to be seen as disaffected malcontents. To reinforce their charade, some married local women and settled down to farm. When they had learned all they could about the local terrain, its defenses, and the enemy's army, they returned home to serve as guides for the Asante army.[40]

On his way to Kumase in 1816, Dutch envoy Huydecoper spent several days living in an Asante military camp. He said it was so large that a man could not walk all the way through it in a single day. While this immense army waited for orders from Kumase, the soldiers spent their time foraging for food, something they did so thoroughly that the surrounding area was soon plunged into famine. The officers had a well-developed interest in alcohol, especially the gin that Huydecoper carried with him in large quantities. A similar fondness for alcohol was shared by the dignitaries in Kumase. A large portion of the palace was used to store bottles of wine, and British visitors were served gin and brandy in such huge tumblers that they could do no more than sip while observing the Asante down theirs with no difficulty.[41] It was with difficulty that Huydecoper was able to save any of his supply of gin to present to the king—or for himself as "solace" on the journey, as he put it.[42] The camp was not disorderly, thanks partly to the use of elephant-hide whips by the officers, but the soldiers sang a great deal and became boisterous at times. Even the otherwise austere officers allowed themselves some pleasure on propitious days. Huydecoper witnessed what he referred to as "general jollification" on a "good

Sunday" (an *Adae* ceremony) when the officers danced to the music of drums, flutes, and horns all night and into the following midday.[43]

In battle the Asante were so brave that they were universally feared by other West African states and well respected by the British. They could also be brutal. They often killed women and children, and enemy chiefs were sometimes tortured to death, their bodies dismembered before being apportioned, much as an animal killed by a hunter would be. As evidence of Asante victory, the jaws of the slain enemies were taken back to Kumase where they were displayed in the palace. But sometimes they treated prisoners with kindness, as some British captives were to learn. They were also greatly concerned about their own dead and wounded. When possible, for example, they smoked the bodies of their own slain commanders over a slow fire to preserve them until they could be returned to their families for burial.[44]

Even when Asante military campaigns were successful, as most of them were, the army often suffered great losses from disease or starvation after the food resources of the conquered area had been exhausted. Nevertheless, the army's return march to Kumase was typically conducted with great discipline. A starving army can easily become mutinous, particularly when so many of the soldiers were slaves taken from other ethnic groups, but the Asante commanders were able to maintain control. Even when a campaign had not been successful, it concluded with a rousing ceremony at the royal palace. The army camped outside Kumase until the time was propitious for it to receive the acclaim of the many thousands who gathered to honor it. When the soldiers marched into the city, they were preceded by their senior officers, who carried hundreds of jaws taken from their high-ranking enemies. On one occasion when the army returned with too few jaws to properly proclaim victory, jaws taken in earlier campaigns were smuggled to them from Kumase so that their entry would appear to be sufficiently triumphant.

When the troops entered the city, they marched through the marketplace, which was filled with not only many thousands of people but every important person in the court, including the king. The soldiers were dirty and disheveled, their hair tied up in long spikes and coils, their beards unkempt—even the officers were much the worse for wear—but they were received with great applause. They fired their muskets in salute to the king, then circled around and repeated the salute. A day of mourning followed, complete with fasting, while the inhabitants of Kumase painted their faces and upper bodies red to symbolize the blood that had been spilled. The following day, rum was available everywhere, as it was during the yam festival, and many people became quite drunk but not too inebriated to be enthralled by the human sacrifices that then took place to expiate the deaths of the great men who had died in battle. Many slaves were required to die for each of the fallen senior commanders.[45] A kernel of corn representing every soldier who died was dropped into a large urn by each senior commander while the king looked on sadly, sometimes feeling a personal loss because among the dead were usually members of the aristocracy or even the royal family. He did not grieve for dead slaves, but he worried nonetheless because slave soldiers would have to be replaced, and heavy losses would invariably strengthen the power of those members of the inner council who regularly opposed the use of force as an instrument of state policy.

Britain and Asante: The Balance of Forces

As the Asante and the British marched toward battle, the Asante had a great advantage in numbers. The British were sometimes able to recruit African allies from coastal peoples, but these soldiers, however numerous, were rarely a match for the Asante in bravery or discipline. The Asante also had an advantage in jungle fighting where it was difficult for the British forces to see their enemy, much less use their usual infantry tactics, such as their famous square formation, or deploy their artillery effectively. Also, the Asante were relatively immune to the malaria that so quickly struck down all but a few Europeans.

British forces were reasonably secure in their stone forts, although not completely so as we have seen, and they were at a distinct advantage when combat took place in open country where they could deliver well-aimed musket fire at far longer range than the Asante could and were able to bring their cannon and rockets to bear long before the short-ranged Asante muskets could take a toll.

These weapons would make the difference in a large battle in open terrain in 1826. As time passed, the British advantage in weapons became even more decisive. By 1853 the Enfield rifle, accurate up to eight hundred yards, was available to British troops, and in 1866 the .577-caliber Snider rifle (that strangely enough had been invented by a New York wine merchant) was adopted. It was this weapon, along with artillery, that gave them success in the great battles of 1874.[46] When the final round of fighting took place in 1900, British forces had still more accurate and longer-ranged rifles, along with Maxim machine guns (like their precursors, the Gatling and Hotchkiss guns, also invented by Americans) and modern 75-mm artillery—weapons that with little modification were used throughout World War I to deadly effect. Most of the Asante were still armed with muzzle-loading, smooth-bore flintlock muskets.

But early in the nineteenth century when the Asante and British first clashed, their arms were relatively similar. Muskets were abundant, at least along the West African coast. The British sold guns along the coast as early as 1646, and in 1829 alone, British traders in West Africa sold 52,540 muskets and pistols and nearly two million pounds of gunpowder.[47] The Dutch sold nearly as many guns and perhaps even more powder. In 1833 alone, the Asante placed an order for ten thousand guns with the Dutch.[48] From 1870 to 1872, as the Asante prepared for impending war with the British, they purchased over eighteen thousand muskets and twenty-nine thousand kegs of gunpowder. The Asante problem was not the availability of guns and gunpowder but their poor quality.

Typically, the muskets sold to the Asante and other West Africans were shoddily made. Their stocks split easily, and their barrels were likely to burst, leading to the development of gun-repair shops operated by Asante blacksmiths to repair them. Most of the gunpowder was low in saltpeter, partly because it had been adulterated by European traders and partly because the Asante preferred weaker powder that was less likely to make the poorly made barrels of their guns explode. However, the low saltpeter content often reduced the explosive power of the powder so much that the Asante had to increase the amount they used in order to give their guns a range of even as much as forty or fifty yards. What is more, they had few bullets, relying instead on the much cheaper slugs of lead, pewter, or iron, but these had such limited penetrating power that they were only lethal at very close range.

European armies loaded their flintlock muskets in several stages. First, powder was poured down the barrel, then wadding was pushed down behind it with a ramrod; finally, a bullet that fit the barrel snugly was rammed in. Later in the century the wadding and the bullet were rammed down as a single unit. The high-quality muskets used by the British before the introduction of rifled barrels—the famous .75 caliber "Brown Bess"—had a deadly range of up to 150 yards. The Asante did not use wadding to compact the powder, nor did they have bullets that matched the size of their musket barrels. They simply poured a huge charge of powder down the barrel, then poured an assortment of lead slugs, nails, and even stones into the barrel. When they fired, this array of projectiles fanned out erratically. The first volley the Asante fired was typically the most deadly because their Dane guns had been carefully loaded before the battle. Reloading was often done by slaves, who hunched down in shelter trenches out of the line of fire and poured powder and shot down the gun barrels as rapidly as they could. The extra powder the Asante used typically caused such an enormous explosion that rather than risk bruising their shoulders, soldiers usually fired from the hip, more or less without aiming. The powerful recoil typically guaranteed that their fire would fly high over the heads of their enemies.

The inability of most Asante soldiers to deliver accurate fire was decisive in almost every battle. When British officers led trained West African or West Indian troops against the Asante, these men too sometimes fired wildly, and when they tried to rely on coastal allies like the Fante, disaster was a common result. But some of their West Indian regiments and virtually all British regiments were so thoroughly drilled in musketry that they fired as accurately as any troops in the world. In battle officers constantly reminded them to aim carefully and fire low. If Asante troops were drilled in musketry at all, there is no record of it. The closest example of target practice was recorded by the young princes of a tributary state who learned how to fire their muskets by using the nipples of young women as targets.[49] In battle after battle, the British were stunned by the volume of fire that harmlessly tore through the leaves above their heads. The Asante did fire volleys on their officers' command, but their marksmanship was dreadful.[50]

Another disadvantage for the Asante was their failure to purchase or manufacture bayonets. Bayonets were not needed against their weaker African opponents, but they could have made a crucial difference against the British. Time and again the British would save the day only by a bayonet charge. The ponderous Dane guns the Asante relied on usually took close to one minute to reload and could never be reloaded in less than thirty seconds. After the Asante fired a volley, they would usually be defenseless against a bayonet charge for a full minute. Lacking bayonets of their own, the Asante often fled. In most nineteenth century wars bayonets seldom played a major role in the outcome of battles, but the British valued them so much against the Asante that they issued a newly designed bayonet for their 1895 campaign. This weapon had a saw-toothed back for cutting jungle foliage and a broad, oval spear tip that resembled a canoe paddle and was capable of inflicting a huge wound.[51] The Asante not only had no bayonets, they did not even use swords or knives in combat, although every man carried at least one knife, mostly to cut off the heads of fallen enemies.

Despite its remarkable discipline the Asante army was anything but uniform in its dress. Officers and men alike dressed quite idiosyncratically in the field. Some wore dramatic feathers, leopard skins, and buffalo horn caps, but others wore nothing but a kind of loincloth. Hair styles varied, too, from long spikes tied up like horns to shaggy braids. The slaves spoke dozens of different dialects of Akan and other West African languages. Some were devout Muslims, and some were teenagers, while others were in their forties. What they all shared was bravery and endurance. At the start of the century this was an offensive army. Its enemies did not attack the Asante; the Asante attacked them. Surprise was much to be desired, but with such large armies, it was rarely possible. Instead, the various units of the army slowly assembled, making ready for a grand assault that would attempt to envelop and crush their enemy. Often they would shout taunts and threats against their opponents for days before the final assault came. When it came, it was signaled by thousands of voices singing defiantly, accompanied by drums and horns. Suddenly there would be a deafening roar as thousands of muskets were fired. If the enemy withstood this fire long enough, the Asante flanking forces would eventually close in and there would be a charge. The Asante army was large, well disciplined, resourceful, and above all, brave. It was more than a match for any West African army, and early in the nineteenth century, fighting in the thick forest its men knew so well, it could also be a match for the British.

✗

4

"The Bush Is Stronger Than the Cannon"

THE LARGE, MAGNIFICENTLY UNIFORMED ASANTE ARMY BOWDICH saw in Kumase in 1817 had just returned from another successful campaign against the Fante. As noted in chapter 1, the devastating military defeat the Asante inflicted on the Fante in 1807 did nothing to resolve the trade route dispute between the two states. The Fante had pledged allegiance to the Asante on several prior occasions, only to forget their oaths as soon as the Asante troops had withdrawn. When disease and hunger forced the Asante to leave the devastated Fante coastal area later in 1807, the Fante immediately boasted to all who would listen, particularly the British merchants, that they had forced the Asante to flee. Predictably, they again closed off the trade routes through their territory, forcing the Asante to trade with the more distant forts at Accra or Elmina. Determined to control trade even outside their kingdom, the Fante next besieged Accra, and although they could not take the fort, they succeeded in blocking Asante trade to the British and Danish ports there. The Asante king was given no choice but to yet again send an army to the coast where, after unexpectedly hard fighting, it drove the Fante and their allies away from Accra.

Despite the victory at Accra, the more direct trade roads through

Fante itself to Cape Coast remained closed until 1814, when King Osei Bonsu again sent a large army to make war against the rearmed and defiant Fante. Led by an aggressive general named Amankwatia IV, the great-grandson of the original general Amankwatia, the Asante won a series of battles that led them close to the coastal forts of the British and Dutch. Amankwatia was under orders not to attack the European traders, but they were sufficiently alarmed by the approach of the Asante army to propose a peace treaty that for a brief period reopened coastal trade. It was after this war scare that the Dutch sent Huydecoper to Kumase, followed shortly after by the British expedition described by Bowdich. On behalf of the African Company of Merchants, Bowdich signed a treaty with King Osei Bonsu that guaranteed peace and free trade. The signing ceremony was conducted with the utmost gravity. Accompanied by the most important men in the realm, Osei Bonsu led the British negotiators to an inner square of the palace where some three hundred of his wives sat "in all the magnificence which a profusion of gold and silk could furnish."[1] After asking Bowdich and the other British officers to stand and swear on their swords that they had told the truth, the king's councillors swore their oaths of agreement to the treaty on their gold-hilted swords before Osei Bonsu himself swore with the utmost solemnity that if he did not keep the treaty, God should kill him. He then declared that anyone violating the treaty would be punished with the utmost severity.[2] For the Asante king, this treaty, like all treaties, was a sacred agreement that everything about his understanding of diplomacy made him feel lawfully bound to follow. For the British governor, John Hope Smith, the treaty was only a means of buying time. This treaty promised peace, but it actually set the stage for war against the British.

Not surprisingly, it was the Fante who precipitated the slide toward conflict. In 1818, one year after the Bowdich treaty had been signed, a rumor circulated along the coast that an Asante army had suffered a terrible defeat in the north and that King Osei Bonsu had died in battle. While the Fante were raucously celebrating this long-awaited event, Asante emissaries arrived at the coast with the unwelcome news that there had been a great Asante victory, not a defeat. They were greeted by the Fante with derision, denied drinking water, and even pelted with stones. When the infuriated diplomats moved on to Cape Coast to complain about their treatment, Governor Hope Smith refused to listen to them, even though the newly signed treaty clearly required him to defend Asante trade interests at the coast by taking action against this kind of mistreatment.[3]

In January 1819, while Osei Bonsu and his councillors were debating their best course of action, the first British official directly appointed to the Gold Coast by the British crown arrived at Cape Coast castle. Joseph Dupuis was to serve as the first British consul at Kumase, a position that was a clear threat to the authority of Hope Smith and the British merchants, who made no attempt to disguise their hostility to him. They were so determined to undermine Dupuis that they took every possible step to prevent him from traveling to Kumase. First, it seemed that supplies could not be assembled, then carriers could not be found, no translator was available, and finally the rains came. Dupuis also suffered several protracted bouts of malaria that further delayed his departure. Frustrated by the obstacles put in his way and furious about the interference with his royal authority, Dupuis freely expressed his contempt for the "servants of a mercantile board."[4] Dupuis's keenly developed sense of self-importance did nothing to smooth relations with the merchants, and it would be twelve long months before he would finally begin his journey to Kumase.

In March 1819, while Dupuis was cooling his heels at Cape Coast, a high-ranking emissary from Osei Bonsu, bearing his golden sword of rank, arrived to ask for a meeting with Governor Smith, known to the king and his council as "Smitty." In a mild and courteous manner the diplomat reminded Hope Smith of the Bowdich treaty provision that called for the king to seek redress from the governor in the event of any aggression against Asante traders by people living under British protection. He requested that the governor punish those responsible for the mistreatment of his messengers so that the king would not have to send a punitive expedition of his own. However, when this speech was translated by a man well-known to detest the Asante, it was given a menacing tone, and the merchants' translator even fabricated an ultimatum to the effect that if nothing were done, the king would invade the coast in forty days. In fact, it was unlikely Smith was deceived by this translation because he actually knew the language well enough not to need a translator. Nevertheless, in his return message the governor not only refused to accede to Osei Bonsu's request, he sarcastically added that for all he cared, the king might come down to the coast "in forty days, or in twenty, or as soon as he thought proper."[5]

For some time the king's emissary remained at Cape Coast, terrified by the prospect of delivering this insulting reply to King Osei Bonsu. When the unfortunate man finally returned to Kumase with Hope Smith's answer, Osei Bonsu refused to believe that the British governor had sent such an inflammatory message and ordered that the messenger be tortured to determine if he had told the truth. The torture apparently proved unsatisfactory, because in June the king sent another senior envoy to the coast to determine whether the first one had told the truth. He was dismissed by Hope Smith with the curt assurance that the message was correct.

The second envoy returned to Kumase with confirmation of Smith's insult and, to make matters worse, reported that he had seen fortifications being constructed to defend Cape Coast in apparent anticipation of an Asante invasion. Osei Bonsu was bewildered and angered by this British treaty violation and troubled all the more because, although his armies were at war to the north, his inner council urged immediate war against the Fante and British. Despite their pressure he resisted precipitous action, insisting on sending yet another emissary to Cape Coast. It was a singular mission. This gold-sword messenger, a diplomat of the highest rank, reported to Hope Smith that the king denied having sent a menacing message to the governor and reaffirmed his sacred commitment to the treaty. He then added these authentically menacing points. The king, he said, could not make war against anyone with whom he had signed a treaty. He therefore sent back the treaty, the "book" as he called it, and asked frankly whether Hope Smith wanted peace or war. If peace, he demanded satisfaction for past insults. If war, then the treaty should be abrogated by the British so that he would be free to attack, no longer restrained by the principles stated by the treaty he had signed and considered binding.

Now properly alarmed, Governor Smith stalled for time, and before war could explode, Dupuis finally found his way to Kumase, carrying among other gifts one hundred kegs of gunpowder, one hundred muskets, and one hundred large kegs of rum.[6] Thoroughly in agreement with Asante demands, Dupuis rewrote Bowdich's treaty to make it more favorable to the Asante and ingratiated himself with Osei Bonsu and his court, with whom he got along famously. The king was in particularly good spirits because his two-year-long war against the rebellious district of Gyaman to the north had just been brought to a triumphant conclusion. Osei Bonsu had personally led an army of perhaps eighty thousand men against Gyaman. Many thousands of rebels were killed, twenty thousand war captives were taken to Kumase as slaves, and enormous amounts of gold were seized. Osei Bonsu used some of it to make a cast of the dead king of Gyaman's head.

Dupuis's treaty explicitly stated that all of Fante land belonged to the Asante Empire by right of prior conquest, a fine point that delighted Osei Bonsu. Unlike Bowdich, who was in such a hurry to get away from Kumase that he left in the middle of the night, became lost in the forest, and very nearly died, Dupuis found himself much in sympathy with the Asante point of view and came very close to championing their cause. He left Kumase not because he was unhappy with the king, although he did find the city squalid, but because he needed to have his treaty ratified. When he left, Osei Bonsu gave him two young leopards in a cage and fifty Asante children. Dupuis accepted the leopards (which the British called tigers) but politely declined the gift of children.

When Dupuis arrived at Cape Coast after a hurried journey, he discovered to his surprise and great distress that Governor Hope Smith and his council of merchants flatly refused to ratify this new treaty, even though it had been negotiated by an appointee of the crown. That was only one of the rebuffs Dupuis encountered. He had returned to the coast with several high-level Asante ambassadors, whom he had invited to accompany him to England for the formal treaty ratification. He had also invited them to present themselves to King George and deliver gifts to him from King Osei Bonsu. The Asante government was delighted by the opportunity to establish direct relations with the British sovereign, and had such a meeting taken place, it might well have opened the door to a lasting peace. But to Dupuis's horror and outrage, neither

Governor Smith nor the British naval officer in command at Cape Coast would hear of any such mission, and Dupuis was forced to sail by himself, leaving the embittered Asante ambassadors and their gifts behind, an insult that greatly strengthened the hand of the war party in Kumase.[7]

The British merchants had clearly overstepped themselves. No sooner had Dupuis returned to London than the British Parliament passed a bill abolishing the African Company of Merchants and transferring all its assets to the crown under the control of Sir Charles MacCarthy, the former governor of Sierra Leone. Unfortunately, this change in governance would not improve British-Asante relations. Sir Charles would soon lead his forces into an embarrassing defeat in which the British would lose prestige and he would lose his head.

MacCarthy arrived at Cape Coast in March of 1822 to a gala reception by the local people grandly accompanied by a royal salute fired from the fort. Sir Charles had been a competent governor in Sierra Leone, and before leaving London to take up his new duties, he had met with Dupuis, who did everything he could to impress upon him the urgency of creating friendly relations with the Asante. But once MacCarthy settled in at Cape Coast, what he heard from the Fante and the merchants who still remained there was decidedly at odds with Dupuis's views. MacCarthy quickly came around to the local opinion that the Asante were untrustworthy, bloodthirsty savages whose power had to be destroyed as soon as possible. Without even sending a courtesy message to King Osei Bonsu informing him that he had succeeded Hope Smith as governor, much less the gifts that custom required, MacCarthy prepared for war.

While Osei Bonsu attempted to restrain the more bellicose members of his inner council, MacCarthy sent a clear signal of his own intentions. He began to fortify Cape Coast, convinced Accra to stop selling powder to the Asante, and began a troop buildup. He was soon able to assemble three companies of British army troops and also had available three companies of the 2nd West India Regiment, former African slaves led by British officers. In addition to these regular troops he began to recruit and arm an African militia officered by some of the British merchants.

Faced with this dramatic evidence of British hostility, Osei Bonsu could hardly have held out much hope for peace, but he nevertheless continued to take extraordinary steps to avoid war, until an unforeseen event overtook him. In May 1822 an African sergeant stationed near Cape Coast quarrelled with an Asante trader so vehemently that he hurled verbal abuse at the Asante king, a capital crime under Asante law. Sometime later, a small detachment of Asante troops captured the sergeant and took him fifteen miles inland to a village friendly to the Asante. Still searching for peace, Osei Bonsu granted a pardon to the man, but members of the war party in his inner council issued orders for his execution, apparently without Osei Bonsu's knowledge.[8] When Governor MacCarthy learned of the execution, he led a force of British regulars and militia to attack the Asante who remained in the village where the execution had taken place. Whether due to treachery, fear of the Asante, or simple ignorance, their guide led the British force away from the village and into a well-prepared ambush. The British troops were forced to retreat with ten dead, thirty-nine wounded, and nothing accomplished.

Even after this armed clash, which he had not ordered, King Osei Bonsu sent out another appeal for peace by offering to negotiate all differences between the Asante and the British. His offer was contemptuously rejected. Only then, in June 1823, did the king allow his army to advance toward the British along several routes. For reasons that remain unclear, their progress was unusually slow, and they did not actually threaten the British at Cape Coast until early January 1824. Governor MacCarthy responded to the Asante advance by dividing his regular troops and now well-armed militia into two columns that marched toward the Asante. Unfortunately for the British, Sir Charles ordered the columns to march so widely separated from one another that they could not possibly coordinate their actions. Then, in a decision that would prove to be even less wise, he personally led a small force of five hundred men detached from his larger column of two thousand five hundred men directly into the main Asante battle force of between ten thousand and twenty thousand men commanded by the redoubtable veteran Amankwatia. Against this powerful army Sir Charles mustered a handful of British army officers all wearing scarlet and white dress uniforms, a regimental brass band, two hundred fifty semitrained Fante militia led by some of the British traders (also in scarlet uniforms), and an equal number of completely undisciplined Fante under their own chiefs, the most senior of whom was so feeble that he had to be carried the entire way. Each man carried only twenty rounds of ammunition, although they were followed by carriers bringing more.

After marching through driving rain and mud, Sir Charles camped on the banks of a small tributary of the river Pra, where he was joined by his chief of staff, Major H. J. Ricketts, and a few men who had marched all night through mud that was often waist deep. Ricketts expressed concern about the exhaustion of the troops and their small numbers, but Sir Charles was sublimely confident, saying that "he was determined to see how the Ashantees liked our balls."[9] (Presumably he was referring to musket balls.) The next day the Asante could be heard moving toward them through the dense forest with drums pounding and elephant horns blaring. MacCarthy's splendid scarlet uniform was splattered with mud, but as a very stout man who stood well over six feet tall even without his plumed hat, he was still an imposing figure. As the Asante came closer, Sir Charles ordered his own brass band to play "God Save the King," and they loudly set themselves to it while he stood at attention. He was under the singularly misguided impression that many of the Asante were eager to surrender to him. To the surprise of no one except Sir Charles, none did, and their drums and horns sounded even more loudly in reply. After several exchanges of martial music with each side attempting to drown out the other, the Asante tired of the musical prelude and unceremoniously opened fire.

Luckily for MacCarthy and his men, the Asante were separated from the British force by a sixty-foot-wide stream that was in flood. The Asante attempted to cross it by felling trees to use as bridges, but leaving themselves completely exposed, they were repeatedly shot down. However, after an hour or so of firing, the British were virtually out of ammunition. Sir Charles had earlier sent for the reserve supply that should have long since arrived. Now quite alarmed by his situation, he was delighted by the arrival of a man named Brandon, who was in command of the ammunition carriers. His joy soon vanished. Unused to the tricks of West African warfare, Brandon had not driven on his Fante carriers from the rear; he had dashed on ahead of them with a couple of men and a few cases of ammunition. Once free of Brandon, the remaining Fante promptly set down their loads and fled. Sir Charles was so appalled that he threatened to have Brandon hanged, but there was no time to waste in hanging poor Brandon; some men were sent back after the abandoned ammunition while others tore open the four cases Brandon had delivered. The ammunition from the first case was distributed while the other cases were being opened. In what was an unforgettably absurd moment, the cases were found to contain not bullets but macaroni.

By now the river had subsided somewhat, and this, combined with the slackened British fire, allowed groups of Asante to cross over. Most of the armed Fante promptly fled, but other groups of MacCarthy's men fought with bayonets, knives, and clubbed muskets. Despite the desperate fighting the battle was quickly over. Taking advantage of the deep underbrush, Major Ricketts and a few of the men were able to escape, but the other British officers were killed or captured, and except for Williams, the colonial secretary (mentioned in chapter 2), who was saved by an Asante officer who knew him, all were beheaded. MacCarthy, or "Mankato" as his name was mispronounced by the Asante, could not have impressed anyone by his leadership in taking such a small force against an Asante army; but he had fought with great courage and, badly wounded, had shot himself rather than be taken alive. In respect for his bravery, after beheading him, Asante commanders cut his heart out and ate it.[10]

In all, 9 British officers were killed along with 178 men. Three officers and 89 men were wounded, some later to die. How many prisoners were taken is not known. Williams was held for some months but then released in reasonably good health despite the well-meant efforts of Asante doctors to extract a bullet from his thigh by squeezing it out with ligatures tied around the leg, one above and one below the wound. The procedure was as excruciating as it was unsuccessful. Another officer named Raydon was killed on the return march because he could not keep up. A merchant named Jones, who was serving as an officer of the Fante militia, was also captured after suffering five wounds. The Asante believed that anyone with five wounds was so defiled that he endangered others and must be sacrificed, and he was.[11] A few weeks later, another large British force, including white troops supported by native militia, fought to a standoff against the same Asante army. On the British side 176 men were killed and 677 wounded. Two white soldiers were known to have been taken prisoner. It seems that three British soldiers had made off with enough rum to make themselves almost insensible when Asante troops found them in the bush. One man drunkenly charged at the Asante with his bayonet and was decapitated. The other two were taken to Kumase where they were well treated by the king. One died of disease after a year. The other, a private named Riley of the Royal African Corps, was released in good health after four years of captivity and returned to Britain.[12] It is not known why these men were taken prisoner instead of being killed or why there was no demand for ransom.

After this battle, the main British forces, complete with their regular troops, withdrew to the coast, and the Asante army made no attempt to interfere. Their inaction was probably due to the death of Osei Bonsu. For many years historians had delighted in reporting the delicious historical irony that he had died on the same day as Governor MacCarthy, but it now seems almost certain that he died sometime earlier.[13] Probably not yet fifty when he died, Osei Bonsu had devoted his reign to peace. The Europeans who came to know him praised the king for his honorable character and his good intentions toward the British. Even some of the British merchants eventually came to respect him highly. John Swanzy, who fought in battles against Asante troops, expressed this opinion before a select committee of the House of Commons: "I think, of all the native sovereigns of Africa that I have either read or heard of, he is the man most likely to act with good faith."[14]

With Osei Bonsu's death the long-frustrated war faction of the inner council succeeded in electing his younger brother to the Golden Stool. There were other possible successors but none as warlike or hostile to the British as Osei Yaw, also known as Okotu (orange) because of the light color of his skin.[15] One of his first proclamations was that he would use the blood of the British to "water" (consecrate) the grave of his brother.[16] By the time Osei Yaw had been "enstooled" in Kumase, the surviving British forces had retreated to the protection of the cannon and the stone walls of Cape Coast castle. It was fortunate for them that they did so, because no sooner had Osei Yaw taken power than he marched south with a large new army to join General Amankwatia's smaller force, which was still in the coastal region. The combined forces, now under direct command of the new king, numbered nearly thirty thousand men.

Demonstrating immediately how different he was from his peace-loving late brother, Osei Yaw sent a messenger to the fort advising the British to build the fort's walls higher and take every available cannon and man from the warships off the coast because he, King Osei Yaw, would soon throw every stone from the fort into the sea.[17] For three nerve-wracking weeks the British forces strengthened their defenses while the Asante army made menacing feints toward Cape Coast. From the fort, smoke from their fires could be seen rising along a line three miles in length, and for two days Asante troops maneuvered grandly just out of range of the fort's guns. The following night Osei Yaw planned to burn the town that lay just outside the fort's walls and in the ensuing confusion storm the fort in the darkness. The plan was betrayed to the British, who preemptively burned the town to the ground during the day.[18] Thwarted, the Asante attempted a weak frontal attack against the town, which was broken off after a stray British cannonball grazed the palanquin in which the king was being carried. Thoroughly intimidated by this evidence of the British ability to locate him despite the thick jungle foliage, the suddenly timid new king ordered his army to return to Kumase. Despite a worrisome outbreak of smallpox among the soldiers, his officers protested this order, and a high-ranking woman member of the royal family sent Osei Yaw a musical instrument, one played only by women, with the message that in exchange for his sword, which he had dishonored, she was giving him a more appropriate implement.[19] This ridicule was too much for the new king, who agreed to continue the campaign until the countryside was completely destroyed, and his army ravaged Fante villages until late in 1824, when disease and hunger again forced the Asante army to withdraw to Kumase.

After a year of peace, the still-combative Osei Yaw again mobilized his army in December 1825. He was determined to punish his former Accra allies, who had been turned against him by Governor MacCarthy. Following the traditional religious preparations he ordered his army south in early January 1826. Once again he took personal command. For seven months he devastated the countryside, meeting no serious opposition. His losses were principally to disease, and he made these up by enlisting the aid of soldiers from the Akim and Assin people, groups whose loyalty was split between the Asante and a newly forged British alliance of coastal peoples. Early in August, his army was camped at Katamanso, just south of a village named Dodowa, a little more than twenty miles north of the seaport of Accra, the target of his campaign. He planned to attack his British-led African enemies on the following Monday, a propitious day for the Asante to give battle—as his opponents knew, and they prepared their defenses accordingly. The day may have been lucky, but the circumstances were hardly ideal for the Asante king. He also chose to attack with only a part of his army. Perhaps not over ten thousand men joined in the attack. His men would be outnumbered by the British force, although some of latter were Akim or Assin soldiers of unknown loyalty. The terrain also favored the British alliance. It was open grassland, and the Asante king's men would be exposed to British cannon fire long before they could charge into their ranks. To the king's advantage was the disciplined courage of his men; how well the British coalition would stand against them was uncertain, but experience must have convinced the king that they would not stand very well at all.

The British-led force of over eleven thousand men consisted of Africans from several tribes, including a contingent of Fante. Sixty British officers and noncommissioned officers led by Lieutenant Colonel Purdon coordinated the defense. Two years earlier the British government had sent three hundred British soldiers to Governor MacCarthy, but their susceptibility to disease proved to be devastating. (The first company of one hundred British troops arrived at Cape Coast in April 1823; eight months later only one man was still alive. The second company of one hundred men arrived in November 1823; one year later only eight men were alive.

Most of the third company died within three months! During the same period fifteen white officers also died of disease. Forty-two wives and sixty-seven children accompanied the men, and they died in similar numbers.)[20] The British government was understandably reluctant to commit more white soldiers or their families to Gold Coast graves. As a result, Colonel Purdon had to depend on the ability of his British officers to train African militia to defend the coastal populations. One of these officers was the same Major Ricketts who had survived the wounds he suffered in the MacCarthy battle to return to the Gold Coast.

Throughout the preceding seven months, while the Asante army was rampaging through the coastal countryside, Purdon and his officers were frantically recruiting, arming, and training men from their African allies. By August Purdon had a reasonably well armed force that, for the moment at least, appeared willing to fight. In addition to the African soldiers' muskets and knives, Colonel Purdon had several cannon and an ample supply of the newly invented Congreve rockets. He also had excellent intelligence about the movements of the Asante, who were uncharacteristically open about their intentions. Purdon took up a defensive position some eight miles south of Dodowa on an open plain. If the Asante meant to attack, as Asante prisoners said would soon happen, they would have to charge across flat and open grasslands. Purdon positioned his men along a line that stretched over four miles. His best trained militia were in the center, backed up by British officers and sixty Royal Marines who had just disembarked with their own artillery and rockets. Large tribal contingents were on each flank under the command of their kings.

It was a colorful army by any standard. Each contingent camped under the battle flag of the European nation to which it felt allegiance: many British, Dutch, and Danish flags waved in the slight breeze. Each man wore white sea shells or a strip of white calico to distinguish himself from the Asante; some tied the calico to the barrels of their muskets. There was much singing, dancing, and drumming, but there was still no certainty that this coalition would stand and fight. The Asante army was in position by Sunday, but on that day everyone knew they would never attack. Hoping that the Asante king would not outflank him tomorrow and that the kings of his coalition would not decamp overnight (something that would almost certainly have occurred if the squabbling kings had been given another day to quarrel among themselves), Colonel Purdon waited for Monday morning to arrive.

He need not have worried about being outflanked. King Osei Yaw's scouts had informed him that the strongest African coalition forces were in the center, reinforced by the British officers and marines. He decided that his honor called for him to attack the center because it was the strongest part of the British line. He rejected the urgings of his advance guard's commander, Yaw Opense, to attack at night under torchlight, insisting instead that he would defiantly show himself to his enemies in the morning light. He also asked his commanders to give up their hammocks and lead from the front rather than push from the rear, an altogether unconventional idea. But then, this would be an unconventional battle. After his men painted their bodies with white stripes, the attack came on Monday morning, at the gentlemanly hour of 9:30 A.M. The Asante moved forward in disciplined ranks, also waving British, Dutch, and Danish flags along with many others of their own design. With drums pounding and horns playing, the Asante charged through heavy cannon fire toward the British center. Many men fell before the front rank drew near enough to kneel and fire a return volley. The British forces returned fire, and before either side could reload their long muzzle-loading muskets, the two shouting and screaming armies were tangled up together in a savage hand-to-hand knife fight that lasted for over two hours. The British militia fought courageously but were being forced back when the British left and right flanks overcame initial defeats and began to drive the Asante flanks back.

Despite these reverses miles away on either flank, the Asante troops in the center appeared to be on the verge of victory. The situation was so serious that several of the African kings made plans to blow themselves up, and one British officer prepared to blow up his gunpowder to keep it out of Asante hands. At this critical point in the battle, Colonel Purdon ordered his Congreve rockets into use and dozens of these new weapons began to arch deafeningly through the sky trailing red sparks and smoke before they landed with tremendous explosions that sent jagged shards of metal in all directions. The Asante might have stood their ground despite the terrible wounds the rockets' fragments produced, but the red flashes followed by the sound of explosions convinced them that the British had called down the force of nature's thunder and lightning against them. This was too much.[21] Slowly, and in reasonably good order, the Asante center fell back.

As the British-led African militia pursued, they ripped open the bellies of wounded Asante and tore out their hearts. They also clubbed their own wounded to death to end their suffering. As it became obvious that the battle was lost, several Asante commanders ignited kegs of gunpowder and blew themselves up, in one instance slightly wounding some nearby British officers. The once faint-of-heart king, Osei Yaw, had been in the thick of the battle, and suffering from seven wounds, he was sitting quietly, preparing to die, because in the confusion of the retreat, the man responsible for guarding his stool had lost it. Several brave Asante officers dashed back into the thick of the battle and returned with it in triumph. Despite his wounds the king would survive the battle.

The Asante rear guard now moved up to protect the army's retreat, but the British-led forces were far more interested in collecting the spoils of war than they were in pursuing the still-dangerous Asante. About two million dollars worth of gold, including one nugget weighing twenty thousand ounces, and other valuables were gathered up along with many prisoners.[22] By now the long, dry grass was on fire, and although it is impossible to recapture the scene of the battle or its sounds adequately, Ricketts recalled the day this way: "the explosion of Asante captains, who at intervals blew themselves up in despair, which was known by the smoke that arose over the trees; the shouts and groans of the combatants, with the burning grass, and the battle raging all around, formed no bad idea of the infernal regions."[23]

At around one in the afternoon, the severed heads of prominent and even royal Asantes were brought into the British camp. A great stir was caused when what was thought to be the skull of Sir Charles MacCarthy was discovered. Carried in a leopard-skin cover, the skull was wrapped in paper covered with Arabic characters and a silk cloth. Ricketts reported that before the battle King Osei Yaw had poured rum on it and invoked it to cause all the heads of the whites to lie beside it on the battlefield. Delighted to have recovered MacCarthy's skull, Lieutenant Colonel Purdon had it sent to England. Embarrassingly, the skull proved not to be that of Sir Charles MacCarthy at all, but that of the late King Osei Bonsu. His younger brother had taken it into battle with him in the hope that it would offset the effect of an omen that had warned the king not to launch the campaign.[24] All that night the wails of Asante women searching for the bodies of their loved ones could be heard in the British camp.[25]

Probably because they fought in front of their men instead of in the rear, at least seventy Asante divisional commanders and princes were killed or committed suicide. Several thousand Asante soldiers died with them, and many others, like the king, had grievous wounds. Despite these dreadful losses the army retreated in order, ferrying its men across the flooded Pra River without incident. There were many reasons for the Asante defeat. Their army was outnumbered by men with better arms, and they attacked the strength of the British line. The British rockets were a terrifying and deadly weapon that they did not understand. Also, smoke from the grass fires and the musketry was so thick that one of the two divisions of the Asante center mistook the other for the enemy and fired on it throughout the battle. Their Akin and Assim allies also fled at the first sign of fighting, leaving the Asante left flank vulnerable. Not least important, the British-trained African militia fought with unexpected resolve. It was a humiliating loss for Osei Yaw, especially because as a result of the defeat, he was forced to re-nounce his sovereignty over six southern states, including his most detested enemy, the Fante.

Though it was clear that Osei Yaw had lost an important battle at Katamanso, Asante military power had not been seriously com-promised. As the new British governor, Sir Neil Campbell, wrote after visiting the battleground and talking to some of the officers who took part in it, the extent of the Asante defeat had been "grossly exaggerated." In his view, despite the size and stalwart de-fense of the British-led coalition forces, the Asante had "repulsed" them and were on the verge of victory; only the rocket fire saved the day.[26] Sir Neil also chided the British officers and the kings of the alliance for allowing their African allies to cut open the chests of the dead and wounded Asante to eat their hearts. The well-intentioned new governor had much to learn about warfare on the Gold Coast.

Not everyone in Kumase was as willing to minimize the Asante defeat as Sir Neil did. So many men and women of influence in Kumase were openly hostile to him that Osei Yaw stayed out of the city and had to arrange to have many of his enemies killed. Believing that Muslim clerics had used magic to ensure his defeat, the king had many of these men arrested, and he banned all Muslims from entering the palace, a step that did much to destroy their influence with the court.[27] Even so, he could not avoid an impeachment contest, and Kwadwo Adusei, a leader of the peace faction in the inner council, began proceedings to have the king removed from his stool. Osei Yaw responded by accusing Kwadwo Adusei of a series of offenses from giving bad advice on strategy to outright treason. After a long and divisive contest Kwadwo Adusei was found guilty and was humiliatingly executed by being pounded to death in a mortar by an elephant's tusk.[28]

But in the political maneuvering that led to the king's exoneration and the execution of his main adversary, Osei Yaw was forced to make major concessions to the peace faction. In addition to agreeing not to launch any more military expeditions to the south, he even authorized a diplomat to approach the British about peace terms. The envoy wore a monkey-skin cap bearing a five-inch by two-inch gold plate on which gold weighing scales were beautifully etched. As he approached the British governor, he laid the cap at his feet as a symbol of submission to the king of England.[29] Even though the Asante king offered an apology and reparations, the coastal chiefs and kings remained skeptical.

Nevertheless, after extensive negotiations a draft of a treaty was formulated, and the Asante peace mission that had taken it to the coast returned to Kumase to be received by two hundred thirty senior chiefs. The treaty called for the king to renounce all warlike acts against the south, as well as the right to tribute from the maritime states under British protection. The king was required to deliver to the British governor four thousand ounces of gold and two members of the royal family as hostages to guarantee the treaty. In return the British guaranteed to restrain the coastal states from all acts of aggression against the Asante state and its traders. The Asante government was disposed to accept the terms of this treaty, but before all of its terms could be worked out, various chiefs of the British protectorate attacked and blockaded Elmina, the Dutch coastal station where the Asante had traditionally conducted trade. When the British could do nothing to lift the blockade, the treaty was left unsigned. In a series of meetings with British envoys in metropolitan Asante in 1828, Osei Yaw made it plain that he did not believe the British were negotiating in good faith. He emphasized his desire for peace but declared that the next move must come from the British.[30]

That move was taken in 1829—the same year that Sir Robert Peel introduced "bobbies" to cope with London's crime—when the British government, frustrated by the futility of its efforts to rule the Gold Coast, gave the administration of the area back to the merchants. The first president of the newly formed merchants' council did nothing even to attempt a peace settlement and was asked to step down from his office. Nothing further happened until February 1830, when Captain George Maclean of the Royal African Colonial Corps became the second president of the newly established merchant council in Cape Coast. Unlike his predecessors, Governor Maclean immediately opened negotiations with Osei Yaw, while he used everything in his power—which at that time consisted more of the force of his personality than military assets—to intimidate the Fante. While Charles Darwin sailed along the coast of South America in the *Beagle*, a treaty consisting of the same terms proposed two years earlier was signed in 1831. Maclean would not change the world the way Darwin did, but he would change the Gold Coast, giving it sixteen years of welcome peace and free trade.

Maclean is one of the most remarkable figures in the history of British colonial relations in Africa. He ruled at a time when the British government had almost no interest in the Gold Coast. He possessed a pitifully small police force of one hundred twenty men to control all of the maritime people of the Gold Coast, and yet he managed to control them with what very soon amounted to absolute authority. He was not only the ultimate policeman, but without any official judicial authority, he quickly became the judge to whom everyone brought the most difficult cases. Known for his scrupulous impartiality, his judgments were obeyed. He was patient, courteous, and wise, the rare British official of that time who actually respected and liked Africans. He was also utterly fearless, often facing down truculent opponents at great risk to his own life. When one local chief defied him, Maclean led his one hundred twenty policemen on all-night marches to surround the offending village. Just before dawn broke, the sleeping offenders were easily taken into custody. Without legal authority over the peoples of the Gold Coast because no official protectorate had been declared by the British government, Maclean nevertheless established his authority over a large and populous area along the coast, and his positive influence was felt throughout the inland area controlled by the Asante and their tributary states. So grateful were the Asante for Maclean's ability to enforce peace that they gave him a nickname that meant "the white man in whose time all slept soundly."[31] The king was so grateful to Maclean for protecting Asante trade interests that he regularly prayed and conducted sacrifices to assure his good health.[32] His good health lasted until 1847 when he died of dysentery.

His remarkable successes on the Gold Coast notwithstanding, Maclean was vilified in some circles in England because his wife, a well-liked poet, died suddenly only a few months after joining him at Cape Coast castle. It was rumored that she committed suicide due to his mistreatment of her or his philandering with African women. A British merchant who was there when she died disputes this, insisting that she was perfectly happy the evening before she died and that she died of a congenital heart defect for which she was taking medication.[33]

Osei Yaw died in 1834 and was succeeded by his nephew, Kwaku Dua I. As much as Maclean was respected in Kumase, he was not the only representative of a European power to receive a favorable hearing there. The Dutch had always been sympathetic to Asante interests, and in 1836 they became so impressed by the success Britain had achieved in recruiting West Indians into their army that they decided to emulate them by recruiting Asante men into the Dutch Army to serve in Dutch colonial possessions in the East Indies.[34] They asked King Kwaku Dua I to receive a high-ranking emissary, Major General Jan Vermeer, who hoped to establish a permanent army recruiting station in Kumase. In return General Vermeer would promise the delivery of firearms. The request was accepted, and Vermeer arrived in Kumase in January 1837 with one thousand men and a military brass band. He reported that he was greeted by a crowd of sixty-seven thousand people, a suspiciously precise number, but the crowd was clearly a large one. Vermeer gave the Asante king two thousand guns in advance, and the king gave Vermeer two of his nephews to accompany him to Holland, apparently as collateral. One of these boys had an unhappy life and committed suicide, but the other became a successful engineer and never returned to the Gold Coast.[35]

The king also sent a few recruits to Elmina who were described as good and strong men, but he asked the Dutch for more muskets and some cannon as well as all manner of presents, including fine silverwork. General Vermeer, now back in Holland, had established as Dutch resident in Kumase the same W. Huydecoper who had visited in 1816. Huydecoper found himself sandwiched between the king, who demanded more and more from the Dutch while he produced fewer and fewer recruits, and Vermeer, who angrily demanded that matters be set straight. Huydecoper was also horrified by the numbers of people who were beheaded, as well as some who were hanged and, Huydecoper wrote, partially eaten. By the time the recruitment station was closed in 1842, largely due to British protests, just under two thousand Asante, almost all of whom were war prisoners, had been recruited and sent to the East Indies. Many of these men later returned and settled around Elmina.[36]

Although there were many threats of war during the reign of Kwaku Dua I, he was devoted to peace and managed, although sometimes with difficulty, to avoid open warfare with the British despite their vacillating policies after the death of Maclean in 1847. Although he did nothing to reduce the numbers of humans who were executed or sacrificed, Kwaku Dua was a wise and prudent king, who continued Osei Bonsu's policy of trade and peace. He even went so far as to consider allowing British missionaries to open a mission in Kumase. In response the Reverend Thomas B. Freeman was the first European missionary to visit the capital. After a preliminary visit in 1839, when he preached the gospel despite his sense of horror at the headless bodies he so often reported seeing in the dirt along the roads, he returned with a large entourage in 1841, bringing with him a carriage similar to the ones used by European aristocracy. Even though the roads were remarkably well maintained, getting the carriage across the two hundred or so streams and rivers was no small achievement, and Freeman was delighted that King Kwaku Dua I was pleased by the gift. So pleased, as it turned out, that he maintained the carriage in immaculate condition for at least five years, although in the absence of horses, it was pulled by men.

The carriage was only one example of a dramatic pattern of gift exchange between Europeans and the Asante kings. Gift exchanges were not present in many parts of Africa, but for the Asante and their European suitors they were obligatory. Early in the eighteenth century the Dutch and English were sending gifts as diverse as plumed hats, gilt mirrors, general's truncheons, four-poster beds, flags, magic lanterns, clocks, silverware, silver-topped canes, all manner of garish uniforms, and, not least, a glass coffin. Much of the material given to Asante kings was little better than junk and was of so little use to them that they stored hundreds of items away in the stone palace, a kind of museum for European exotica. In return Asante kings often presented gifts of far greater value to the Europeans. For example, former Royal Navy Commander Governor Sir William Winniett, who replaced Maclean in 1848, gave King Kwaka Dua I £300 worth of gifts in return for which the king sent 550 men to him bringing bullocks, sheep, pigs, fowls of various sorts, and all manner of food. Winniett characterized the gifts as "magnificent."[37]

Kwaku Dua invited the missionary Freeman to a sumptuous dinner, to which the king wore an elegant European brown velvet suit with silver lace, a white linen shirt, white satin trousers, and a silk sash around his waist. Two golden knives were suspended from a chain around his neck, and another large gold chain coiled six to eight times around his neck before hanging down to his waist.[38] A middle-sized man of about thirty-six who, unlike most wealthy Asante, neither smoke nor drank, the king was courteous to Freeman and was satisfied about the missionary's good intentions. Freeman returned to the coast convinced that a mission would be established, but in his absence conservative Asante resistance to Christian influence grew, and it would be more than a half century before a Christian mission actually opened in Kumase.

During Governor Winniett's visit to Kumase in 1848, King Kwaku Dua took him to task for British newspaper accounts that characterized the Asante as bloodthirsty savages addicted to human sacrifice. Winniett was surprised that the King knew anything about the British press and was not able to appease Kwaku Dua.[39] From this time on, relations grew more troubled, but no serious rift took place until 1862 when an elderly and wealthy Asante citizen was accused of hoarding gold nuggets rather than conveying them to the king, their rightful owner. Rather than risk facing trial in Kumase, this man fled to the British protected territory along with many of his retainers. King Kwaku Dua requested his extradition, as he had a treaty right to do, but Richard Pine, the new governor, was convinced of the man's innocence. A lawyer himself, Pine was torn between the treaty, which required extradition, and his conscience. Pine refused extradition, and Asante pleas went unanswered.

That there had been no armed conflict between the Asante and the British since 1826 is truly extraordinary. During this thirty-six year period the world was hardly a peaceful place. America fought a war against Mexico and began its terrible civil war, much of West Africa was torn by tribal wars, and Britain fought colonial wars in Canada, Aden, Afghanistan, Lebanon, India, South Africa, Burma, Persia, China, New Zealand, Bhutan, and Ethiopia, as well as the horrible Crimean war against the Russians. The Asante fought states to the north during this period, including a three-year war against the Gonja that was raging while Freeman and Winniett were in Kumase. The Asante and the British were anything but unwilling to wage war, but until Pine's fateful decision, they had lived in peace with one another for over three decades.

Reluctantly, King Kwaku Dua I, fundamentally a man of peace, felt obliged to assert his treaty rights. Over the objection of his councillors, who recommended further negotiation, the king uncharacteristically called for mobilization, and the inner council finally agreed. An army of as many as sixty thousand men commanded by Owusu Koko, the son of King Osei Bonsu, moved south with little opposition. After brushing aside some troops from a rival state, advance units of the Asante army came up against a native army bolstered by four hundred disciplined troops led by a British major named Cochrane. Instead of facing the Asante as his men urged, Cochrane ordered a retreat, leaving behind a rear guard that was easily overrun. This shameful performance left the Asante with a clear path to the coast. But before launching a major invasion of the south, General Owusu Koko offered Governor Pine another choice—extradition of the wanted man or war. Pine chose war, declaring that he would fight "until the Kingdom of Ashantee should be prostrated before the English Government."[40] For someone with very little military force, this was an incautious threat. But before the Asante general could make up his mind to order an attack, the rains came, and he withdrew his army to Kumase. The king was so angry that he ordered a court of inquiry into the conduct of Owusu Koko and his senior commanders, at least one of whom was executed for dereliction of duty.[41]

Pine was aware that his luck could run out if he did not establish a strong military force. The cost of maintaining a large native militia was beyond his means, and Britain rejected his appeal for two thousand regular white troops. Still, Pine was determined to show the flag, and he eventually decided to march the troops he had— men from the 2nd, 3rd, and 4th West India Regiments, six hundred in all—to the Pra River. The troops marched during the dry season and built a fortified camp well supplied with arms, ammunition, and food; but even during the dry season neither the West Indian troops nor their white officers had great enthusiasm for their role. A force of this size could not possibly cross the Pra to invade Asante territory, nor could it hope to stand very long against a determined Asante attack. More likely, an Asante army would simply bypass their position and sweep on to the coast. When the rains returned, the health of the men quickly deteriorated, and soon many were down with malaria and dysentery. As soon as the rains abated enough to allow travel, the entire force straggled back to the coast, leaving behind their only partially destroyed supplies, cannon, and stores of ammunition. Not a shot had been fired. King Kwaku Dua was amused, remarking that "the white men bring cannon to the bush, but the bush is stronger than the cannon."[42] Pine's failed gamble left British prestige at a new low. A noted Gold Coast historian wrote, "Never did any enterprise end in such utter failure."[43]

It was a costly failure for the British, and it left them in a politically precarious position, to be sure, but it was to have tragic consequences for the Asante as well. It led them to doubt the willingness of the British government to send white soldiers to the Gold Coast, and when a powerful British force threatened to invade the Asante homeland a decade later, the Asante rulers underestimated the killing power of British weapons and the resolve of their leaders.

Pine's war was such a failure that the British government was at a loss as to how to proceed. Simply to withdraw from the Gold Coast was an unacceptable alternative, but the Asante and British were still technically at war, and there was little hope that their differences could easily be reconciled. Trade was disrupted everywhere, the Asante war faction was stronger than ever, and the entire Gold Coast was on the verge of war when in April 1867, at the age of seventy, King Kwaku Dua I died suddenly in his sleep. While various political factions struggled to enstool their respective favorites as king, many people, including some members of royal family, had to be sacrificed to accompany Kwaka Dua to the next world. One of those killed was the nephew of Asante's most powerful general, Amasoa Nkwanta, who had reorganized larger Asante units into twenty-man platoons and had invented the rapid reloading procedures for muskets by using slaves. Nkwanta was so outraged that he threatened to raise an army and march on Kumase. He finally agreed not to do so after a close relative of the man who had killed his nephew had been executed in retaliation, but he refused to have anything further to do with the army for almost six years.[44]

After three months of bitter infighting, a successor to the kingship was chosen—Kofi Kakari, Kwaka Dua's sister's daughter's son, a legitimate heir but hardly the only contender. Deciding on a new king always brought powerful factions into competition, but in the end the new Asante king was chosen by an electoral majority, if not a consensus. This time the second most powerful man in the kingdom, General Owusu Koko, was in no mood for democracy. He arranged to have Kofi Kakari kidnapped and held in seclusion while he pressed his own claim to the stool. Koko was found out, convicted by a court, and sent into exile.[45] Only then did Kofi Kakari become king. Known to the British as "King Coffee," Kofi Kakari was thirty years old when he was enstooled. He was of medium height, had a full beard, and was said to be handsome except for some smallpox marks on his face. He was typically pleasant, courteous, and considerate to his European prisoners, who came to know him well. But the Asante court was no place for a pleasant young man with no military experience. His predecessor Kwaku Dua I was a much older, widely respected sovereign, who was gifted at the palace intrigue necessary to control the aggressive and competitive generals and war hawks who sought to control policy. When necessary, he could dominate them by the force of his personality and authority. Kakari was incapable of controlling his "elders," as he called them, and he was fearful that he would appear weak before the generals who had chosen him to be their king. Puzzled and intimidated by the intrigues of the royal family and the great men who elected him to office, he told the captive missionaries, Ramseyer and Kühne, that his ascendancy to the throne "was like a dream to him."[46] He was also dominated by his priests and Muslim advisers, whose insistence on divination, human sacrifice, and religious ceremonies was usually repugnant to the men of the inner council, who much preferred secular political decision making.

The new king soon made more enemies through his wanton sexual debauchery. He not only collected a huge harem of legitimate wives, he often made sexual advances to the wives of powerful men. To secure the favors of these women, he lavished so much gold on them that the previously vast treasury was quickly depleted. His uncomplimentary nickname was Osape, "one who scatters gold."[47] When he was enstooled, it is said that he promised his people, "My business shall be war." Whether he actually said this is not certain, but he did wear a cap covered with flints, a traditional symbol of war, and war would in fact prove to be his business.

Kofi Kakari's first crisis was the Fante blockade of the Elmina people who lived in the area surrounding the Dutch fort of the same name. The Elmina were ancient allies of the Asante who had long provided them with military protection in return for tribute and free trading access to the Dutch. In 1868 the new king sent two large armies, one of which he commanded in person, along with a smaller one to relieve the Elmina and destroy the Fante coalition of allies. Fante resistance was unexpectedly resolute, and desultory fighting dragged on into 1869. In the course of events, one of several Asante forces took two mission stations, capturing a French trader and two European missionaries, one of whom had a wife and infant. Once these people arrived in Kumase, Kofi Kakari treated the hostages well, but although the Asante soldiers who escorted them proved to be quite kind, the officer who commanded their escort to Kumase was so harsh that all the adults suffered badly and the baby boy died. Asante villagers were kind to the white captives throughout their long and hard march, and when the Ramseyer's son died, they somberly placed flowers in his hands. These Europeans were valuable pawns for Asante diplomacy, and while the war was bogged down in inconclusive battles, the king attempted to trade their freedom to the British for an end to the Fante blockade of Elmina. The British felt great concern for the hostages' welfare, but these people were not British subjects, nor were they captured in British protected territory. As a result, the British were uncertain about what steps they should take. Before negotiations could advance very far, the situation took a dramatic change. The Danes had sold their fort at Accra to the British in 1851, and now in late 1869 the Dutch decided to sell them their fort at Elmina.

The unending warfare near Elmina had completely disrupted Dutch trade, and it was now threatening Dutch authority altogether. The Dutch government decided to cut its losses and leave the Gold Coast to the British, who despite the turmoil, were interested in the Dutch proposal. When the Asante government learned of the negotiations between the Dutch and English, it quickly protested, pointing out that the Elmina fort was the king's possession and the Elmina people were his subjects. In support of his position was the fact that the Dutch had paid rent to the Asante every year since 1702, and the Elmina people recognized the Asante state as their protector. Indeed, the original treaty signed by Bowdich and the Asante in 1817 explicitly acknowledged Asante sovereignty over the Elmina people. Undaunted, Dutch authorities permit-

ted the Fante to seize and deport the senior Asante representative
to Elmina along with his large staff, all of whom were forced to
leave their possessions behind. The Dutch handed the job of over-
seeing the deportation of the Asante mission to a British Royal
Marine colonel, whose men treated them roughly. When they later
told their story in Kumase, the Asante government was furious.[48]

British negotiators were concerned about the Asante claims of
dominion over Elmina, but the Dutch airily dismissed them, asserting that the money paid annually to the king was not rent but
wages, because he was their employee. The British disingenuously
accepted this patently absurd Dutch explanation, and the treaty
was signed. In response Kofi Kakari sent another message to the
Dutch protesting the treaty and reasserting his rights to Elmina. In
what was scarcely better than an insult, the Dutch sent a young,
semiliterate African clerk named Henry Plange to Kumase to induce the king to waive his rights to Elmina. We know from the European hostages in Kumase that Plange did arrive in Kumase and
meet with the king on more than one occasion. He also left a
crudely written journal purporting to describe his negotiations.
However, when he returned to Elmina, what he presented to the
Dutch was anything but crudely written. It was an elegantly
phrased "certificate of apology" in which Kofi Kakari waived all
rights to Elmina. The certificate was a preposterous forgery, but it
was happily accepted by the Dutch and British, who ratified the
treaty early in 1872.[49] Shortly thereafter, the British took over
Elmina fort, and after 274 years of continuous residence, the
Dutch left the Gold Coast. The seeds of war had been sown.

The Asante had been stockpiling muskets, gunpowder, and lead
in earnest since 1870, and there could have been few people in the
Asante government who did not believe that war was near.[50] One
of the many reasons why some Asante wanted war was the senior
generals' jealousy of a somewhat junior commander, Adu Bofo,
who had achieved a signal success in a relatively small campaign to
the east. The Ewe people of what is now Togo to the east of the
Gold Coast had been openly rebellious toward the Asante, and
their discontent was threatening to spread to other districts closer
to Kumase. With an army of fifteen thousand men, Adu Bofo
crossed the Volta River, utterly smashed several Ewe armies, and

returned to Kumase with tons of booty and thousands of prisoners, including the French merchant Marie-Joseph Bonnat and missionaries Johannes Kühne, Friedrich Ramseyer, his wife Rose, and their infant son.[51] When the Europeans protested that they had nothing to do with the war, Adu Bofo disingenuously replied, "I am the slave of my King. I must send you to them."[52]

The power of the Asante state had declined since the visits of Huydecoper, Bowdich, Dupuis, and the others earlier in the century, but the pomp of the king and his court was as majestic as ever. Soon after their arrival in Kumase, the ragged European prisoners were led toward the king by an officer carrying a gold-hilted sword in a leopard-skin scabbard and wearing a magnificent fan-shaped tuft of eagle feathers in his cap. After bowing to the king and removing their hats, the prisoners were allowed to sit while a seemingly endless procession of notables passed before them. The loud, clear tones of elephant-tusk horns vied with flutes and drums as the silk-robed, gold-bejeweled chiefs passed by. Heralded by eighty men—each wearing a monkey-skin cap adorned with gold—dwarfs, buffoons in red flannel shirts, and sixty boys—each wearing a Koranic charm sewn into leopard skin—King Kofi Kakari arrived, carried in his throne chair under a rust silk umbrella as pages fanned him. His arrival was marked by even louder music, including thirty boys who kept time by shaking calabashes filled with pebbles. He was followed by hundreds of executioners of all ages, each with two knives slung around his neck, who danced along behind him to the dismal three beats of a drum that signified death.

Boys with swords, fans, and elephant tails danced around the king, shouting at the tops of their voices, "He is coming, he is coming. His majesty the lord of all the earth approaches!" The king wore golden sandals, a richly jeweled turban, a yellow silk toga, and dozens of golden bracelets and pendants. Six pages guided him along, crying out, "Look before thee, O lion! Take care, the ground is not even here."[53] King Kakari stood staring at the Europeans, apparently the first whites he had seen, before dismissing them with a kindly expression and moving on. This panoply of regal power was nothing out of the ordinary. King Kofi Kakari was not personally fond of pomp, but such processions were commonplace in Kumase where there always seemed to be an occasion to reaffirm the king's supremacy. This was often done by displaying an assortment of European clothing and musical instruments. On one procession there was a fife-and-drum corps dressed in Danish and Dutch uniforms, a band playing cymbals, clarinets, and European snare drums, while various dignitaries marched along wearing fragments of European clothing. According to the captive missionaries, ". . . one had a scarlet coat, but no trousers; another wore a long dressing gown, reminding one of a German university professor; one of the generals was in a brown velvet dress and sash, another had proudly donned a field marshal's hat and white cockade, while to the lot of a third had fallen a woman's undergarment, in which he found it somewhat difficult to walk."[54] One supposes that the impression made on the Asante audience was rather more favorable than that made on these Europeans.

Wearing a cap with bull horns and falcon feathers, the general, Adu Bofo, soon after returned to a huge welcoming celebration in Kumase that lasted five days. The shaggy-haired returning soldiers, dressed in oddments of Asante and European clothing, followed their officers, who wore battle-soiled red and yellow coats covered with amulets and antelope-skin caps decorated with feathers, gold emblems, and religious charms, past a huge throng of people who overflowed the vast marketplace. As each unit passed before the king, the men stopped and fired a salute. As usual, the onlookers were streaked with red paint to symbolize the blood of the men who had died, and as the magnitude of the losses became clear, many sobbed and shrieked in mourning. The next day was spent in mourning. The red painted men and women of Kumase fasted, cried, and drank large amounts of brandy provided by the king.[55] Although 136 senior officers had died in the campaign, Kofi Kakari rewarded General Adu Bofo with gold, many slaves, and large tracts of land.

Generals senior to Adu Bofo furiously demanded the opportunity to demonstrate their own military genius and to achieve the same honors and wealth. The British at Elmina were an obvious target. They made their case to the king and inner council by assuring one and all that the British were incapable of opposing them.[56] With the help of many well-placed friends, Amankwatia IV, the son of general Amankwatia III, lobbied successfully for his own command to reoccupy the British protected southern states lost after the defeat of 1826. For the Asante inner council the decision for war was not difficult. Their economic interests were at stake, the coastal people were too weak to resist, and the British did not seem to have the resources or the will to intervene.[57] Governor Pine's humiliating defeat was to have a terrible legacy. Even so, it was not until October 1872 that the national assembly called for war and the generals announced that they would march to the coast. The king grandly replied, "If you go, I shall go with you."[58] After prolonged ritual preparations an Asante army that may have numbered eighty thousand men marched south in December 1872. Despite his pledge the king did not accompany them. In fact, he was personally opposed to the war and was angry when his council overrode him. By September this huge force was encamped only five miles from Cape Coast. Led, as expected, by General Amankwatia IV, the army was so well established that it had replanted abandoned Fante farms and built huge camps. At that time there was no food shortage.

They soon began to launch a series of small-scale forays toward Cape Coast itself. Newly arrived troops of the 2nd West India Regiment, along with British marines and sailors led by a valiant and intelligent Royal Marine lieutenant colonel named Festing, did what they could to oppose them, but Festing had such limited troop strength that he could do little more than defend the fort and Elmina town. Later, some hot skirmishing developed, and the Asante learned a deeply troubling truth: while they were still armed with their cumbersome, inaccurate, and short-range muskets, the British marines and West Indian soldiers now had powerful artillery and carried rapid-firing, breech-loading rifles that could kill at long range. One senior Asante general was so appalled by the disparity between the weapons of the two armies that he urged peace. Asante soldiers complained that the new British rifles could kill five men at long distance with a single bullet, while their own flintlocks were worthless beyond point-blank range. Nevertheless, other officers and men were more than willing to fight and were frustrated because no general attack had been ordered against Elmina.[59] While Amankwatia hesitated, the food supply gradually became exhausted, and by October disease was again ravaging the army. According to one Asante prisoner, their situation had become desperate.[60] Their major camp at Mampon was a mile square and probably held twenty thousand men. Supplying that many men for a long period was a logistical impossibility. For a while crops could be stolen, purchased, or even grown, but all too soon food would run out. Eventually, too, large camps would breed disease. Amankwatia's son died of smallpox shortly before the general finally agreed to retreat.[61]

Amankwatia had long refused to attack Elmina, and now he appealed to Kumase for permission to withdraw his sick and dissension-ridden army from the coast. King Kakari rebuked him with this harsh reply: "You wished for war, and you have it; you swore you would not return till you could bring me the walls of Cape Coast, and now you want me to recall you because many chiefs have fallen and you are suffering. It was not I; it was you who wished it."[62] The king also insisted that he would not recall his disgraced general until the many chiefs who advocated war agreed to repay him for the costs of outfitting the army. They finally agreed, but when Amankwatia heard the king's message, he drank himself into a stupor and had to be carried to his quarters. Nevertheless, despite being harassed by small British forces that initiated several sharp skirmishes, the orderly withdrawal was carried out with such skill that a British officer wrote that any European army would have been proud of the accomplishment.[63] By early December 1873 the entire army had crossed the Pra River into metropolitan Asante.

The Asante army had not suffered defeat, but neither had it accomplished anything of note, and King Kakari now faced a dangerous political climate. His dispirited generals and soldiers were demobilized and some were so rebellious that they openly threatened not to go to war again. Members of the peace faction were again listened to in the inner council. And although the king did not yet know it, while his troops had been threatening the coast, officials in the British government had decided not to negotiate peace with the Asante in good faith but to destroy their power once and for all.

5

"Does It Not Make One's Heart Ache?"

WHILE GENERAL AMANKWATIA IV WAS CONSIDERING WHETHER HE should withdraw his army to Kumase and the king and his inner council were debating their options for peace or war, the British government had been implacably preparing for war. In late July 1873 the colonial secretary, the Earl of Kimberly, received a letter from a former Royal Navy captain, John Glover, recently an active entrepreneur on the Gold Coast, offering to raise an army of Africans and lead them up the Volta River to the east of the Asante and eventually attack Kumase from the northeast. Glover had earlier demonstrated his ability to raise and lead native troops in the area, and Lord Kimberly eagerly accepted his plan, agreeing to supply arms, money, and a few British officers to serve under the captain. But before Glover's expedition could get underway, the government decided to appoint a British army officer to command all British armed forces in the Gold Coast, including those led by Glover, and to serve as civil governor as well. The man chosen was Colonel Sir Garnet Wolseley, who, while in the Gold Coast, would hold the rank of major general and the title of governor.

Wolseley's selection came as no surprise. As early as August 1873 he had been asking everyone he could in London for information about the Asante, and he soon became convinced that Asante imperialism badly needed a stern lesson in the folly of opposing British military might. He proposed the idea of leading a punitive expedition to Kumase to his patron Sir Edward Cardwell, Prime Minister Gladstone's secretary of state for war. Colonel Wolseley had been Cardwell's principal adviser as he pushed through far-reaching reforms in the British army after its many weaknesses had been exposed in the Crimean War, where, incidentally, Wolseley had been blinded in one eye by a shell fragment. Cardwell convinced Lord Kimberly that the expedition was needed and that Wolseley was the man to lead it. The decision was a fait accompli. Remarkably, there was no cabinet discussion of the expedition until two months later, and Parliament was not consulted at all.

Many in the army were less than thrilled by Wolseley's selection. He was seen by many of his superiors as too young at forty (King Kofi Kakari was thirty-seven) for this rank, too brash, and worst of all, largely responsible for the reforms that most older officers detested. Yet no one could deny that he had fought bravely in four campaigns, had been heavily decorated, and had been wounded many times as well. In addition to his blind eye, he still occasionally suffered great pain from a leg wound, received in Burma, that had never fully healed. Short, slight, with a receding chin, he did not look the part of a distinguished general, but those officers who had served with him earlier could not wait to volunteer for this campaign, and hundreds of other officers applied for temporary leave from their regiments to serve as special-service officers under the young general. Wolseley handpicked his officers from candidates representing the most distinguished regiments in the British army. Those he finally selected were mostly young men he already knew well, and he proved himself a great judge of talent. Without exception the men who served with Wolseley proved to be energetic and brave, often astonishingly so. Many were also notably intelligent, a trait less common among British officers of that time than bravery; it was a common joke among European armies to refer to the British army as "lions led by donkeys." Most of the officers who survived the Asante war went on to perform with great distinction in Zululand, the Sudan, South Africa, and World War I, and almost all of those who survived achieved high rank.

Wolseley and his "ring," as his young special-service officers were known to sneering senior officers, immediately attempted to learn everything they could about the Gold Coast and the Asante. They discovered precious little. Asante—or Ashanti as it was then known—was hardly a household word in Britain, even among highly educated people. When one of Wolseley's officers mentioned to a civilian shipmate that he was on his way to fight the Asante, the man, who had been educated at Rugby and Cambridge, asked "What part of India is Asante in?"[1] It was especially irksome to Wolseley's officers that there were no decent maps of the Gold Coast available, and although they read Bowdich's, Dupuis's and Hutton's accounts of their trips to Kumase a half century earlier, they somehow missed their description of hills and rolling terrain near the coast. As a result, Wolseley intended to build a railway inland from Cape Coast and actually had many tons of rails shipped there from England. It was to prove a comic and costly misadventure. However, Wolseley's men did learn that during the rainy seasons no European army could hope to campaign effectively on the Gold Coast and that disease was a terrible threat.

Perhaps no military commander before or since has given disease so prominent a role in planning his campaign. Wolseley was well aware that the Gold Coast was known as the "white man's grave," and as he went forward with planning his campaign, he was seldom allowed to forget it. For example, when he asked an old West African hand what he should take to the Gold Coast, the answer was "a coffin, you won't need anything else."[2] He also learned to his dismay that earlier in the nineteenth century the surgeon general of the British army estimated that the life expectancy of a British soldier on the Gold Coast was one month! Elephantiasis and Guinea worm were endemic at the coast, and both smallpox and yellow fever were common. Many died of dysentery, but the greatest killer of Europeans was malaria, or fever as it was simply called. At the time, no one knew that malaria was carried by anopheles mosquitos, but the disease's association with rainy weather, swamps, and tropical vegetation was widely observed. Most contemporary physicians believed that it was caused by poisonous vapors exuded by swamps and rotting vegetation, but others believed it to be the result of a lack of ozone in moist and fetid tropical air. Some seriously recommended the use of a Rube Gold-berg–like instrument called an ozonometer to measure the ozone content of Gold Coast air.[3]

Mosquito-repellent oils and lotions were available to the British army, but only a few officers used them. Some officers carried mos-quito nets, and one officer wore a brown veil during the campaign, but the veil was intended to filter out poisonous vapors, not defend against mosquitos. There were no nets, veils, or repellant oils for the soldiers. Wolseley's ignorance about the role of mosquitos in the transmission of malaria can hardly be held against him since the scientific community did not become aware of it until more than twenty years after this campaign.[4] What is more, Wolseley's personal experience gave him good reason not to suspect mosqui-tos as disease vectors. A few years earlier he had led the British troops on a summer campaign in the mosquito-infested forests of Canada without a single man falling victim to fever.[5]

It had been known for centuries that quinine offered some pro-tection against malaria, and Wolseley would order all his white troops to take quinine under supervision every morning. It is not clear how large a dosage they took (probably one grain), but it would prove not to be enough. Wolseley also planned his invasion for the dry season when fever was said to be less common, and he arranged that his troops would spend the shortest time possible in the Gold Coast. He also made elaborate preparations to provide healthy campsites for his men. Every night on the march the men would sleep in roofed huts on bamboo beds raised off the ground so that they would not become wet or chilled (both were thought to bring on fever), and each camp was provided with a huge sup-ply of logs so that immense fires could be kept burning throughout the night to dry the air and keep the deadly vapors at bay.

Captain Huyshe, an otherwise healthy young officer who had served with Wolseley in Canada, believed in the prophylactic pow-ers of cold tea. He died of malaria. Captain Maurice, an intellectual officer who survived the campaign to write a book about it, be-lieved that the key to avoiding fever lay in not drinking too much alcohol—or too little.[6] Maurice also recognized the value of qui-nine but, like many other officers, stopped taking it because of its side effects, which included dizziness, deafness, loss of memory, and a pounding sensation in the head.

When malaria struck, it did so suddenly, almost without warning. One moment a man was capable of performing his duties, the next he was incapable of any activity except writhing in his bed with a fever of 105° or 106°, followed by agonizing chills that no number of blankets could assuage. Sleep was impossible for days at a time, and those who recovered commonly referred to their bout with fever as the most painful experience of their lives. Too weak to care for any of their needs, unable to eat or sleep, they experienced terrifying delusions of being attacked and devoured by horrific demons or beasts. They also became obsessed with the need to carry out some trivial task that they were too weak to perform. When the fever finally abated and the delirium was replaced by sleep, men were so grateful that they often wept. Wolseley himself had a severe case of malaria. After terrible suffering he returned to duty, but not until two weeks had passed. He had been delirious for six full days.[7]

Wolseley's precautions undoubtedly saved many lives, but malaria remained a terrible enemy. Before he even left the coast, he had to leave two hundred men behind because they were too ill to march inland, and after the campaign's last battle as many men had to be invalided to the coast for malaria as for battle wounds (12 percent in each category), and more men died of malaria than of their wounds. Fully 59 percent of the European troops contracted malaria, and 71 percent suffered from some debilitating illness.[8] One who died of malaria was the popular Captain Alfred Charteris, the oldest son of Lord Elcho, who collapsed soon after making a heroic long run in great heat to deliver a message. Taken on board a hospital ship, he received the preferred therapy of having his head shaved and a huge blister raised on it to reduce the fever. He died soon after.[9]

In November 1873 Gladstone urged Wolseley to make peace without entering Kumase, but Wolseley had already decided in favor of destroying Asante power, not simply by defeating its army in a decisive battle, but by destroying Kumase, thereby "leaving our mark of victory stamped in the country."[10] To accomplish his mission, Wolseley was not prepared to rely on African soldiers, as Glover proposed to do; he wanted "English" troops, as British battalions were typically called in those days. He asked the government for two battalions of British infantry (one thousand three hundred men), sixty men of the Royal Artillery with four mobile mountain howitzers, and forty Royal Engineers to join his fifty volunteer special-service administrative officers from various regiments.

Wolseley's request for British troops alarmed the government, which was all too aware of the dangers of disease. But he did not stop there. Instead of asking for two regular battalions, he made the extraordinary request for handpicked officers and men, that is, those best suited for combat in the tropical rain forest of the Gold Coast. In many armies this would have been a reasonable request, but not in the British army, which had always been organized by battalions (two to a regiment), each of which had long traditions, enormous pride, and the belief that it was the finest fighting force on earth. The idea of breaking up the regiment, much less the battalion, was akin to breaking up a family. Wolseley's scheme was rejected. If he was to receive British troops at all, and this issue was still in doubt, they would fight as battalions.

In the end the government was unwilling to commit British troops to Wolseley at all, and the general was told that he and his ring were to sail to the Gold Coast alone. If Wolseley found that he could not defeat the Asante with the troops available at Cape Coast, he could again request British troops, but only with a compelling justification of why they were needed, how their health would be safeguarded, and how victory would be assured. Before sailing, Wolseley drew up a remarkable list of supplies to be shipped to Cape Coast. In addition to 6 howitzers, 1,000 Congreve rockets, 4,000 Snider rifles, and 3,200,000 rounds of Snider ammunition, he asked for 30 foghorns and 100 railway guard whistles. The abortive railroad plan explained the whistles, but the foghorns remain a mystery.

Instead of their scarlet tunics or their kilts, Wolseley wisely decided that all officers and men (if any were to be sent) would wear uniforms of drab gray homespun, cork sun helmets, and long hobnailed boots. This was the sort of break with tradition that infuriated many senior officers. Officers were also to leave their swords behind, carrying sword bayonets instead, weapons that could also be used to hack away jungle vegetation. No officer could bring more than fifty pounds of gear, the maximum that Wolseley believed a native carrier could manage, but Wolseley and his officers did not impose any such limit on themselves. A reporter who sailed with them wrote that "no equal number of men ever started upon a warlike expedition with so immense a train of impedimenta," including generous supplies of whiskey, champagne, and wine.[11] He did not note, however, that they were denied the right to a soldier servant, an unusually spartan way to go to war.

Wolseley's orders were to demand that King Kakari withdraw his forces from the British protectorate, make reparations to the Fante and other coastal peoples for injuries and losses, and give securities for lasting peace. If diplomacy should fail, Wolseley was to threaten war, secure in his government's promise of sufficient force to compel the Asante to agree to British terms. Wolseley was given discretion to negotiate peace terms as he saw fit, and he was given permission to ask the Asante for high-ranking hostages to be held until their promises were kept. He was also told to do what he could to put an end to human sacrifice and the slave trade in the Asante kingdom (no mention was made of ending these practices in the British protectorate where they were also commonplace). There was no mention of marching on Kumase, much less destroying it, but that is what Wolseley was determined to do.[12]

Wolseley, his officers, and several newspaper reporters, including the famous Henry Stanley who had found Dr. Livingston, sailed from Liverpool on September 12th on board HMS *Ambriz*, a ship that disgusted even the most stalwart of these hardy souls. The berths had been painted with enamel only twelve hours earlier and smelled appallingly, there was foul-smelling bilge water several inches deep in the cabins, and the old ship tossed sickeningly. The voyage south was the most miserable any of them had ever experienced. While Wolseley and his shipmates were enjoying a welcome stopover at Madeira, they learned of an incident that put the Gold Coast on the front pages of newspapers all over Britain. In July Royal Navy Commodore Commerell arrived at Cape Coast aboard HMS *Rattlesnake*, the first of several ships to arrive with fresh Royal Marines and West Indian troops. Early in August it was rumored that Amankwatia was moving troops close to the Pra River near the coast and was planning to cross the river in force. Unable to obtain any useful intelligence from Fante spies, who were terrified at the thought of approaching closely enough to Amankwatia's army to learn anything of significance, Commerell decided to make a reconnaissance up the river in small boats. Hugging the right bank of the river to stay as far away as possible from Asante scouts thought to be on the left bank, Commerell's boats were about a mile and half upriver when a fusillade of shots erupted from the right bank at a range of only ten yards. Four men were killed and six officers and fourteen men wounded, Commodore Commerell among them. British public opinion blamed the Asante for this ambush, but in fact the shots were fired by men of a coastal people sympathetic to the Asante.[13]

When the *Ambriz* finally arrived in Sierra Leone, several officers were sent off to recruit African soldiers and supply carriers. Wolseley had his first contact with Africans there, and it confirmed his prejudices. He wrote to his wife that "the Negroes are like so many monkeys; they are a lazy, good-for-nothing race."[14] Soon after arriving at Cape Coast, he declared that "the African" was an "objectionable animal" who was intended to be "the white man's servant."[15]

Wolseley and his men had arrived at Cape Coast on October 2nd to find it in a state of panic. The Asante army had crossed the Pra River and was encamped nearby, and there were no more than one hundred West Indian soldiers to defend the town. Wolseley had counted on finding three hundred well-trained Hausa soldiers armed with powerful .57-caliber breech-loading Sniders at Cape Coast, but these men had been taken up the Volta River by Captain Glover, who had arrived there ahead of him. The general was not pleased. The one hundred men Wolseley did find belonged to the 2nd West India Regiment, small detachments of which were stationed elsewhere on the coast. These were well-armed and disciplined troops, even though their uniforms did much to belie it— they wore scarlet fezzes and jackets with yellow braid, baggy black pantaloons and yellow gaiters. These uniforms were so unsuited to tropical warfare that they were replaced by the same gray homespun and pith helmets to be worn by British troops. The West Indians were proud of their new uniforms. However, they continued to amuse British officers by their practice of carrying loads on their heads with their pith helmets perched precariously on top.

As might be imagined from his comments about Africans, Wolseley had little confidence in them or other black soldiers as fighting men. However, he did attempt in vain to recruit fighting men among the Fante, which is perhaps just as well, because he had few weapons to arm them with and they had no will to fight. When skirmishes did break out, they regularly fired at other British-led African militia rather than the Asante, and they were characterized by one British officer as "infinitely worse than useless."[16] He rapidly sent word to the fleet offshore that he was in urgent need of men and weapons. Marines and sailors armed with Sniders came ashore, bringing with them artillery and rockets. Cape Coast was quickly entrenched, and General Wolseley soon felt secure enough about his defenses that he actually hoped the Asante would attack against his massed firepower.

Instead, without orders from Kumase, General Amankwatia decided to attack the fort at Elmina. He provided his men with at least one thousand boarding ladders to scale its walls but failed to understand how murderous British cannon and rifle fire could be. At least one thousand men died in the assault on Elmina castle, and many others died in several smaller battles that followed. Small numbers of Royal Marines, sailors, and West Indian soldiers engaged small units of Asante troops in battles that invariably began with the sounds of the Asante's characteristic "singing cheer," followed by the voices of their officers urging them on. When the firing ended, hundreds of Asante lay dead. The first of the *Ambriz* officers to die was Lieutenant Eardley Wilmot, whose arm was so badly shattered that surgeons later said it would have had to be amputated had he lived. Yet he led his troops for a full hour with his arm dangling in excruciating pain until he was shot through the heart.[17]

After one of these battles, an incident took place that illustrates the favorable attitude that many Asante had toward the British at that time. A British officer came upon a half-dozen men from the British-led African soldier militia grappling with a short, powerful Asante soldier whom they had disarmed but could not quite kill. The Asante soldier fought them off with amazing strength as some men battered at his skull with their musket butts while others tried to hold him down. A uniformed Hausa soldier was so intent on finding an opportunity to slit the man's throat that he did not notice a British officer's arrival. The white man immediately punched the Hausa in the ear with such force that he toppled over, and the Asante took the opportunity to hurl himself at the British major and grasp his hand. The Asante thought that the white man would save him, and he was right. It was obvious that most Asante, at least, were sincere about not wishing to fight the white men, and British officers still believed in taking prisoners.[17]

While Amankwatia negotiated with Kumase for permission to withdraw his sick and hungry army from the coast, many of his men conducted trade with their allies the Elmina and again threatened the small British garrison at Elmina fort. Wolseley boldly decided to disrupt their trade. Gathering 150 Royal Marines, 29 sailors, 126 Hausas (an ethnic group from northern Nigeria, but also the name the British applied to many Africans from that general area), and along with nearly 200 men of the 2nd West India Regiment accompanied by 300 African supply carriers, he marched his men twenty-one miles along the beach toward Elmina. The marines who had been on board ship under dreadful conditions quickly became exhausted, but a large case of red wine was sent ashore, and they were soon said to be "new men," as a newspaper correspondent who marched with them wrote.[18] This was not quite right. The sweat-soaked, dehydrated men were barely able to stagger into Elmina fort, and all of the officers with them soon fell ill.

The battle that followed was inconclusive, but it thrilled a veteran newspaper man who witnessed it:

> It is difficult to describe that human tornado which raged for half an hour over half a mile of African bush. The enemy were on all sides, and the firing incessant. The air was all flame and smoke, and filled with various sounds—the booming of guns, the whizzing of rockets, the cracking of Sniders, shouts, groans, laughter, the whistling of slugs; Haussas chanting verses from the Koran, English hurrahing; and then, as the village began to burn, the roaring of flames, explosions of powder, and blazing of rum.[19]

Despite the heavy firing there were apparently few casualties on either side, although Wolseley's chief of staff, Colonel John Mc-

Neil, suffered such a severely shattered wrist that he had to be invalided home. Wolseley was sickened by the sight of McNeil's mangled wrist, but McNeil stoutly tried to stay in the fight. His only comment to Wolseley was, "An infernal scoundrel out there has shot me through the arm."[20] Wolseley used this encounter to confirm his convictions about the uselessness of African troops. The Hausas had fired wildly, and to some extent so had the West Indian troops, leading Wolseley to write to the secretary of state for war that he could not defeat the Asante without English troops. Insisting that their health would not be jeopardized, he asked that these troops be sent at once.

Wolseley could not estimate how long it would take for his message to reach London or, for that matter, what the response would be. As it happened, his dispatch sat at Cape Coast for two weeks before a ship arrived to carry it to Madeira where there were telegraphic facilities. While he waited, Wolseley encouraged his officers to intensify their attempts to recruit African soldiers and supply carriers. It was an unrewarding effort. One Fante chief's response to a request for men was characteristic: "I have got smallpox today but will come tomorrow."[21] He did not.

Early in October Wolseley wrote to King Kakari, demanding that he withdraw his army, release all captives, and guarantee indemnification. If he did not agree to do so within twenty days, Wolseley warned him to expect "full punishment."[22] He sent three copies of the letter, all of which were intercepted by Amankwatia's men. Instead of forwarding this ultimatum to the king, the general wrote his own reply, in quaint English, asserting that his quarrel was not with the British but with four tributary states that had fled Asante rule to live under the protection of the British. He concluded by saying, "There is no any quarrel with you. I send my love to you."[23] Wolseley wrote back, thanking the general for his friendly disposition, but reminded him that the original letter was meant for King Kakari.

As this confused correspondence passed back and forth, the British officers continued their efforts to interest coastal people in fighting the Asante. One officer's comments typified the experience: "I had the greatest trouble with him as he is a true type of the lazy, palm-wine-drinking, good-for-nothing African, who, like all the other native petty princes, has got the idea into his head that the European officers are to do all the real hard work of running about all over the country collecting troops, while his majesty lies all day on his back smoking and drinking. Their total apathy, indifference, and want of energy, is almost maddening to me at times, for neither princes nor people appear at all anxious to go to war."[24] Despite this widespread lack of enthusiasm for war, some men, many of them Fante, began to arrive at Cape Coast to serve as supply carriers. Fante men were universally scorned for their indolence and cowardice; their most remarkable trait was said to be an ability to sleep so soundly that no amount of physical pummeling could rouse them.[25] Fante women, on the other hand, were praised for their cheerfulness and their willingness to carry heavy loads. One Fante woman attracted special attention. Young officers persisted in visiting the newsman Winwood Reade to ogle his voluptuous next-door neighbor, a young woman named Jessie who proved to be frustratingly faithful to her absent husband.

Wolseley did not yet know whether an army would be sent from England, but he knew that he would have to prepare for one by collecting large numbers of Africans to carry supplies and make a road for the army to march along. Beginning as soon as they could, his engineering officers supervised several hundred men in widening and clearing the same road that Bowdich and Dupuis had used on their journeys to Kumase. Not only was the road badly overgrown, it had to be widened to allow four men to march abreast. There were few tools at first, few men as well, and heavy rains often slowed their work. No fewer than 237 streams and rivers had to be bridged if Wolseley was to reach Kumase, and the challenge of chopping down huge trees, then sawing them into usable lumber in 90° heat, put the British engineering officers to a life-threatening challenge. Exhausted, they nevertheless pushed ahead, never doubting that British soldiers would soon need the road they were building with their malaria-racked bodies. Many would die of the disease. Voracious biting ants sometimes interrupted the work, grunting leopards made men nervous at night, huge spiders spun webs that could envelope people as they slept, and slate-colored rats as large as rabbits scrabbled away at them in search of food. Their almost frantic efforts were not helped by African militiamen who tore down bridges for firewood as soon as they were built, defecated on the road, and left tree trunks lying across the road after felling them to no useful purpose.

General Wolseley's hopes for a railroad had to be abandoned when it was discovered that the astonishing amount of six and a quarter miles of rails already delivered could not be laid because the land was far from being level. A railway engine was converted to use tractor tires, but it had only gone a few yards before it tumbled over into a muddy ditch and was abandoned. The railway was set aside, much to the derision of newspaper men who wondered why the idea had been entertained in the first place. That Bowdich, Hutton, and Dupuis had all noted the presence of valleys and hills was not lost on the newsmen, and the decision to build a railroad when time was so much of the essence and laborers were so difficult to obtain was also ridiculed.[26] It was not one of Wolseley's better ideas.

As the Asante army slowly withdrew to the north, Wolseley fumed in his dispatches to London that he lacked the troops to strike a serious blow at them. The best he could do was use men of his West India Regiment, supplemented by Royal Marines, sailors, and native recruits, to nip at their heels—to "keep them moving," as he put it. Occasionally, the Asante rear guard stood to fight, and the two sides exchanged fire. Fortunately for the British, almost all of whom were solidly hit by Asante slugs, these were fired at such long range that, except for one sailor who was hit in the eye, they did no more than sting. The African allies the British had pressed into service had even less stomach for combat than the starving and dispirited Asante. British officers flogged men with sticks and umbrellas (which they actually carried into combat), but they would not advance. Many dead Asante were found, apparent victims of starvation, and numerous starving and diseased prisoners of the Asante were left behind to be taken by the British. They were described as living skeletons.[27] As Captain Maurice was marching behind some Hausa soldiers under a Captain Gordon, he came upon "a poor little sick boy" who was apparently wounded and starving as well, lying by the side of the road. A Hausa "ran his spear in mere wantonness into the stomach of the poor little wretch. I don't suppose I shall ever forget the look of agony with which the poor creature drew together his limbs and rolled himself over."[28] Maurice could not identify the Hausa, and Gordon had no time to stop his column to investigate; so the troops moved on.

As General Amankwatia slowly withdrew toward Kumase, he decided that he would vent some of his rage on the rebellious king of Abra by attacking his capital, Abrakrampa. Amankwatia boasted so publicly about his intention to destroy the king of Abra that his plans became known to Wolseley, who reinforced the British garrison there. Some one thousand armed men, including Marines and Hausas, sited rocket launchers, built stockades, dug shelter trenches, loopholed houses, and converted the brick Wesleyan chapel into a fort. The brush was cleared away for one hundred yards in all directions. The force was commanded by Major Baker Russell, one of Wolseley's favorites. A cavalryman from the 13th Hussars, Russell was an instinctively effective leader who loved battle. He was noted for reminding the men of the 13th Hussars, a famous regiment, that it was their duty to "look pretty in time of peace and get killed in war."[29]

Amankwatia's decision "to plant his umbrella" in the Abra king's capital caused widespread dissension among his junior officers and soldiers, who were hungry, sick, and tired of war. A threatened mutiny was barely averted by the senior officers, who reluctantly supported Amankwatia. Abrakrampa was so heavily fortified that, by the time the Asante attack finally took place on November 5, it was tantamount to suicide. Still, with their ivory horns blaring out martial music, their drums pounding heavily, and thousands and thousands of men chanting in unison, the Asante soldiers made a valiant charge. But they had to cover one hundred yards in the open and were shot down in such numbers that the charge was beaten back. Despite severe losses they continued to blaze away at the British position for thirty-six hours. When Wolseley was informed about the fighting, he decided to march to the rescue of the garrison with the few men he still had available. When his small force arrived, the Asante had withdrawn, and Baker Russell urged Wolseley to send the marines and Hausas after them to strike at their rear. Wolseley listened, but to Russell's dismay he delayed for hours while he carefully sited his cannon to the south, not north toward the Asante, and stared in that direction with a fixed expression.[30] Wolseley was in the grip of malaria. He gave no orders to the marines or Hausas, but he did finally send his undisciplined coastal allies after the Asante. The Asante badly mauled them, sending them scrambling back in disorder.

While the meager British forces tried to hurry the Asante withdrawal, work on the road was accelerated so that it would be twelve feet wide, free of roots, dry, and level. Without skilled labor Major Home, the senior Royal Engineer, and his handful of Royal Engineers had to improvise at every step and do backbreaking work themselves. One crew of Africans cut back the brush, another dug out roots. A third group, more skilled and closely supervised, dug culverts and drains so that the troops would not have to march with wet feet. Another crew built bridges. Major Home reported with chagrin that it had taken twelve hours to bridge a stream that was only six feet across. Home's men also had to set up supply depots. All of this had to be done while heavy rains fell and Home had only 220 laborers. Despairing, he asked for an additional one thousand men, but it was weeks before any could be found.

Wolseley, Home, and Surgeon Major Gore also had to prepare campsites for the troops along the line of march. Eight sites were chosen along the route of march to the Pra River. Each camp contained housing for at least 450 men. There were eight large huts with wattled walls and thatched roofs, each capable of sleeping fifty men on comfortable split bamboo or palm-stalk beds raised two feet above the ground. There were smaller huts to house officers and even smaller ones for senior commanders. Deep latrines were dug, one for officers and the rest for the other ranks. Each camp had a small hospital (the largest one bore a sign reading The Forlorn Hope), and some had post offices and telegraph facilities. Four of the camps even had bakeries. The campsites were placed on elevated, well-cleared land with a good water supply, but even if the water appeared to be uncontaminated, it was not drunk until it had been filtered through a large mobile filter tank. There was also a large commissary filled with food supplies, a roomy, open-sided mess hall, and a canteen that sold wine to officers.

Correspondent Winwood Reade was so impressed by these camps that he wrote, "In no campaign has the British soldier ever had such comforts and luxuries on the march. Each camp was like an hotel, and some were almost elegant, with neatly swept roads, and boards fixed up pointing the way to the Water, the Latrine, etc."[31] Other correspondents agreed with Reade, but if they had seen these camps before the troops moved in, they would have received quite a different impression. Before the British troops arrived, African laborers were joined by people from nearby villages in making themselves very much at home in the camps. Some huts were used to slaughter sheep, and others as toilets. One of the larger huts had been converted into what one British observer discreetly referred to as a harem.[32]

Wolseley distributed information to his officers and men instructing them about means for preventing illness, the need for kindness to carriers, and various infantry tactics. Then he made this astonishing declaration: "It must never be forgotten by our soldiers that Providence has implanted in the heart of every native of Africa a superstitious awe and dread of the white man that prevents the negro from daring to meet us face to face in combat."[33] Colonel Torrane, Sir Charles MacCarthy, Captain Ricketts, and Colonel Purdon, among many others, would have been surprised to learn this.

As ever, the health of the men Wolseley hoped to command was uppermost in his mind. He was determined to get his European troops to the point of battle as rapidly as possible and, of course, in a condition to fight. He ordered that every man take quinine daily, that they avoid chills at all costs, and that they be warm and dry when they slept. He also ordered, with the approval of his medical officers, that wherever the men slept, they protected themselves against malaria by burning huge fires to dry the poison-laden air. At each camp huge piles of logs were stacked up so that when the troops arrived, gigantic fires could be lighted to burn away the noxious vapors that were thought to threaten the men's health. These fires certainly made the camps colorful, and they probably drove away mosquitos, thus perhaps inadvertently reducing the chances of malaria. The general was also greatly concerned that the troops he hoped to receive not overexert themselves, something that was thought to assure an attack of malaria and, in many instances, appeared to do so. This caution did not apply to his officers. They performed exhausting physical labor from 5 A.M. to 5 P.M. every day, and all except one contracted malaria.

Although officers were expected to run every risk, the troops were to be protected at all costs. Small hospital facilities were provided at each camp, and a major one hundred-bed hospital facility was built at the most advanced camp, where it was expected that casualties from the first battle would be treated. Even better facilities were available at the coast, where survivors would be cared for. There would be no fewer than sixty surgeons with the army. It was also arranged that hospital ships would be offshore, ready to care for the sick and wounded and, when necessary, transport them to England.[34] Incredibly detailed arrangements were also made for carriers to be provided with stretchers and hammocks to carry wounded from the battlefield to the nearest treatment center and, if need be, to the coast. Not surprisingly, these arrangements were calculated for European troops only. Sick or wounded African troops and carriers would be cared for as circumstances allowed.[35] Despite the thought given to these matters, Wolseley did not provide enough hammocks for the sick and wounded, and his campaign was seriously jeopardized as a result.

Wounds and malaria were not the only concerns. When some Europeans aboard ship were found to be suffering from yellow fever, a strict quarantine was imposed on all ships. Even so, some naval officers died of the disease while these ships sailed home. Dysentery was a killer, too. Reade, the correspondent, suffered a terrible bout of dysentery but survived. He also wrote movingly about Captain Huyshe, one of Wolseley's favorite officers, who had served with him so courageously in Canada. Sick with ghastly diarrhea almost from the moment he stepped ashore, he nevertheless found the strength to save a fourteen-year-old Asante boy from certain death at the hands of Africans allied to the British, and he then treated him gently. But Huyshe continued to suffer so terribly from dysentery that when newsman Reade stopped by his sickbed, he could barely manage these last words: "Goodbye, we shall meet at the front."[36]

Whatever the cost, Wolseley was determined that his men would be well provisioned. On the recommendation of the surgeon major, the soldiers' daily ration would be enormous: each man was to receive 1 1/2 pounds of biscuit or freshly baked bread, 1 1/2 pounds of fresh beef or canned Australian beef without bone, two to four ounces of rice, potatoes, peas, or other vegetables, plus salt, pepper, tea, and three ounces of sugar. In addition to these prescribed rations, a large amount of sausage and cheese would also be available. Lime juice with sugar was to be provided four times a week. Preserved vegetables were so scanty and unappreciated by the men that a soldier's diet effectively consisted of 1 1/2 pounds of bread plus cheese or sausage and beef three times a day, washed down by very sugary tea. This was considered to be an ideal diet for troops marching and fighting in ninety-degrees heat and tropical humidity. Even well-filtered water tasted foul in the men's wooden canteens, so they carried lukewarm tea, which proved to be a little more palatable.

Wolseley's otherwise meticulous preparations all hinged on the availability of transport, and here his plans miscarried so badly that the outcome of the campaign was significantly affected. There were no navigable rivers that approached Kumase and no beasts of burden. Everything depended on African labor, and in making his plans, Wolseley ignored what past experience had taught earlier British officers—namely, that neither the Fante nor other coastal people were eager to carry loads, especially not into the heart of the Asante kingdom. When he sent his officers out to round up men to carry British supplies, they usually returned empty-handed.

Despite nearly three quarters of a century of experience on the Gold Coast, the British had somehow not yet understood that carrying heavy loads was not men's work there, it was women's. When they finally began to recruit women, they found that Fante women were not only willing but capable carriers. It soon became commonplace to see long lines of Fante women cheerfully chatting as they walked along, each with a sixty-six-pound box of Australian beef on her head and most with a baby on their back. For carrying this load over one hundred miles to the base camp at Prahsu, a woman would earn a maximum of ten shillings, the price of half a dozen chickens. A special correspondent to the *Daily Telegraph* was touched when one of the slave women carrying his goods recognized her mother among another company of carriers and rushed over to embrace her. As mother and daughter embraced, they sobbed and laughed with such joy that all the other women stopped to watch. The two women had been enslaved by the Asante seven years earlier and had not seen each other since.

The British had reservations about relying on women as carriers. For one thing, they were reluctant to put women in the line of fire, and too many women in camp at night could lead to disruptive temptations, not only for African men, but for British soldiers, sailors, and marines who had been away from women for a dangerously long time. So British officers continued to search without success for more men to carry the masses of supplies that were piling up at Cape Coast. Desperate, Wolseley turned to a special-service officer, Colonel George Pomeroy Colley, perhaps the most brilliant staff officer then serving in the British army. Superbly organized and tireless, Colley saved the day.

When Colley took over, he found himself in command of 201 African carriers and 583 deserters, hardly a happy circumstance. There were several reasons for these mass desertions. Some British officers and African overseers were not disinclined to kick, beat, and even flog carriers. Moreover, relatively little food was available to carriers, and that was largely rice, a foreign food these men thoroughly disliked. Not least, their pay was late in coming. When a few men walked away in disgust, mass desertions followed. Colley first tried to use soldiers of the 2nd West India Regiment as carriers, but they were unable to carry the loads that Fante women could, and when one soldier actually collapsed under his load and died, Colley resorted to kidnapping.[37]

Colonel Colley asked Wolseley's permission to hunt down the deserters and to capture new carriers by force. Wolseley quickly agreed, and British officers, including several from the fleet offshore, led dozens of expeditions that burned villages where deserters lived and carried off nearly the entire adult populations of others, leaving only grandmothers behind to care for the small children.[38] Colley soon put these thousands of men, women, and children (who carried smaller loads) to work under close guard. Force was used when officers felt the need for it, but Colley favored persuasion and was wise enough to organize the carriers on a tribal basis, with each group having its own interpreter. He also paid them reasonably well and allowed them a day off for every four worked. Colley and his officers worked so hard that all came down with dysentery and malaria, but they soon had over two thousand carriers efficiently moving supplies up the road toward

Kumase. By late December the number rose to six thousand, of whom one thousand six hundred were women. To command this large number of men and women, Colley never had more than sixteen officers, all of whom were dreadfully ill much of the time.

On December 9 Wolseley was surprised by the arrival of a large British troopship that anchored off Cape Coast. His telegram requesting British troops had reached London on the seventeenth of November, and later that same day the Cabinet approved his request. With an unaccustomed sense of urgency, orders went out that night, and two full-strength battalions sailed on the nineteenth. A third battalion that Wolseley had not asked for sailed a few days later. Wolseley knew nothing about the dispatch of these troops until the first ship arrived, and although he was delighted to have them, he was far from being ready for them. Fearful above all of needlessly exposing the men to disease, he sent the ship back to sea. It held 30 officers and 652 noncommissioned officers and men of the Rifle Brigade, including Prince Arthur, son of the queen; 4 officers and 68 men of the Royal Engineer; and 70 or so other officers and men, most of whom were medical personnel. There were two chaplains as well.

Three days later another ship arrived with the second battalion of the 23rd Regiment, the Royal Welch (then written "Welsh") Fusiliers, half a battalion of Royal Artillery, and more medical officers and chaplains. Five days later, to Wolseley's great surprise, yet a third battalion arrived, the 42nd Highlanders (the famous Black Watch), accompanied by several senior staff officers, another forty medical personnel, and supplemented by a draft of 169 Scots from the 79th Highlanders. Wolseley now had not two but three battalions of English troops, even if the Black Watch consisted of Scots, the Royal Welch were largely Welshmen, and the Rifle Brigade had many Irish. The Cabinet's rapid response to Wolseley's telegram would prove embarrassing to the general. Because there was nothing for the troops to do until the road had been completed, camps prepared, and supplies stockpiled, nearly two thousand men would cruise aimlessly in the sun until the end of December. Christmas passed almost as unnoticed aboard the ships as it did on shore,[39] and the news that Charteris had died aboard ship and that Neill's shattered arm would require surgery in Britain did nothing to raise the spirits of the men who were trying so hard to put a military campaign together.

By the time the British troops finally landed on New Year's Day, Wolseley, despite his intense distaste for Africans, had assembled several large contingents of African soldiers. Wolseley's views were widely shared. Captain Maurice, the same man who was horrified when a Hausa speared a helpless boy, wrote this comment about New Year's Eve: "A nigger company, not requiring paint to make them look it, performed round a camp fire for our benefit, a small boy beating an old empty store box by way of castanet with wonderful skill."[40] It was a rare British officer who did not express racist views about Africans, yet a vital role in Wolseley's campaign would be played by two large brigades of African militia that would be led by British officers. Baker Russell of the 13th Hussars would command one brigade and Colonel Evelyn Wood, who earned a Victoria Cross for bravery in the Crimean War, would command the other. In addition, Captain Glover had raised several thousand Africans to march on Kumase from the east, and Major W. F. Butler, one of Wolseley's favorite officers, would attempt to raise an African army to drive toward Kumase from the southeast. Finally, there was a small unit of scouts commanded by Lieutenant Lord Gifford, a lean, handsome, recklessly brave twenty-three-year-old, who would spend the campaign scouting far in advance of the troops.

In late December, wearing their drab gray uniforms instead of their traditional kilts and green or scarlet tunics, the British troops came ashore in small boats rowed by Africans. The notoriously ill-tempered goat that served as the regimental mascot of the Royal Welch Fusiliers did not get very far. No sooner had the battalion formed up and begun to march across the beach than he fell dead. He was not a lovable mascot, but this was not a good omen. As soon as the battalions were assembled, British troops began their march north toward their base camp at Prahsu, just south of the Pra River, which marked the southern boundary of metropolitan Asante. The soldiers were joined by a naval brigade of 250 sailors and marines wearing broad-brimmed straw hats, who marched into Prahsu camp in perfect order, singing "When Johnny Comes Marching Home." Newsman Henry Stanley, a veteran observer of military campaigns including the American Civil War, was greatly impressed by the robust health of these men, their high spirits, and the athletic way in which they marched.[41] The 2nd West Indian Regiment came next, slouching in a leaden careless walk, according to Stanley. Stanley did not realize that they were brave, disciplined soldiers who were devoted to their British colonel, a man appropriately named Bravo. Each force was followed by hundreds of carriers, at least one for each soldier.

When the entire British force assembled at Prahsu in January, the camp held 3,520 combat troops, about 2,500 of them British, over three thousand carriers, and hundreds of tons of supplies. Another five thousand carriers were at work bringing more supplies up from the coast. As might be imagined, a military camp this size was a lively place. Men of the Naval Brigade were inveterate pranksters, not only among themselves but with officers as well. During one inspection tour by General Wolseley, they convinced a small African boy whom they had made their mascot to wear a full naval uniform with a wooden sword, step forward, salute, and introduce himself as "Mixed Pickles, Sir." This was apparently such a screamer that even Wolseley, who was not known for his sense of humor, admitted he was amused.[42] The Naval Brigade also had many pets, including a young chimpanzee and a small crocodile who lived in a canvas bathtub.

The troops especially enjoyed watching an elephant bathing in the Pra River, a novel sight because the recent retreat of the massive Asante army had left the forest almost empty of animals. After dinner officers bathed in the river. At night sentries fretted about the exotic night sounds, but the camp itself was a picture of peacetime soldiering. Huge fires blazed everywhere, and the British units vied with one another in singing their favorite songs for Wolseley and his staff. The Naval Brigade was said to sing best, but they refused to do so until they had their nightly ration of rum.[43] The British army men were not pleased that the sailors and marines had rum because unlike most campaigns, where they received a daily ration of liquor, Wolseley had ordered this one to be dry (except for officers, of course, who were not without requisite bottles of whiskey and champagne). The African carriers gambled long after everyone else was asleep.[44] Virtually all of the officers had already suffered at least one attack of malaria, and now some of the newly arrived troops began to fall victim, even though officers handed out quinine every morning and the men obeyed orders to avoid chills at all costs and to wear a hat whenever they were in the sun. Oddly, only one correspondent, who happened to sleep under a mosquito net, reported being troubled by mosquitos, and several newspapermen reported that they never saw a single one.[45]

Patrols that crossed the Pra reported no sign of Asante troops. The southernmost portion of metropolitan Asante was deserted. The events that took place in Kumase in 1873 and early 1874 have been chronicled by the missionaries Ramseyer and Kühne and the French businessman Bonnat. Although they were often away from the court, living on plantations a few miles outside of the city, they were in continual touch with influential Asante and could share experiences with J. S. Watts, a part-African catechist of the Wesleyan church who was also being held in Kumase. Besides, they were frequently in the company of the king, who needed their services as interpreters for the many notes that were delivered from concerned church groups and British authorities at Cape Coast. The Ramseyers were particularly welcome because King Kofi Kakari had grown fond of their daughter, who would run to him and sit on his leg while he played with her. He was also fascinated by Rose Ramseyer's blond hair.

In July 1873, as General Amankwatia's army was crossing the Pra on its march to the south, life in Kumase continued as before. Despite the absence of as many as eighty thousand people—officers, soldiers, sutlers, carriers, wives, priests, and others—large festivals still took place. In one the son of King Kwaku Dua I organized a festival to thank Kofi Kakari and others for their many gifts and human sacrifices given to celebrate the deaths of his mother and brother some years earlier. A large party of his soldiers, painted red to symbolize the blood that had been shed, fired salutes to the king for at least fifteen minutes before more gifts were exchanged and several men were sacrificed. One of these victims had managed to hide a knife on his person and made an attempt to fight back before he was disarmed and executed. Ramseyer was appalled to see many Asante standing near the headless bodies "laughing and joking."[46]

In September a far grander and more terrifying funeral took place to celebrate the death of a sixteen-year-old crown prince. Executioners rushed through the city seizing slave victims for sacrifice, some 150 in all. With their cheeks pierced and their arms bound behind their backs, they were taken away to await their turn to die. The king sent word to the Europeans not to worry for their own safety, but he warned that the sacrifices would not be pleasant. As various chiefs presented the king with gifts of silk cushions, clothing, gold ornaments, sheep, and slaves, the prince's pages, who had attended the coffin, were beheaded as muskets fired to signal their doom. They had known what their fate would be since the prince had died three days earlier. The sacrifices continued for ten days, and several members of the royal clan were slain by the king himself. Their bodies were left exposed to the royal vultures.

Following another funeral during which over two hundred people were executed—several by the king himself, who ordered that the victims be made to stand so that he would not have to stoop as he beheaded them—Kofi Kakari stopped before the horrified missionaries, performed a ritual dance, then offered each of them his hand as a public display of his friendship. He then asked them to draft letters for him to British authorities. The king continued to display great affection for the Ramseyer's daughter, but when their son was born, he and all other Asante ignored the boy, because it was an evil omen for captives to give birth to a son on Asante soil. There were evil omens aplenty in Kumase as 1873 drew to a close.

In December, as Amankwatia's shattered army was returning from the coast, a yam festival even grander than the one described by Bowdich took place. Great chiefs and their wives—the women's bodies painted with green powder and all wearing dozens of gold ornaments—passed along the streets. Executioners, painted red, danced with long chains of jawbones clattering around their necks. On the following day, everyone except the most powerful drank themselves insensible and were permitted to break most rules of decorum, to have virtually indiscriminant sexual relations, and even to mock authority. But on the day after that, those designated for death by the king and his councillors were suddenly seized and beheaded.

The executioners danced ecstatically with the severed heads, painting the foreheads white and red, kissing the mouths, and mocking one dead man for his alleged treachery. One executioner roasted a victim's heart, then ate it along with his maize bread as if it were his ordinary breakfast. The display of wealth by the king was dazzling. The European captives had no idea that the Asante possessed so much gold. That evening the skulls of their most famous enemies were taken from the mausoleum at Bantama and placed before Kofi Kakari, who solemnly enquired about the state of their health. Among the skulls was that of Sir Charles Mac-Carthy, killed a half century earlier. On the final day of the festival, the queen mother led hundreds of richly gowned women, including 250 or so of the king's wives, on a promenade that Asante men were not permitted to watch. Between each group of women of all ages walked obese eunuchs and small children carrying small boxes of toys.[47]

In November and December Kumase was alive with reports from the coast about British activities, including their attacks against Amankwatia's retreating army, but it was difficult for the king and his council to form any clear picture of British intentions. Wolseley's demands that they leave the protectorate were known, and Amankwatia was already moving out of British territory as he and his officers glumly swallowed their pride and prepared to make the payment to the king that he had demanded. When Wolseley's note demanding the release of prisoners and the payment of indemnification arrived in Kumase, the issue was hotly debated, and the king was under intense pressure from all quarters. As early as February 1873 one of the king's senior Muslim advisers had consulted his oracle, which informed him that the Asante must release the European prisoners. The king and inner council ignored this warning, but to the annoyance of many of his councillors, he continued to seek out religious and magical solutions to the growing British threat.[48] He also took the extraordinary step of sending a message to the king of Dahomey, a traditional enemy, asking him to join the Asante in the coming war against the British. The king of Dahomey sent a message back declining the request because his "great fetish" had indicated that the Asante were sure to be beaten.[49]

On November 20, 1873, before the first British troops had arrived, King Kakari and his inner council had begun a series of conferences to assess the impending crisis. The king began by arguing for war, insisting that Kumase had never been invaded and never could be. Many of his councillors disagreed, pointing out that British weapons were so superior to those of the Asante that there could be little hope of victory.[50] The queen mother, then fifty-five, was a shrewd and energetic woman who exercised great influence. In the past she had often counseled war, but now she was so certain that war would be ruinous that she made an impassioned plea for peace. Saying that she was old and did not want younger generations to blame her son for plunging the Asante people into a calamitous war, she argued that "from olden times it has been seen that God fights for the Asante if the war is a just one. This one is unjust."[51] She argued that the European prisoners be released and the indemnity paid. The queen mother was a powerful person, but there were other powerful councillors who were unwilling to make these concessions, and it was these men, a militaristic oligarchy, who dominated the Asante government. One of the most outspoken was Adu Bofo, the newly victorious general whose successes had driven Amankwatia IV to demand the right to lead the current campaign to the coast. Adu Bofo was the son of the former powerful treasury minister and noted general Opoku Frefe, whom he had succeeded in both roles. He passionately declared that he would never countenance the release of the European captives. His voice carried weight under ordinary circumstances, and in this instance it was particularly persuasive because it was Adu Bofo who had captured them.[52]

As usual, the king stalled for time. His councillors had decided that the prisoners would remain in Kumase and there would be no payment to the British, but Kofi Kakari did send messengers permitting Amankwatia's army to return to Kumase. Worried by reports that were circulating in Kumase about the army's failures, he declared it a capital offense for anyone even to hint that the army had achieved nothing.[53] When the army returned to Kumase on December 22, the extent of their losses could not be hidden. Only about half the army had survived, and 280 senior officers had died.[54] Disgruntled soldiers described the destructive power of the new British rifles. Some of these men said vehemently that they would not fight again "as we are sick of it. The white men have guns which hit five Ashantees at once. Many great men have fallen."[55] Hoping to put the best possible face on the matter, the king sent messengers throughout Asante land to announce a great victory, but the demobilized soldiers told a different story. At the same time that he declared victory, the king continued to demand that the officers who had insisted that the campaign take place pay huge sums to offset the cost of the war. One officer had to sell not only his slaves to pay the debt but his wife and a young son as well, who were said to have cried bitterly. The European missionaries who were witness to these events in Kumase wrote feelingly that "there were many upright, quiet men who had wished for peace and free trade, who lost half their families by the war, and were afterwards obliged to sell the other half to pay for it."[56] The king's hold over his country and his army had never been so tenuous.

Exasperated by Kumase's failure to respond to his ultimatum, Wolseley sent a letter from Prahsu camp to Kumase on the second of January that not only repeated his peace demands but increased the indemnification to the immense sum of fifty thousand ounces of gold. He declared further that he intended to march his army into Kumase to sign the peace accord. Wolseley bluntly added that the Asante were powerless to stop him. Several councillors now joined the queen mother and Prince Ansa, who had recently returned from a stay in England and was well aware of British power, in urging compliance with Wolseley's terms; but many senior councillors, or elders, as they were also known, continued to resist. These insular old men had no knowledge of British firepower and continued to think of Kumase as the center of the universe.[57] King Kofi Kakari lacked the support to openly challenge the elders, most of whom indignantly insisted that to yield to threats of force would violate Asante honor.[58] The king feared that his weakened and rebellious army would be unable to stop Wolseley, but he also knew that if he yielded to the threat of force, his councillors were very likely to depose him in disgrace. Wolseley did not realize it, but his threat to use force left the Asante with no honorable alternative but to fight.

On the same day that Wolseley's ultimatum arrived in Kumase, a ferocious windstorm knocked down the sacred tree in the central square that symbolized the well-being of the nation. Kofi Kakari called his priests together to ask what this ominous happening portended. They instructed that two men should be bound to trees in the nearby forest, their cheeks pierced with knives. If they died quickly, the Asante would have victory. The portent was not good: one man lived five days, the other nine.[59] The king attempted to appease his war party by ordering that ammunition be stockpiled, and he began courting favor with some of his senior army commanders. But at the same time he surreptitiously released one of the European missionaries, the German Johannes Kühne. Fearful that members of his war party would learn of Kühne's release and see it as an act of weakness, he ordered Kühne to leave unobtrusively during the night. Before Kühne left, the king told him to tell Wolseley of his desire for peace, and he had a letter sent to Wolseley, signed by six Asante dignitaries, expressing the same wish. Kühne did quite the opposite. He told the general that the king could not be trusted and that his army was too demoralized to offer any serious resistance. Wolseley, needless to say, was greatly encouraged.

Kofi Kakari once again turned to his Muslim religious advisers for help in preventing the British invasion. Although he had not acted on their earlier warning to release the European prisoners, he now paid considerable sums to several Muslims to conjure up magical means of turning back the invaders.[60] One of these men, the scholar-priest Sulayman Kumatay, actually confronted Gifford's scouts with solemn curses designed to drive them off. When Gifford's men responded with gunfire, he disappeared but left behind a manifesto written in Arabic: "This is a prayer to God, and a wish that the white men would fight among themselves, and return to their own country. May pestilence and disease seize them! The writer of this is the great High Priest, who invokes God to do these things. Europeans never possessed any land in this country, and all the angels of heaven are invoked to drive them out."[61] The British were amused.[62]

Kofi Kakari was not the only Asante to place his faith in Muslim charms. All officers and most soldiers purchased Koranic charms and talismans consisting of pieces of paper containing protective incantations and tied together with colored threads. Many officers wore hundreds of these so-called *saphi* on the chest to ward off harm. Some of the charms were outrageously fraudulent. One was found to contain a page from the Bible, and another was torn from a British governor's proclamation made at Cape Coast.[63]

Despite the growing crisis the king was sometimes preoccupied with ceremonial or private duties, leaving the affairs of state to others. He spent one full day attending to the legal matters involved in elevating one of his three hundred or so wives to the status of paramount wife, a transaction that called for her to be given autocratic powers over at least six villages and six hundred people. This extremely important event cost the king one hundred ounces of gold dust.[64] But Kofi Kakari could not afford to be distracted for long: he had to put his army back together or face destruction. As people all over Kumase busied themselves making bullets of lead and iron and drying corn and cassava for provisions—the record about how this was done is vague—the king managed to convince the king of Mampon, the traditional commander of the Asante army, and another famous nobleman, the long-disgruntled General Asamoa Nkwanta, to lead the army of resistance. Nkwanta, who was known to the troops as their guardian spirit, was probably the only man who could have inspired the footsore, sick, and demoralized soldiers to shoulder their arms again.[65] There were severe shortages of food and salt in Kumase, and so many men were without muskets that two or three often had to share a weapon; but in an act of supreme patriotism, the sick, wounded, and dispirited Asante soldiers came together again, ready to defend their nation's borders and their own honor, this time with little hope of plunder or success.

The king also chose to make a last-minute gesture to the advancing British army. On the twenty-first of January, he released the Swiss missionary Friedrich Ramseyer, his wife, and their two children, along with the French merchant Marie-Joseph Bonnat. Their release was mediated by Joseph Dawson, whom Wolseley's predecessor had sent to Kumase some months earlier. The son of an English father and Fante mother, Dawson spoke Asante and English and was in regular contact with the king and his inner council. He continually pressed the king to release the prisoners, even saying that he himself would remain behind as a hostage if this were done. After much haranguing and to the surprise of the Europeans who also served him as interpreters, the king one day fell silent, "gazed vacantly before him, then suddenly turned and said, 'Go, go, and tell my good friend the governor [Wolseley] that I did not march against him. Amankwatia attacked the fort [at Elmina] contrary to my commands [something that was apparently true], I have nothing against the white men, go and speak a good word with the governor.'"[66]

Dawson then demanded to know whether the Fante and other African prisoners were to be released, as Wolseley insisted, or only the Europeans. "'What', the King angrily exclaimed, 'Is it not enough if I send *you*, am I to give up the Fantees too?'" The queen mother also was excited, and the entire council rose in consternation, "swearing and shouting in the wildest confusion."[67] In a rage the king shouted that no one would be set free. Terrified, the Europeans sat meekly, praying for deliverance. To their great surprise it came. After some time Kofi Kakari softened and said, "Oh, I have nothing against you. . . . Go speak a good word, I have now done what I can. If the governor will not wait, I must leave the matter with God."[68]

As the Europeans prepared to leave, they were surprised and pleased to receive valuable gifts from the king, including an Asante silk dress for Ramseyer's wife. After 9 P.M. they were summoned to the palace, where they feared the worst but found a deeply depressed King Kofi Kakari, who appeared as if their liberation had cost him dearly. He looked at Ramseyer's wife and, addressing her by her Asante nickname, complimented her on her new silk dress: "Well, Susse, you know how to wear the national dress."[69] Reverend Ramseyer and the French merchant Bonnat both felt such sympathy for the king at this moment of parting that they again promised to do everything in their power to bring about peace. "He smiled and dismissed us with the words, 'Yes; it is alright, go, do as you say.'"[70]

The Ramseyers and Bonnat were escorted toward the British troops, now only a few miles away. When they came to a town called Dompoase, only three miles from the British advance guard, they found it swarming with Asante soldiers under the command of a middle-level commander named Obeng—by coincidence the same man who had treated them so badly on the way to Kumase after their original capture that they had suffered greatly and their infant son had died. Though they feared for the worst, they were pleasantly surprised at being greeted politely. They assured Obeng that they would urge Wolseley to seek peace. The Asante officer asked that a good word for his men be expressed as well, saying that he, like the king, had "no quarrel with white men," adding that war was an altogether bad thing. "Look at this village, it is quite deserted; does it not make one's heart ache?"[71]

6

"The Most Horrible War"

As the European captives were being warmly welcomed by some of Wolseley's junior officers, the king was desperately attempting to muster enough troops to confront the British force. While urging his men to mobilize, he tried to buy time and perhaps to forestall an invasion altogether by sending Wolseley another appeal to halt and negotiate. Wolseley had already planned to halt on January 24 for four days at a town named Fomena because he wanted to build up a ten-day supply of food and ammunition before attacking, but he deceitfully wrote to the king that he would agree to make a peace gesture by halting. Thirty years later Wolseley confessed his lie, writing "may God forgive me that fib—the halts were absolutely necessary."[1] However, before he would agree to negotiate, he demanded that he be sent six of the highest-ranking men and women of the Asante royal family, including the queen mother, as hostages, be paid a huge down payment on the fifty thousand ounces of gold indemnity, and be promised safe passage to Kumase for his staff and five hundred troops, where he would sign a peace treaty. Once again he declared that it was his intention to march to Kumase and it was for the king to decide whether he did so peacefully or not. He also specified the routes that he, Glover, and Butler would follow in their advance, hoping to force the Asante to divide their forces. In reality, he had little confidence that either Glover or Butler would advance at all, as both forces were stalemated to the east and southeast of Kumase.

King Kofi Kakari and his councillors were appalled by Wolseley's harsh conditions. For one thing 50,000 ounces of gold was worth £1.5 million (or over $6 million), substantially more than the cost of the entire British military campaign and far more gold dust than could possibly be delivered on short notice. Furthermore, such high-ranking members of the royal family could not possibly be surrendered. To do so would mean handing over the core of the royal family to British custody, an unimaginable betrayal. Without any reasonable hope of negotiating peace, the king ordered Asante commanders to redouble their efforts to block all the British routes of advance and be prepared to fight if the British attacked. Nevertheless, he sent two more letters again asking Wolseley not to advance and to allow more time for negotiation. He knew that the rains were due soon, and if he could delay until they began, he might be safe. This time Joseph Dawson, who as usual did the translation, included a note of his own, acknowledging some money sent to him by General Wolseley. The note concluded, "Please see 2d Corinthians, chap. ii, ver.II." Grabbing a Bible from a nearby soldier, one of Wolseley's staff officers deciphered Dawson's warning: "Lest Satan should get advantage of us, for we are not ignorant of his devices."[2] Wolseley's reply was curt: "I halted four days at Fomena to please your Majesty. I cannot halt again until you have complied with my terms." Then, as if to test the king's grasp on reality, he concluded, "I am, King, your true friend."[3]

Initially, the Asante military commanders had planned to set up a defensive position at the crest of the one thousand six hundred-foot Adansi Hills, forcing Wolseley to attack up the steep escarpment, something that would have been difficult, especially for the men who would have to haul his artillery. This would have been a very strong position. In fact, it was so formidable that the king's advisers, including some of his Muslim councillors, feared that the British would find this defensive line so impregnable that they would retreat before the Asante could surround them and capture all their weapons and supplies, something that at least some Asante leaders regarded as perfectly feasible. Persuaded by this argument, the king, who planned to go to battle with his commanders, agreed to leave the Adansi Hills unguarded, surprising the British to such an extent that many officers took it as a sign that the Asante would not fight at all. Henry Stanley agreed with them and cursed the Asante for their cowardice. Wolseley's intelligence officer, the indomitable Redvers Buller, who would become a great hero in the British war against the Zulus five years later, knew better. His spies told him that the Asante army would fight at a place called Amoafo. Wolseley was pleased by the intelligence and wrote in his memoirs that the Adansi Hills were "delightful."[4]

The Asante army was willing to fight, but there was great controversy about what strategy to follow. In an attempt to vindicate himself, Amankwatia proposed that the entire Asante army mass near Amoafo and, instead of following their usual enveloping tactics, launch a surprise frontal attack against the British. The powerful king of Dwabin with his army of ten thousand men agreed to this plan, but King Kakari insisted on the traditional battle plan proposed by the charismatic Asamoa Nkwanta, Asante's greatest and highest-ranking general, and perhaps the only man who could inspire the troops to fight. Neither the king nor the Asante troops had confidence in Amankwatia. He was the son of a famous general and the darling of many of the older war hawks, but he had insisted on the invasion of the coast that had not only failed to reap dividends but cost him half his army and, what was worse, brought Wolseley's army into the Asante kingdom on his heels. Amankwatia also ordered the costly frontal attacks on Elmina and Abrakrampa, decisions Kofi Kakari insisted were against his orders.

The king of Dwaben was so enraged by this decision not to make a frontal attack that he held his men out of the battle. (These men later served the Asante cause by holding back Captain Glover's force advancing from the east, but their absence at Amoafo was crucial.) Another ten thousand disciplined troops attacking the thinly manned British front could have made a decisive difference.[5] Instead, their seventy-year-old, gray-haired, and long-bearded commander, General Nkwanta, chose to fight a defensive battle at a position just south of Amoafo. To attack the Asante line, the British would have to advance through marshy land, drop down into a ravine, and then climb a ridge. The brush was so thick that the Asante troops would be nearly invisible to them. The main Asante force would lie flat on a broad front across Wolseley's line of march. Two flanking armies would circle the British and attack their rear. One of these would be commanded by Amankwatia. At least ten thousand men assembled at Amoafo, and as the British would soon learn, their failure to fight in the Adansi Hills had nothing to do with cowardice.

Although their will to resist had miraculously been rekindled since their humiliating withdrawal from the British protectorate only a few weeks earlier, the Asante were so short of powder and shot that many men would have to load their Dane guns with pebbles or even snail shells.[6] A handful of Asante had modern breech-loading British Enfield rifles that fired deadly bullets, but the only other additions to the antiquated Asante weaponry were one thousand well-worn French smooth-bore muskets originally used in 1814 at Waterloo! Ironically, the brunt of the Asante fire at Amoafo would be taken by the Black Watch, a regiment that had lost 330 men at Waterloo, perhaps to fire from the same muskets.[7]

Hoping to surprise the British, the Asante assigned highway police to prevent anyone from approaching Amoafo by road, but a spy hired for £20 was able to slip through, and he reported to Wolseley exactly how the Asante troops were deployed.[8] In an attempt to gain more information, Wolseley offered large rewards to anyone who could bring in an Asante prisoner, but there was little success, partly because the African advance troops of Wood's and Russell's brigades preferred killing Asante prisoners to handing them over for questioning.[9] For example, on one occasion Colonel Wood's aide, Lieutenant Arthur Eyre, ran to the colonel, asking him to hurry along with his pistol so that he could shoot some of his Mende troops who were practicing their sword strokes by seeing if they could cut an Asante prisoner in half with a single blow. When Wood arrived, he found that the man was dead but cut only three quarters of the way in half. Wood could not find the culprits because the African sentry who witnessed the act said he could not tell one Mende from another.[10]

Wolseley never failed to send African scouts under British officers in advance of his main body, and far in advance of these men was Lord Gifford with forty picked men from various tribes, including some Mende. They wore short pants, had no shirts, and were barefooted; but some sported monkey-skin or buffalo-horn caps, others had long feather headdresses that stood straight up, and others had their own hair braided into long spikes that stood out in all directions.[11] Gifford and his men had survived many harrowing encounters with Asante scouts, including one particularly frustrating episode in which Gifford challenged an advance party of armed Asante to fight, only to be indignantly told that they could not because they had no orders to fight white men. He did not realize that these men were highway police, not soldiers, and thus quite properly refused to fight without orders.[12]

Early in the morning of January 30, Gifford cautiously led his men through the gloomy, shadowless forest so dark that a man could not read written orders, toward the small village of Egginassie, a mile south of Amoafo. Throughout the advance Gifford's men had come upon magical and religious paraphernalia intended to deflect the British from their purpose or send them away. One was a long white thread, apparently mimicking the telegraph wire that was thought to be British magic. Earlier that morning the scouts found an emasculated slave impaled on a bamboo stake. Disgusted, but lacking any tools to dig a grave, Gifford threw the man's body down a deep ravine. As Gifford's scouts moved closer to Egginassie, a sudden roar of Asante musketry dropped three of Gifford's men; he quickly withdrew, sending word back to Wolseley that the enemy were in strength and had opened fire. Later that day another British patrol stormed an Asante village, capturing fifty-three muskets, twelve kegs of powder, and the umbrella of Essaman Quantah, a venerable Asante general who had taught Amankwatia the art of war. The old general barely escaped capture.[13] It was an impressive little victory but not without loss. Captain Nicol, a brave officer whom Wolseley characterized as elderly, was shot dead as he led his men into the village. Some of Wolseley's young officers blamed Nicol's death on the general's order to his men not to fire first. One went so far as to refer to it as murder.[14] Later that day General Wolseley ordered that a general advance against Amoafo would take place on the following morning, January 31.

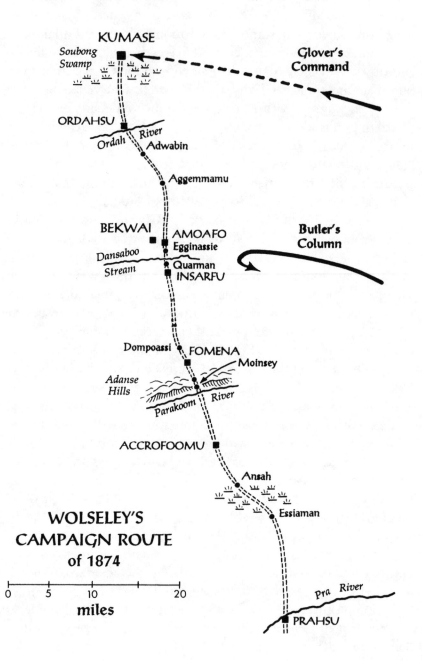

KUMASE

*Soubong
Swamp*

Glover's
Command

ORDAHSU

Ordah   River   Adwabin

Aggemmamu

BEKWAI   AMOAFO

Egginassie

*Dansaboo
Stream*   Quarman
INSARFU

Butler's
Column

Dompoassi   FOMENA

Moinsey

*Adanse
Hills*

Parakoom   River

ACCROFOOMU

Ansah

Essiaman

WOLSELEY'S
CAMPAIGN ROUTE
of 1874

0   5   10   20

miles

Pra   River

PRAHSU

As far as the jungle would permit, a traditional British square would advance along a six hundred-yard-wide front. Royal Engineers and African laborers would do their best to open up the brush enough for the men to move forward. The 42nd Highlanders, bearded veteran troops led by clean-shaven officers who seemed to Henry Stanley to be mere boys, would be in front, closely followed by Rait's Hausa artillerymen with their cannon and rockets. The front line would be commanded by Brigadier General Sir Archibald Alison, a veteran who had lost an arm in the Crimean War twenty years earlier. The left flank, which would extend very loosely for over two miles to the rear, would be manned by half of the Naval Brigade followed by Russell's African troops. The right flank, equally long and vulnerable, would be led by the other half of the Naval Brigade followed by Wood's African brigade. The Rifle Brigade would be the rear guard. Wolseley and his staff would direct the battle from the middle of the square, which would also hold the supply carriers and the 23rd Royal Welch Fusiliers led by their aggressive colonel, the aptly named Honorable Savage Mostyn. Because the serious thigh wound he had suffered years earlier in Burma had been causing him great pain, Wolseley had ridden all the way to the battleground in a rickety American-made buggy pulled by four Africans, but once the battle started, he would be on foot like the other officers.

Lord Gifford's advance guard once again came under Asante fire at the village of Egginassie, but reinforced by two companies of the Black Watch, he pressed forward until he ran into the main Asante line. By 8:15 A.M. the entire front was engulfed in pungent sulfurous smoke from thousands of Asante muskets. There was no wind, and the smoke hugged the ground, obscuring everyone's vision. Under the command of Colonel Cluny MacPherson, whose name left no doubt about his Scottish ancestry, the Highlanders did everything men could to press forward against the Asante fire. The sound of the weapons was so intense—the Dane guns booming, the Sniders much sharper—that the Scots could not hear the skirl of the bagpipes that always accompanied them into battle. The Highlanders came under tremendous fire before they could see anyone to fire at, and they began to take heavy casualties. Lying down, they returned fire in the general direction of the Asante smoke, but they could not advance. Sir Archibald Alison, who had campaigned in India and the Crimea, wrote, "The Ashantis stood admirably, and kept up one of the heaviest fires I ever was under."[15] Wolseley's written assurance that the Asante would never dare to stand against white men must have caused a few dark thoughts among the troops.

After an hour the battlefield resembled a scene from the Western front in World War I. All the bark and leaves had been stripped off the trees, but as usual the Asante fired high, sparing most of the men who were lying down.[16] The Asante also launched a series of attacks against the Highlanders' flanks, forcing Alison to move up his reserve companies. Others climbed trees to fire down on the British, most of whom, except for officers, were now returning fire while lying down. At 9:30 A.M., after an hour and fifteen minutes of intense fighting, Alison sent a messenger to Wolseley, reporting that his reserves had been committed and he was heavily engaged: "The enemy is holding his ground stoutly in the front and left flank; some relief to my men would be advantageous, if possible, from the Rifle Brigade, as they are getting tired from this continuous fighting. Our loss in wounded is pretty severe."[17] If the king of Dwaben had allowed his ten thousand Asante troops to add their fire at this point, it might well have changed the course of the battle. The British infantry had been stopped cold, and they were beginning to waver.

The Royal Engineers were also under heavy fire, and unlike the soldiers, they had to remain standing to cut brush and command the African laborers, most of whom had either thrown themselves down or left the front altogether. Captain Buckle was killed while trying to rouse these men. At the same time the advancing left flank of the Naval Brigade came under such heavy fire that it was forced to lie down and return fire. Wolseley sent a company of the Royal Welch Fusiliers to aid Alison at the front just as Alison's dispatch arrived asking for surgeons to treat wounded Highlanders. The Asante now opened fire up and down both flanks. At 10:30 A.M. General Alison again reported that he could not advance and asked for half a battalion of the rifles. At the same time Colonel MacPherson was carried back to Wolseley's headquarters with three wounds, the one in his ankle being incapacitating. He confirmed Alison's report that the infantry could not advance.

Hard pressed on all sides and with virtually no reserves remaining, General Wolseley was faced with a difficult choice. His men had been stopped in their tracks, casualties were mounting, and Asante fire showed no sign of slackening. He could have fallen back on a nearby village and formed a strong defensive position, but he refused even to consider such an action for fear that it would encourage the Asante to fight even harder. The sound of Asante musketry continued to be deafening, as Wolseley later wrote, but he calmly ordered Major Rait, his favorite artillery officer, to have his Hausa gunners manhandle their cannon across the swamp and fire at point-blank range into the Asante front line. With great effort and many casualties they managed to bring their guns to bear at close range, and their fire of rockets exploded against tree trunks with deafening crashes while their canister and explosive shells caused such appalling casualties that Asante fire began to slacken.

Seizing the opportunity, Alison ordered the Highlanders to charge with fixed bayonets. Unable to defend themselves against bayonets because it took them so long to reload, a portion of the Asante line retreated, drawing other Asante on their flanks back with them to a nearby ridge where they took up another strong position. Rait's artillery pursued, and once again the Asante front was driven back with great losses. As the Highlanders and Royal Welch moved forward, they passed by hundreds of Asante dead, all so terribly mutilated by the cannon fire that the correspondents who saw them were moved to comment on their horrible wounds. The huge .57-caliber Snider bullets had torn fist-sized holes through the dead, while the rockets and shells had left arms, heads, torsos, legs, and entrails in piles on the ground with blood and chunks of flesh scattered through the brush and trees.

By midday, after four hours of fierce combat, General Alison had pushed his men into the town of Amoafo. Hearing heavy fire on both flanks and knowing that his men were done in, General Alison halted his advance and took a defensive position while he awaited orders from Wolseley. The Asante strategy had always called for allowing the head of Wolseley's column to advance, although obviously not without stiff resistance, while the crucial attacks would be made on the flanks and the rear of the British army. The Asante flanking armies, especially the one led by Amankwatia, who was desperate to salvage his reputation, continued these attacks without letup, probing for weak spots that they could exploit. At one point earlier in the day, Colonel Wood, on the right flank, had been so annoyed by the inability of his men to advance or even to see the enemy that he rushed ahead and began to push the brush away with his hands. Fortunately for Wood, Lieutenant Eyre, his adjutant, almost tackled him to hold him back because an Asante soldier was in the brush only a few yards away. The man fired and somehow missed as Wood was pulled down. Later, as the Asante fire increased, Wood was hit above the heart with a nail head and fell heavily. The surgeons could do nothing and were so certain Wood would not live that they sent word to Wolseley that Wood was dying. Wolseley adamantly refused to believe them, but the doctor in charge, Surgeon Major Mackinnon insisted, "No, Sir, you never yet saw a man live with a shot in his pericardium."[18] Dosed with brandy, Wood lay on a stretcher guarded by his Sierra Leone servant, who sat beside him armed with a Snider. To the astonishment of the surgeons, Wood recovered and rejoined his command the next day.

At the peak of the fighting, Wolseley strolled about without apparent concern, smoking a cigar, appearing to be wholly fearless.[19] Asante slugs were cutting the air all around him, but he shrugged them off, telling his staff that nearly everyone had been hit by a slug or a pebble, usually without harm. However, he later wrote that it was a strange sensation to realize that there were thousands of people trying to kill him and his men, yet none of them could be seen. He also added that if the Asante had been armed with Sniders, the British force would have been annihilated.[20] The General was quite impressed by newsman Winwood Reade, who rushed to the front to join the Highlanders' attack, and by the veteran African explorer Henry Stanley, who was cool under fire and shot back like a veteran, which for all practical purposes he was. But Wolseley called one unnamed newsman a craven coward.[21] By 2 P.M. the firing in front stopped, but the Asante now enveloped the British rear and overwhelmed a supply column led by Colonel Colley. The unarmed carriers threw down their loads and stampeded, trampling Colley as they ran for their lives. Troops from the Rifle Brigade and the 2nd West India Regiment arrived just in time to save Colley, but many of the supplies were lost. The West Indians fought gallantly, but Wolseley never praised them, perhaps because his prejudice blinded him to their courage.[22] There was no more heavy fighting that afternoon, but bursts of fire continued at various places along the British flanks until sunset.

British officers and newsmen generally agreed that between two and three thousand Asante must have been killed, but to everyone's amazement, after twelve hours of fighting by over one thousand five hundred British troops and seven hundred Africans against endless Asante fire, they had suffered only four dead, three of them British. However, there were at least two hundred wounded, many of them in serious condition. Surgeons worked throughout the day and into the night extracting slugs, nails, and a few Snider bullets (usually the unintended result of British troops being unable to see one another's positions) and bandaging wounds as best they could. The British doctors had morphine and used it liberally, but many of the wounded were nevertheless in great pain. Observers were struck by how well they endured their suffering. When one young lieutenant was carried in with a severe shoulder wound, a surgeon left a wounded Hausa soldier whom he had been treating to attend to the British officer. The officer refused to be treated until the doctor had done his best for the wounded African.[23]

Even before rations were handed out, rum was served to the troops and brandy to the officers. The general's sense of victory overcame his insistence on a dry campaign, but class distinctions were, of course, maintained. Soon after, torrents of rain and tornadic winds struck, the first serious storm since the British force had invaded Asante land. The troops had no tents or cover of any kind, no fires could be made to burn, and the ground soon became a morass of mud. The wounded lay uncovered on their stretchers all night in misery that it would be difficult to exaggerate. The engineers were equally miserable as they worked throughout the night to bridge a rapidly rising stream that the army would have to cross the next day. Everyone in camp went without sleep, and few men even bothered to lie down in the mud. Wolseley called the rain the heaviest he had ever been under.[24] He was greatly concerned about his exhausted men but still determined to march on Kumase in the morning.

The Asante army spent an equally miserable night, although not for quite the same reasons. Many were able to find shelter from the rain, and the old campaigners were accustomed to rain, mud, and the lack of cooking fires. They were dispirited more by the knowledge that British firepower was too destructive to stand against than they were by the elements. Their greatest concern about the rain was keeping their powder dry. If the rain continued into the next day and the British advanced as they were expected to do, their ancient flintlocks would be extremely difficult to fire. The Asante were also disturbed by the heavy losses they had suffered. Many were seriously wounded, including the king of Mampon, and General Amankwatia had been killed. To inspire his men to fight harder, the general had stood on his stool, an act that was intended to make his men fight more fiercely. As he exhorted his men, he was shot through the back and died on the battlefield.[25] Their morale did not improve when it was rumored that King Kofi Kakari had left the battlefield early in the day.[26] When the decision for war was made in 1873, King Kakari had ordered his retainers to recite praise songs for his martial valor. His favorite was, "Kakari the hero, the champion who will fight at the cannon's mouth." Although far in the rear during the fighting, actual cannon fire did not please him. He fled with a few slaves whom he then had executed in a vain attempt to prevent word of his cowardice from spreading. His actions were widely considered to bring disgrace to the Asante nation.[27]

In Kumase a fearful populace was making ready to flee, and they were not pleased when the severed head of a Highlander was triumphantly displayed. Many worried that this was a bad omen. This Scottish soldier, whose name is unknown, resisted his death so resolutely that the fingers on his hands were found to be almost entirely severed as he tried in vain to prevent the Asante from taking his head by fending off their knives.

After the terrible night of deluge, the British were not able to organize themselves to advance until one the next afternoon, giving the Asante time to fortify the next town along the road to Kumase and dry their powder. Houses were loopholed, and a huge tree trunk was dragged across the road. When the British advanced, fire from the houses and the tree wounded seventeen of

Gifford's scouts, and he was forced to withdraw. With the help of artillery fire, men of the Naval Brigade were able to drive the Asante back, but one sailor was killed and several wounded. At the same time, supply convoys in the rear of Wolseley's army were harried by a series of attacks. Many of these carriers had been ordered to carry wounded back to Cape Coast, but when they were fired on by the Asante, they dropped their charges and fended for themselves, to the great suffering of the wounded men. One large group of African carriers refused to carry even their own wounded, insisting that it was customary for them to leave wounded men behind to die. Colonel Wood who had argued and pleaded with them to no avail, finally had their leader flogged "until I was nearly sick from the sight."[28] It was not until he had given a second man twenty-five lashes, a terrible, back-scourging punishment, that the African carriers finally agreed to carry their own wounded away.

Wood was concerned by another problem common to his African militia: they insisted on carrying everything balanced on their heads—rifles, ammunition, cooking pots, blankets, food, and what all. Whenever a shot was fired from the bush, the men ducked, and everything fell down with a crash, leaving them defenseless until they could crawl around and recover their weapons. Wood solved the problem by ordering them to wear military crossbelts on which their equipment could be neatly hung. One man refused to comply and continued to carry everything on his head. Wood fined him, to no effect; so he called a doctor to witness punishment and ordered the man flogged. His comrades implored Wood not to carry out the punishment, but Wood explained that the man must obey orders. Frustrated and puzzled, he asked the man why he would not obey orders and was told that the belts were painful. Wood examined the man and to his horror found that he had a gaping slug wound in his chest into which he had shoved a wad of grass. Wood and the doctor were properly impressed. The doctor treated him and the man was not punished.

Wolseley's army spent the night of February 1 in a large, comfortable town that impressed the officers with the beauty of the bas-relief ornamentation of its houses. It provided ample, clean, and comfortable housing for the exhausted men. Correspondent Henty of the *Standard* found the Asante houses so well made and their furniture so finely carved that he could not comprehend how these people could endure the rigors of campaigns in the unforgiving jungles near the coast. Perversely, that night, when the troops had cover, there was no rain. Much better rested, the troops moved out at daybreak on the second. After crossing a river on a bridge elegantly built by the always remarkable engineers, they encountered a series of ambushes, but the Asante opened fire at such long range that they did no damage. The British returned fire but made no serious effort to attack. Earlier in the day the Asante had made an attack on the main British supply depot, an attack so ferocious that the carriers now refused to leave the fortified camp. Short of supplies, Wolseley camped in the early afternoon, hoping that a convoy would reach him. When he learned that night about the disruption to his supply system, he made the audacious decision to attack Kumase with no more than his troops could carry. This meant that he would have to get to Kumase and back to his supply dump at Fomena in five to six days without expending too much ammunition. Colonel Wood concluded that no other British commander would have had the confidence and courage to make this decision.[29] Wolseley had both, but he also knew that with the rains now upon him, he could not long afford to be on the wrong side of flooded rivers, nor could he safely expose his troops to malaria for much longer. He took the gamble.

Wolseley's advance guard moved out early on the third and quickly encountered heavy Asante opposition. British artillery fire drove them back, but they re-formed again and again, and the firing continued while the British slowly advanced north on the road to Kumase. At mid-afternoon an Asante messenger arrived carrying a white flag of truce designed by Joseph Dawson. The gold-breast-plated envoy presented Wolseley with yet another disjointed appeal to halt and negotiate but did nothing to comply with Wolseley's demands. Dawson, in fear of his life, wrote a separate note appealing to the general. He insisted that the king now truly wanted peace, that the Asante were beaten, but that members of the royal family could not be handed over as hostages and the king needed time to raise the gold. All this was true, but Wolseley sent back a brusque note rejecting the king's request, and he ordered his troops to press on. (This time he said nothing about being the king's true friend.)

That night they camped on the south bank of the formidable and rapidly rising Ordah River. Heavy rain fell all night, and as the Royal Engineers worked to bridge the river, the rest of the troops tried, without any semblance of success, to stay dry by crouching under large plantain leaves. It was another sleepless night.

At dawn the men tried to dry themselves around large fires, but few succeeded. Soon the scouts were across the new bridge, and the main body followed. Asante prisoners had said that an army of ten thousand men was ahead of them but that it was under orders not to fire unless fired on.[30] As the British advance approached, however, the Asante opened a deadly fire that stopped the white troops in their tracks. The Rifle Brigade was sent forward, but it could not advance either. As the men lay down to exchange fire, the Asante launched a strong attack against the Highlanders on the British right flank. The attack was so persistent that Wolseley was worried, but once again, when artillery was brought into place, the Asante attack was held off. Wood's adjutant, Lieutenant Arthur Eyre, was standing upright as most officers did, but the firing was so heavy that Wood told him to kneel down. He had no sooner done so than he was shot through the bladder. Despite morphine he was in such agony that a shaken Wood, who loved him like a son, was relieved when he died two hours later, his last wish being that his rings be given to his mother.[31]

While Eyre lay dying, the battle was not going well for Wolseley. Russell's African regiment in the front wavered, firing aimlessly, and even a company of the Black Watch lost its discipline and fired wildly at nothing. Amid loud singing, cheering, and drumming, the Asante pressed attacks on both flanks with such determination that the usually staunch Rifle Brigade also began to lose its composure. The Asante charged so close to the British lines that officers shot them down with their revolvers.[32] One officer who saw an Asante unit in the open was astonished to see that they marched in perfect order, their muskets all held at the same angle. He said that they were "disciplined, under command and well in hand."[33] As casualties mounted, Colonel John McLeod, or "Old Jack" as he was better known, rushed about giving a copy of the Book of Psalms to wounded officers. McLeod's faith in the healing powers of the Scriptures was so well known that many officers found his actions hilarious. One seriously wounded officer had such a laughing fit when McLeod approached him that he claimed it stopped his bleeding and saved his life.[34]

Just as Wolseley had decided to send the Highlanders to the front to replace the shaken Rifle Brigade, a slug hit him in the head with enough force that it knocked him down, but the thick leather strap on his helmet deflected it enough that he was able to carry on. The bearded, sweat-soaked Scotsmen, their numbers now reduced by 25 percent, moved up the road toward yet another Asante roadblock, an immense tree that sheltered riflemen. This time they did not wait for Rait's artillery. With their pipers playing as loudly as possible, their officers leapt up and led the cheering men on a bayonet charge that broke the Asante line. After two hours of valiant fighting, the Asante finally fled, leaving behind chiefs' umbrellas and war chairs, drums, muskets, powder, and many dead and wounded. The Black Watch attack was so successful that the men trotted and walked forward for four miles, firing as they went, before sheer exhaustion forced them to a halt. As the Scots rested, they congratulated themselves on a fine fight, although one man insisted that if they had been able to wear their traditional green coats and their "kilts and bonnets," they would have routed the Asante easily. They also discovered that all had been hit by Asante slugs and compared their cuts and bruises with good humor, except for one man whose beard had been partly sheared off by Asante fire. He complained that his girlfriend would be furious about the loss of his "manhood."[35]

At 1:45 P.M. General Alison sent word to Wolseley that the road was open and that if he were supported from the rear, he would be in Kumase that night. When Wolseley shared this news with his men, they erupted in an enormous cheer, and those Africans among them who could speak Asante shouted the news as loudly as they could. The Asante gunfire on the flanks immediately halted. Knowing that the battle was lost, the Asante began to withdraw toward Kumase on parallel paths to the road that the now-triumphant British hurried along.[36] The Black Watch, now led by Colonel John McLeod and followed as closely as possible by Sir Archibald Alison, reached the outskirts of Kumase at 5 P.M.

Many Asante greeted them by saying "thank you," the only English they knew. They were also greeted by a high-ranking As-

An Asante warrior stripped for battle holds a long musket, his primary weapon. The Asante had a near monopoly on guns among the Gold Coast Africans which gave them an enormous advantage over their neighbors in fighting the British. Their muskets, "long Danes," were, however, vastly inferior to British weapons; some of them had been used by the French at Waterloo. (Basel Museum)

Dense undergrowth characterized the Asante forest. Walking through the clearing pictured above, soldiers would have been unable to see anything on either side, making them vulnerable to ambush. (Doran Ross)

THE ILLUSTRATED LONDON NEWS.

REGISTERED AT THE GENERAL POST-OFFICE FOR TRANSMISSION ABROAD

No. 1793.—VOL. LXIV. SATURDAY, JANUARY 3, 1874. WITH EXTRA SUPPLEMENT SIXPENCE. BY POST, 6½d.

The terrain determined the fighting style of the Asante and British. In this drawing, taken from *The Illustrated London News*, the Asante are waiting in ambush, unable to see more than a few feet in front of them. Peering through the brush at top center, one can see Africans approaching. Non-Asante Africans always preceded the British columns, scouting for Asantes. The Asante preferred to save their ammunition for British soldiers but, for the most part, battles began suddenly when the Asante collided with the scouts in the thick forest. *(The Illustrated London News)*

The 42nd Highlanders, or "The Black Watch" as this Scottish regiment was commonly called, was one of the most famous in the British army. They had a reputation as the toughest regiment and accounted for most of the British casualties in this campaign. *(The Illustrated London News)*

Here, the African allies of the British are scouting in advance of the British army. Lord Gifford, left of center in the front line of soldiers, is leading the scouts into an Asante village. Asante huts line their path on either side and the furniture clustered around the tree indicates where Asantes cooked and ate their meals. Twenty-three and handsome, Lord Gifford was not only unbelievably brave but also incredibly lucky. Though he served in the exceptionally dangerous position of chief scouts officer during the Asante war of 1873–4, he was never wounded. He was also the only British soldier who didn't contract malaria in this campaign. *(The Illustrated London News)*

After the British defeated the Asante in battle outside the capital city of Kumase in 1874, they took over the city itself and its largest architectural structure, the king's palace. In the conversation taking place in the palace courtyard pictured above, the British are trying to convince the king's emissary to surrender. Not long after, the British burned down the palace. *(The Illustrated London News)*

The British retreat from Kumase to the African coast with their
wounded and war dead. Had they waited any longer, they would have
had too many people to carry. The victorious Asante panicked when
they thought they saw another army approaching—it was only a negli-
gible column of soldiers. They chased after the retreating British and
signed a treaty promising to pay them an indemnity of fifty thousand
ounces of gold. *(The Illustrated London News)*

When the Asante rebelled in 1900, the British locked themselves up in their fort at Kumase while the Asante tried to starve them out. Down to little ammunition and no food, the British, in true Victorian style, carried their women out of the fort. A combination of sheer luck and the stupidity of an Asante officer saved them. While the Asante soldiers were busy looting British luggage which, in their weakened state, the British porters were forced to leave behind, the prisoners all but strolled to safety. (Armitage and Montanaro)

This log stockade, one of dozens surrounding Kumase built during the war of 1900, was probably a quarter of a mile long and the product of much labor. Most of the war was fought with the Asante firing at British troops from behind the walls of a stockade. This method of defense was extremely effective until the British learned to blow them up with artillery and charge them with bayonets. (Armitage and Montanaro)

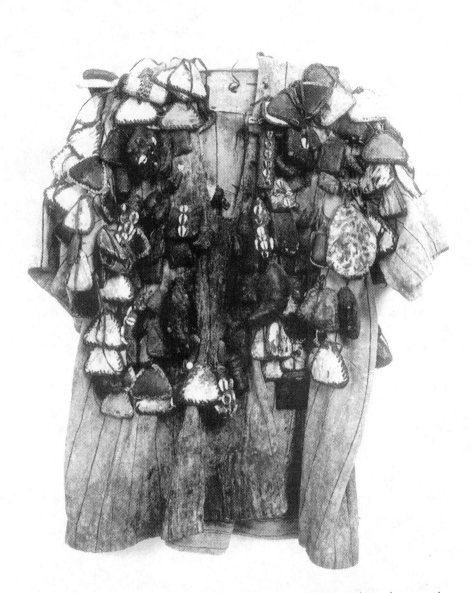

All Asante officers and many of the soldiers wore shirts, such as the one pictured above, as they walked to battle before stripping down to fight. Most were made of cotton, although some were animal skins and a few officers wore silk warshirts. The shirts were decorated with animal teeth and small pouches. The triangular and rectangular pouches were believed to hold Islamic charms acquired from the Moslems who had been conquered by the Asante, but many of the amulets proved fraudulent. One was found to contain a verse from the Bible, and another contained a fragment of a proclamation posted by a British governor. (Fowler Museum, UCLA)

ante officer in a leopard-skin uniform, who begged the scouts to stop and allow for a proper truce. Because his men needed a rest, Sir Archibald agreed. He needed one as well. Only a few minutes earlier as he was riding across the fetid swamp that lay before Kumase, his wretched mule slipped, pitching the general into the vile water before collapsing on top of him. The one-armed officer was vainly trying to extricate himself when his adjutant came to his rescue. Covered with fecal-smelling water, he tried to gather his wits and his dignity while his men restored their strength. All the while, Asante soldiers with loaded guns stood nearby, their faces contorted by anger. The British soldiers were nervous until Asante officers spoke to the men and they reluctantly moved away.

At 5:30 P.M., less than an hour before darkness would fall, Alison received Wolseley's order to move into Kumase. His men were greeted by large crowds of credulous Asante eager to see the white men. A court buffoon danced and tried to amuse the British by kissing them, a courtesy that was not well received. It was a tense moment as the advance guard of Highlanders, who numbered only 340 men at best, moved along, surrounded by several thousand Asante soldiers whose numbers increased by the moment. The powder-stained men were all fully armed and clearly capable of further hostilities. As Alison and McLeod looked on, hundreds of men and women passed by them carrying food, powder, guns, and boxes on their heads. The British conquerors could do nothing to interfere.

Shortly after six Wolseley rode into Kumase on another less-than-splendid mule followed by his staff and very eager newsmen. For reasons that are still unclear, when British envoy and interpreter Joseph Dawson met Lieutenant Lord Gifford on the outskirts of Kumase, he did not lead him to the king's palace as ordered but instead took him on a thirty-minute wild-goose chase that ended with Gifford threatening to shoot Dawson and Dawson claiming to be confused. It seems likely that the avaricious Dawson had been paid to delay the British as long as he could. As a result, much of great value could have been removed from the palace before the British could find it. When the British did locate the palace, they quite inexplicably did not place guards around it.[37]

As the remainder of Wolseley's force of barely more that one thousand white troops made their way into Kumase, he ordered sentries posted on all avenues of approach to the central square, where he billeted his men. He sited cannon to command every street that hostile Asante soldiers might use in an attack, something the seemingly terrified Dawson had warned him was very likely to take place that night. Large supplies of gin were discovered, and when medical officers declared it to be fine Hollands gin, it was served out to the troops, a greatly appreciated reward for taking the city. At 8 P.M., well after dark, Wolseley sent a messenger, whom Dawson had provided, to the king, assuring him that if he returned to Kumase to make peace, his palace and the city itself would be left untouched. But he also warned the king that if any Asante were to shoot at the British troops, the city would be burned and everyone in it killed.

By Wolseley's order the Fante prisoners were located and freed, often to touching scenes of kindness as Fante carriers tenderly ministered to the wounds of their long-fettered and mistreated countrymen. Wolseley also decreed that anyone found pillaging would be executed. The general's orders notwithstanding, the city soon burst into flames as the newly-released Fante prisoners wreaked vengeance on their captors, whose powder-filled houses caught fire and exploded. As the fires spread, engineers and troops were called out to pull down neighboring houses in an attempt to contain the blazes, but parts of the city burned all night. Against orders, pillaging also took place. Several carriers caught looting were flogged, and when a seventeen-year-old Fante policeman was caught with a stolen cloth in his hand, he was promptly sentenced to death. The young man was hanged from a tree, but his hangmen neglected to tie his hands. His agonizing efforts to avoid strangulation were so loud that many people rushed to the scene. Let down, he was hanged again, but the rope was now tied across his mouth to silence him. It took another 15 minutes of appalling agony for him to die. Asante who witnessed this event were disgusted and later pointedly wondered why the British thought the Asante's method of executing their criminals was so barbaric.[38]

The execution did little to prevent arson or looting that night because very few men were aware that the hanging had even taken place, but it served some small purpose the next morning. When Captain W. T. Dooner marched his African soldiers from Russell's brigade past the hanged man, he warned them that they would suffer the same fate if they were caught looting: "To my amazement they then emptied their haversacks on the road, and out came beautiful silks and cloths of all kinds, and there we left them."[39]

Despite their exhaustion few among the British invaders, including General Wolseley, slept more than a couple of hours that night. The exciting strangeness of Kumase and the uncertainty about what tomorrow would bring preyed on their minds. Their sleep was also disturbed by the nauseating smell of putrefying human flesh that came from the nearby "place of the vultures" where the headless torsos of executed Asante were left to rot. The smell was so offensive to the British that they lit fires hoping to cleanse the air, but to no avail. In this predeodorant age these men had not bathed or changed their filthy, sweat-encrusted uniforms for many days; still, this new odor was too much for them.

Everyone was awake before daybreak, eager to see more of the exotic city. Though Wolseley still hoped that the king might return to Kumase and agree to peace terms, he feared that the fires set last night had made Kofi Kakari even less inclined to trust him than before, and he was right.[40] Wolseley was only too aware that if the king did not return to Kumase soon, the heavy rains and the lack of food would compel him to march back to the coast the following day. It was not yet clear what the valor of his men had won for him.

Wolseley began the next day by issuing an order praising his troops for their courage and devotion, which, he said, had "been rewarded with complete success."[41] As his officers well knew, success was far from being complete. Wolseley had enough food for his men to remain in Kumase for at most two days; but as he looked at the leaden, drizzly sky, he could not avoid worrying about the swollen rivers in his rear. More heavy rain seemed to be on the way, and he feared that his army could be trapped.[42] He was also greatly troubled by a shortage of hammocks for carrying his sick and wounded. If he had to fight another battle, he would not be able to carry them all. His only option was to find some way to lure King Kofi Kakari back to Kumase to sign a peace treaty in a day or two at most or withdraw without a fight and without a treaty.

While he waited for word of the king's intentions, the general and some of his staff officers visited the still-unguarded palace. It was obvious at a glance that much of value, including the gold dust, had been removed during the night. They nevertheless noticed boxes and crates filled with silks, gold and silver treasures, leopard skins, and many curiosities of European manufacture, including a music box that played "O rest thee babe" and "Adeste Fideles." They also found many enormous umbrellas, some of the king's pet cats (a passion that Asante kings had maintained throughout the century), and his huge four-poster bed, covered in silk. Offended by some ritual objects and a number of executioner's stools covered with clotted blood, Wolseley stayed only long enough to glance around. Belatedly he ordered that a guard be placed around the large building. It took one hundred men to guard all the entrances.[43]

As the clouds darkened ominously, some of the newspaper correspondents explored the deserted city, which was so large that one of them believed it would ordinarily have held forty thousand people.[44] Yet anyone who had seen it in Bowdich's time would have found it badly down at the heel. All of metropolitan Asante had suffered a population decline, and Kumase was no longer the imposing capital that had dazzled earlier European visitors. While these men were exploring the empty city, various Asante messengers arrived bringing word that the king was on his way. Wolseley was cautiously delighted, but time passed and the king was nowhere to be seen. However, two of these high-ranking messengers were later discovered gathering guns and ammunition to be carried out of the city. They were placed under arrest. Frederick Boyle, special correspondent of the *Daily Telegraph*, recorded the following anecdote about one of these messengers:

> One of them is a prince, whom we call Bosomnogo, the most courteous and charming of savages. Tied to him is a captain, Cocoforo. . . . Both of them were captured in the act of removing guns and powder from the palace, after bringing to the General a message from the King. The prince has an excellent face, very good-looking and intelligent. There is something quite high-bred about his manner, but the Ashantees especially pride themselves upon their courtesy. When taken, he wore a bracelet of strung nuggets, sandals heavily plated with gold, and in his hand a bag of dust worth nearly £500; so, at least, he complained to Monsieur Bonnat. Both he and the captain

were dressed in clothes of native manufacture, strikingly clean, and arranged like an ancient toga. They were white, handsomely marked with a blue pattern. The prince showed himself particularly indignant at the manner in which he was carried down. "Here am I," said he to Monsieur Bonnat, "a prince of Ashantee, tied like a slave to one of my captains. That third man is only a warrior! It is infamous!" Monsieur Bonnat reminded him that the Ashantees had kept their prisoners, whites and one a woman, seven weeks in irons, without any cause at all. But an Ashantee prince could not see the parallel.[45]

More messengers arrived to declare the king to be on his way, but by then even the ever-hopeful Wolseley knew that the game was up. Shortly after noon the city had been inundated by thunderstorms that knocked over the troops' newly arrived canvas tents like houses of cards and left everyone thoroughly intimidated by the fury of tropical rain and wind. By mid-afternoon the general made his decision. He sent so-called prize-agents to the palace to remove everything they could that was of value. Led by intelligence officer Captain Redvers Buller, these men spent all night removing valuables while nursing the only four candles they had. They found pure gold masks, one weighing forty-one ounces that represented a ram's head and other smaller ones representing men and other animals. There were necklaces and bracelets of beads, gold and silver, silverplate, swords, gold- and silver-embossed cartridge belts, caps mounted in solid gold, stools mounted in silver, calabashes covered with silver and gold, silks, and all manner of European gifts from earlier times. The prize-agents worked throughout the night, and although it took thirty Africans to carry away the loot, they were still unable to remove everything of value.

While these exhausted officers robbed the palace, Royal Engineers obeyed Wolseley's orders by mining the building so that it could be completely destroyed. While these destructive steps were being put in place, the rain continued to pour, and the British troops sought shelter without much success. As the day passed, it became obvious to everyone that the king had no intention of negotiating with General Wolseley, and it was not only those closest to the general who realized how much this refusal compromised the complete victory Wolseley had announced. Winwood Reade reported that every officer he spoke to expressed disappointment because the king had not capitulated or paid even an ounce of gold. They were also concerned that if the Asante army attacked them as they withdrew from Kumase, it would appear that they had been driven out.[46] It was a cold, wet night spent in largely sleepless despondency by the British staff officers. They had won Kumase but not the peace. Unless there was a miracle, tomorrow the general would order the destruction of Kumase, and they would all march back to the coast, possessors of a Pyrrhic victory at best. If they were attacked, there might be no victory at all.

At daybreak Wolseley ordered the mines to be fired, and they went off in a spectacular eruption. Unfortunately, the walls of the palace were still standing, but engineers confidently said that they were too badly damaged to do so for long. At the same time troops were ordered to deploy throughout the city with firebrands, torching the tinder-dry undersides of the houses' roofs. Within minutes the city was an inferno. Wolseley believed that destroying the palace and the city would demonstrate British might and Asante weakness. Brutal as these actions were, they would prove to have the desired effect. The Asante were appalled by the destruction of the city. While Kumase was being burned and the palace destroyed, many high-ranking British officers paid a visit to the place of the vultures. Holding their noses, they found an area at least an acre in size filled with bodies in various stages of decay. On top of uncountable numbers of skeletons and partially decomposed bodies, lay fourteen bloated bodies, including at least one woman and a child, all writhing with worms. Disgusted, the white men quickly left.

By 8 A.M. the troops began to move out of Kumase toward the coast, and by nine the rear guard of Highlanders had left the burning city. The first obstacle they came to was an expanse of water two hundred yards wide that had been a narrow stream only three feet deep when they crossed it three days earlier. With the help of a large tree used as a bridge, the troops managed to wade across. The river Ordah, which they came to next, was even more difficult to cross, as Wolseley had feared. Remarkably, the bridge the British engineers had built was still standing, even though the flood waters were two feet above it and still rising. Most men made it across the bridge, but it collapsed before the 42nd Highlanders reached it, and they had to strip naked and swim across, with their clothes and equipment being carried by Africans. It was nightfall before all the men were safely on the south bank of the river. With fires blazing, they spent the night in relative comfort in a large, well-fortified camp that had been constructed while they were in Kumase.

The troops that marched south the next day were happy to be headed home, but in addition to the hundreds of sick and wounded who had to be carried, many had minor but painful wounds, and others suffered from fever and dysentery. The rough joking that had earlier taken place around the subject of men suddenly plunging off the road to empty their bowels had long since ceased. Some men openly wondered what they had accomplished by their gallantry and suffering. They were a victorious army, but when they camped at the end of the day's march, there was no singing. To the Asante, who could not understand why the British were retreating, the long column of tired, filthy, and increasingly glum men looked more like a vanquished army than a victorious one. Wolseley could not help worrying about the reception he would receive in England if many more of his exhausted men fell ill on the return march.

But on the ninth of February, Wolseley was blessed by an apparent miracle. To everyone's surprise a messenger from King Kofi Kakari arrived in camp with an offer to accept Wolseley's peace terms. He begged the general to halt Captain Glover's forces, which he said were advancing toward Kumase from the east. Wolseley, who had all but forgotten the seemingly inert force that Glover was attempting to lead, was astonished but somehow managed to maintain his imperious poker face. He agreed to remain in camp at Fomena until the night of the twelfth, and if the king sent him a down payment on the indemnity of fifty thousand ounces of gold dust, he would sign a treaty of peace and order Captain Glover to halt. The messenger returned in haste while Wolseley and his staff were left to wonder what on earth was happening. To the best of Wolseley's knowledge, none of the three British officers who had attempted to mount diversionary attacks had been able to achieve anything. A captain named Dalrymple had run into a stone wall of fear and indifference as he tried to raise an army and had long since been written off as a threat to Kumase. Glover's dispatches had been promising great things, but so far his activities were largely unknown. And much more had been expected of an African force raised by Captain W. P. Butler.

Butler was a physically powerful, adventurous man who had served with Wolseley in Canada and was one of the general's most trusted officers. In 1873 he had crossed Canada from east to west by dogsled and foot, then hiked down the Pacific coast to San Francisco, where he learned of the impending Asante expedition and rushed by train to New York and by ship to London in order to join Wolseley again. Wolseley gave him the unenviable task of raising an African army from the people to the east of Cape Coast and marching this force northwest toward Kumase on a path parallel to the one taken by Wolseley. Despite his gifts of rum and gunpowder, his promises of plunder, and the force of his personality, it was only with the greatest difficulty that he was able to assemble some one thousand four hundred armed men like the one he described as follows:

> He was a large powerful negro, armed with a flintgun; he was utterly destitute of clothing, unless a square black Dutch bottle could be construed into a garment. . . . The gun was balanced upon his head; the bottle was worn after the manner of the Old Hussar jacket, suspended from the left shoulder. His whole appearance fulfilled the requirements of what is termed "an Irregular." He was, I think, the most irregular-looking soldier I had ever seen.[47]

By January 30, as the battle of Amoafo was about to begin, Butler managed to cajole his irregular army to a position only a few miles southeast of the town, when suddenly "a complete panic" took place and the entire force fled, leaving Butler alone and completely unable to support Wolseley.[48]

While the sick and wounded continued to be carried to the coast, Wolseley remained at Fomena, hoping that the king's latest peace offer was not another delaying tactic to allow the Asante army to regroup and attack. The tenth was spent in growing anxiety as no word came from the king. The eleventh was equally silent and even more nerve-wracking. Though there was no messenger from the king, Wolseley could take some comfort from the reports of his scouts that they could find no sign of the Asante army; so perhaps the king's message was not a ruse to hold the British in place until they could be attacked. The morning of the twelveth passed without event until noon when, as Wolseley's staff sat down to lunch, an exhausted British officer on an emaciated horse staggered into camp at the head of twenty Hausa soldiers, who somehow had kept up with his pony on foot! The officer was Captain Reginald Sartorius of the 6th Bengal Lancers, whose previous reputation for great bravery would not be diminished by his amazing ride.

It seems that Captain Glover's force had been thoroughly blocked by an Asante army of between five thousand and ten thousand men under the king of Dwaben. The loss of this powerful army against Wolseley's advance was critical, but the men from Dwaben had nevertheless managed to play an important role in the war by preventing Glover's advance. Several small battles took place without success for Glover, whose men took some serious losses. On February 2 Dwaben scouts discovered that the body of Glover's army, which was only then ready to attack, consisted of men from the Akyem Abuakwa kingdom, with which Dwaben had a reciprocal peace treaty that forbade them to fight each other. The troops from Dwaben promptly withdrew, and so did Glover's Akyem men despite Glover's best efforts to restrain them. Left with his surviving Hausas and a couple of thousand Africans from other tribes, Glover cautiously moved ten miles closer to Kumase before camping on February 10 at a place he estimated to be seven miles east of Kumase. Deeply concerned about the condition of his nearly starving troops, he sent Sartorius to Wolseley with a message that he would remain where he was until he received further orders. He added that his men had been given only one ounce of salt meat a day since the eighteenth of January and that Captain Sartorius had done "excellent and hard service." Leaving without provisions, Sartorius and his Hausa escort set out for Kumase, finding that it was not seven miles away but eighteen. He was fired on but pressed ahead and slept that night in the bush four miles from Kumase. The next day, the eleventh of February, he entered Kumase, finding it deserted except for a few apparent looters, who fled when he approached. Moving on, he met an Asante woman who told him that the king and his soldiers had entered Kumase and were anxious for revenge. He reached Amoafo that night to find that it too was deserted. The next day, having traveled fifty five miles without food and very little water, he found Wolseley.

Wolseley and his staff fed the famished Sartorius and his men, but after the excitement of his arrival wore off, they still waited impatiently for the king's messenger. What they did not know was that at 1 P.M., as they were eating, Glover's force had entered Kumase. Horrified by this new invasion, the distraught King Kofi Kakari and his councillors decided that further delay was impossible, and they sent messengers to Wolseley with some gold dust. It was dark before two gold-breastplated envoys accompanied by a suite of carriers arrived at Wolseley's camp. There followed one of the least dignified treaty signings on record.

First, the envoys blithely declared that they had only one thousand ounces of gold with them and that no more was available. They then asked to see Joseph Dawson, who first pocketed some of the gold, then oversaw what followed. The Asante envoys had brought not only gold dust—which was carefully scrutinized and weighed by a gold tester from Cape Coast who somehow happened to be with the general—but many solid gold masks, ornaments, and nuggets as well. The British gold tester weighed and inspected everything while Dawson, the ever-present former hostage Bonnat, and various Fante assistants kept up a spirited dialogue worthy of the most raucous fish market in East London. What little dignity remained to either side was lost when the British inspected the folds of the Asante envoys' garments in a search for more gold dust. In fact, they found an additional forty ounces.

Finally convinced that there was no more gold to be had, Wolseley called these demeaning proceedings to a halt and sent back a draft of his treaty to King Kakari for his signature. Amazingly, the signed treaty was quickly returned, and Wolseley was triumphant. The Asante king had made his submission and the general could not be happier. When Glover received Wolseley's dispatch telling him that a peace treaty had been signed and to halt hostilities, he was only too happy to march south where food was waiting. Wolseley, wasting no time waiting for Glover or smoothing his way, marched off toward the coast as rapidly as possible, leaving Glover's wretched men to their own devices. Glover's eleventh hour actions had saved Wolseley's campaign, but sharing the glory with Glover was not one of the general's priorities. Not only did

Wolseley do nothing to thank Glover at the time, his memoirs pointedly ignored Glover's vital role in the peace process. As one of Wolseley's biographers later observed, they were not the best of friends.[49]

Wolseley was convinced that by signing this treaty, the Asante would lose their ascendancy. That indeed appeared to be the result, as it soon became apparent that the coastal people were greatly encouraged. Of course, their confidence was likely to be fragile at best. As the British forces crossed the Pra River, they met a Russian prince, well known in London, who was hoping to participate in great events. He was, as he put it, "just in time to be too late." The returning British troops, on the other hand, were just in time to receive a glorious welcome at Cape Coast, complete with a triumphal arch of flowers, townspeople singing hymns, and a salute from the ships offshore. While the troops were ferried out to waiting ships, the valuables taken from the king's palace were sold at public auction. Wolseley personally bought the king's crown and orb, which his daughter later used as a rattle, and a Georgian silver coffeepot. All told, the palace's treasures sold for less than £5,000, a trifling amount compared to what could have been raised if the sale had been held in Britain or Europe and a tiny fraction of the cost of the campaign, about £900,000.

The cost to the British in men was regarded by the War Office and the public as quite low. Still, sixty-nine had been killed and some four hundred wounded, 135 of these from the Black Watch. Over one thousand men had to be invalided home due to wounds or disease. Seventy-one percent of the army units had suffered some form of severe illness, and 95 percent of the Naval Brigade had done so. Of the thirty officers who sailed to the Gold Coast with Wolseley, seven were dead and seven others wounded. The only one who had not been incapacitated by fever or diarrhea at least once was Lord Gifford, who had not been sick at all. For conspicuous bravery Wolseley recommended him, along with five others, for the Victoria Cross.[50] One so decorated was Lance Sergeant Samuel McGaw of the Black Watch, who had led the charge at Amoafo, and Captain Sartorius (the son, incidentally, of a prominent admiral), whose brother had been awarded a Victoria Cross in an earlier battle.

The first troops to return home to a tumultuous welcome were the Royal Welch Fusiliers. Through no fault of their own, they had seen little combat but had suffered a greater percentage of casualties from disease than any other battalion. Next to return were the 42nd Highlanders, who were delighted to be wearing their bonnets, kilts, and green coats once again. They were received with even greater enthusiasm.[51] When the Rifle Brigade arrived, there were feasts, balls, and honors all over the country. Every officer was decorated and almost all were promoted.

One member of Parliament was not impressed by Wolseley's campaign, saying that it reminded him of the famous rhyme,

> *The King of France with twenty thousand men*
> *Marched up a hill and then marched down again.*[52]

However, most in the government could not be happier that their faith in Wolseley had been vindicated. Disraeli and Gladstone competed with each other in search of ever more extravagant words of praise for their general, and the country joined in. Queen Victoria reviewed those troops able to leave the hospital in Windsor Park and bestowed the Grand Cross of the Order of St. Michael and St. George and a Knight Commander of the Bath on General Wolseley. He was also offered a baronetcy, which he contemptuously refused; he expected soon to be offered a peerage and become known as Lord Wolseley of Kumase.[53] The lord mayor of London presented him with a sword of honor, both the universities of Oxford and Cambridge awarded him honorary degrees, and the House of Commons made him a personal grant of £25,000, a phenomenal sum at a time when a fine riding horse could be purchased for £20. When Captain Glover returned to England some weeks later, all he received was a word of thanks from Parliament.

"So ended," Wolseley was later to write, "the most horrible war I ever took part in." So ended, too, by far the luckiest of his many campaigns. If the disgruntled King of Dwabin had not withdrawn his ten thousand men from the battle of Amoafo, Wolseley could have been stopped cold or, at the very least, accumulated so many more casualties that he could not have carried them. If the Asante had attacked as he marched back to the coast, he would have had the same problem; and if the king and his inner council had not panicked at the forward movement of Glover's almost starved force by unnecessarily sending gold dust to Wolseley and signing a treaty, it is likely that Wolseley's campaign would have been reckoned a failure. As British correspondents and members of his own staff acknowledged, despite his many brilliant preparations for the campaign, Wolseley's utter failure to anticipate the need for more African laborers delayed his march inland by a full month, putting him into the drenching start of the rainy season, when despite the great bravery of his officers and men and the luck of Glover's advance, he was within an ace of defeat.[54]

7

"Britannia Waives the Rules"

WOLSELEY WENT ON TO LEAD BRITAIN'S IMPERIAL ARMIES TO MORE victories, including an undeniably brilliant campaign in Egypt in 1882. He was later promoted to Field Marshal, raised to the peerage, and made commander in chief of the British army. However, his memory now largely lost, the last twelve years of life were lived in obscurity. On the eve of World War I, at the age of eighty, he died in bed, not the soldier's death he had longed for. His country did not forget him. A grateful War Office conducted his funeral with the utmost ceremony. Troops from all the regiments he had served with or commanded were there to honor him, and he was buried close to his hero, Wellington, something he would probably have considered his greatest honor.

King Kakari's fortunes took a very different course. Kumase was in ruins, his palace was looted and destroyed, his reputation badly tarnished, and his empire on the verge of dissolving into the chaos of secession and civil war. His militaristic councillors, who had so long dominated him and had led him into the calamitous war, were only too willing to blame him for everything. When the increasingly hostile kings and chiefs of the empire refused to pay any portion of the indemnity of fifty thousand ounces of gold demanded by the

British, Kakari had to dip into his own greatly depleted resources to pay small installments in May and June 1874. His hopes that these payments would influence the British to support him were not fulfilled. By the middle of June, his enemies made his position so precarious that he considered leaving Kumase to escape them.[1]

King Kakari had long offended some in the kingdom by his insatiable appetite for women. In addition to his hundreds of wives, he seduced many other women, including the wives of many powerful men. Neither his charm nor his power were enough to guarantee such conquests, however, so he relied on gold taken from the state treasury to captivate women, publicly handing out handfuls of gold dust and nuggets to women who caught his fancy. As a result, he was known among members of Asante's elite as *osape* (scatter of gold) and *axyempo* (he who gives away nuggets).[2] Now, desperate for money to pay Wolseley's indemnity and to support his appetite for women, the embattled king did the unthinkable. He rifled the tombs of his grandmother and other close relatives buried in the royal mausoleum at Bantama. The right to remove this buried gold, part of the national treasure, could only be granted by a vote of the national assembly. To open these tombs like a thief was not only unconstitutional, it was sacrilegious. To compound this reckless behavior with stunning stupidity, Kakari actually gave some of the beautiful old jewelry to various of his wives and girlfriends.

When the queen mother learned of her son's utter folly, she led the chorus of voices calling for his destoolment—largely, it would seem, because she knew he could no longer be king and in the hope that by doing so, she could preserve the line of succession for her lineage. Before the king could destroy the Golden Stool and kill himself by blowing up a keg of gunpowder, the Golden Stool was seized and Kakari was charged with bringing the kingdom to its ruinous state. Despite his quite reasonable rejoinder that it was not he who wanted war but the militaristic oligarchy, after five days of intense negotiation, he was forced to abdicate on October 21, 1874. Accompanied by sixty of his wives and five hundred of his closest followers, he was allowed to live in state in a small village though in very modest circumstances. He was succeeded by his younger brother, thirty-five-year-old Mensa Bonsu, whom his supporters hoped would restore Asante to the glorious past of his grandfather, Osei Bonsu. Instead, he ruled over a steadily diminishing empire torn to bits by civil wars.

The Civil Wars

In 1873 Royal Navy Captain Glover was commissioned to lead a military expedition up the Volta River valley. Wolseley suspected that its purpose was not primarily to aid his invasion of the Asante kingdom. He was right. The British government had hoped that Glover would be able to open up trade with the interior by circumventing Asante control, an economic vision that the British Government had long endorsed and that even Wolseley could appreciate. British lust for the wealth of the Asante kingdom was often expressed in the starkest imperialistic terms. Before Wolseley's invasion, Henry Stanley wrote that "King Coffee [Kofi Kakari] is too rich a neighbor to be left alone with his riches, with his tons of gold dust and accumulations of wealth to himself."[3] He added that the gold that a Wolseley victory would yield could pay the cost of the British military expedition "twenty times over." At the same time the *African Times*, usually a reliable voice of merchant interests, published an article under the caption "The Ashanti War—Gold, Gold, Gold," claiming that victory would bring thirty or forty million pounds of gold per year to Britain for years to come. It added almost breathlessly that the British troops were marching "into one of the richest gold fields in the world."[4]

It was a grand vision, but many doubted that it would ever be realized. Wolseley's inability to crush Asante resistance and the alarming effects of disease on his troops led many in Britain to despair of ever turning the Gold Coast into a profitable colony. To benefit from Asante gold, an army would have to occupy a very large area—an obvious impossibility in the face of disease and Asante truculence—or some new trading scheme would have to be devised. But as government officers fretted and merchants schemed, the conditions within the Asante kingdom became so desperate that it began to appear that Asante gold might well be Britain's after all. The Asante economy had collapsed, Kumase was a burned-out ghost town, and all the tributary states were seeking, or in some cases already declaring, their independence from the central government in Kumase. The district of Adanse was the original Akan-speaking state in the union and was considered by most Asante to be the birth-place of Greater Asante. It also had the richest gold deposits of any of the metropolitan states, and its high hills, left unprotected against Wolseley, were a great barrier to invasion from the south. Adanse was not powerful militarily, usually being able to muster only one thousand soldiers, but it nevertheless declared its independence from Kumase. The state of Dwaben, enormously wealthy from its dominance over the kola nut trade to the north, also left the union, taking with it its large army of up to twenty thousand men. Only Kumase itself might be able to mobilize as many. In 1869 European visitors had found the Dwaben capital larger and grander than Kumase had been before Wolseley destroyed it.[5]

Faced by impending chaos, King Mensa Bonsu appealed to the new British government at Cape Coast for "peace, trade and open roads," none of which the Kumase government could then provide for itself.[6] Instead of backing Kumase, the British sided with Dwaben as their new and preferred entry point into the interior of the Gold Coast. Emboldened by the open support of the new British governor, G. E. Strahan, and European missionaries and adventurers, such as the ever-entrepreneurial former French prisoner, Marie-Joseph Bonnat, and by the weakness of Kumase, the Dwaben king, Asafo Agyei, claimed not only independence from Kumase but supremacy over it. He began by declaring that he would block Kumase's trade routes to the north, cutting off its only remaining source of income. Despite Kumase's weakness, he overplayed his hand. His position was weak because he had no legitimate claim to the Dwaben stool, having been appointed to it by King Kwaku Dua I, who had executed a more legitimate claimant. The Kumase government now used Asafo's illegitimate claim to his stool against him, and his own excessive use of terror drove some former supporters into the Kumase camp. Opposition to Asafo Agyei soon became so heated that a council of kings from still-loyal states authorized Mensa Bonsu to depose him by force if need be.

Beginning at the end of August 1875, it took only two months to mobilize and ritually prepare an army of fifteen thousand men led by five veteran generals, including Adu Bofo, the hero of the Volta River campaign of 1869–1872, and Asamoa Nkwanta, still Asante's most beloved commander. On the thirty-first of October, the Asante army marched into the Dwaben capital where it was met by tenacious defenders who first stopped them cold, then surrounded and threatened to annihilate them. The situation appeared so hopeless that many senior officers, including the gray-haired, seventy-year-old Asamoa Nkwanta, blew themselves up with gunpowder.[7] When the battle seemed to be lost, the young general Adu Bofo sat on his golden stool and threatened to die then and there unless his demoralized troops fought to defend him. Somehow they rallied and drove the Dwaben army back in flight.

Dismayed by the prospect of a Dwaben defeat, Governor Strahan sent Dr. V. S. Gouldsbury to Dwaben to negotiate peace with Kumase. Even before he could reach Dwaben, he found King Asafo Agyei and his followers in flight, "helpless and terror-stricken."[8] Gouldsbury could do nothing while the Kumase forces punished Dwaben relentlessly. Virtually the entire population was killed, captured, or driven away to the British protectorate—which since 1874 had been called the Gold Coast Colony—where some fifteen thousand refugees settled. Every town and village in the formerly large and rich kingdom was burned to the ground.[9] Governor Strahan was dismayed by the Kumase victory. He informed London that he had hoped the Dwaben forces would hold out long enough to make his intervention "not only possible but even agreeable." The Colonial Office agreed that the surprising success of the Kumase troops was "unfortunate." The power of this Asante army in defeating an elite Dwaben army again emphasizes Wolseley's good fortune that it did not attack him as he withdrew to the coast.

The shattering defeat of Dwaben did not end rebellion within the teetering Asante Empire. Encouraged by Governor Strahan, state after state broke away from Kumase in search of its own economic autonomy. British policy was centered on the isolation and destruction of Kumase as the center of trade in the Gold Coast, and with the help of long-disaffected chiefs and kings, it was successful. Kumase no longer controlled its great roads or the traders that used them. Highway police were replaced by brigands. The once great market at Kumase that had so impressed Bowdich a half century earlier was now empty, and famine was reported in many areas. The British were unabashedly delighted by the results of their policy. The colonial secretary, Lord Kimberly, called for continuing efforts to encourage the independence of states now in rebellion against Kumase, and his undersecretary, the acerbic Evelyn Ashley, wrote, "It is their turn to be bullied—and, till they have changed their nature, it is better for us that they should be 'down' and not 'up.'"[10]

To the surprise and dismay of the British, the success of the Dwaben war reunified part of the Asante kingdom, and King Mensa Bonsu used the newfound spirit of hope and confidence to institute a number of reforms. Much of the impetus for change came from his brother, Prince John Owusu Ansa. Ansa had been educated in England and was a true believer in the principles of Western democracy, a devout Christian, and a caricature of an English gentleman. When one British visitor to Kumase encountered him on the street, he was so startled by his appearance that he "stood still and stared open-mouthed at this amazing apparition. . . . He wore a shapely 'bowler,' and a well-fitting, fashionably cut suit of clothes; his cuffs, shirt-front and high collar were faultlessly got up; his patent leather boots were a miracle of polish, and in one of his kid-gloved hands he carried a modish walking cane. But the most astonishing thing was that he wore his clothes and carried his cane with the unmistakable air of a man who was accustomed to them. . . ."[11]

Mensa Bonsu accepted Ansa's radical idea that European civil servants be hired on a contract basis to take important roles in the government. Unfortunately for the new king, there were no trained civil servants available; so he was forced to make do with a collection of shady European expatriates and adventurers, including Marie-Joseph Bonnat, and various Danish, Canadian, and Scottish gold prospectors. These men were more interested in becoming wealthy than they were in governmental reform, but even if they had been devoted civil servants, there was little that they could have accomplished in the face of conservative Asante opposition. Prince Ansa had been away too long, and he did not understand how dangerously his innovative ideas would clash with Asante culture. Prince Ansa's cherished dream of the establishment of Christian missions and schools in Asante was rejected out of hand. Ansa's ideas threatened the traditional balance of power in Kumase, a reality he consistently failed to grasp. He also did not anticipate that his own brother, General Owusu Koko, would become his most outspoken opponent.

A few important changes were made, among them a change in the law making homicide the only crime punishable by death, but Mensa Bonsu was never able to overcome the opposition of the senior members of the military oligarchy that had put him in power and that, he well understood, could depose him just as easily.[12] Instead of presiding over a reformed government, as he and Prince Ansa had hoped, Mensa Bonsu found himself largely ignored by his inner council. The great men of the kingdom still had power, including private armies as large as two thousand five hundred men. Like the king's own army of six hundred men, some of them were armed with Sniders. These powerful men, many of whom were members of the royal family eager for more power, continually vied with each other for control of the king and the government.

In 1879 a conservative religious cult dedicated to the restoration of the power and glory of the Asante past tried to influence the ever-buffeted king to become even more traditional. When Mensa Bonsu showed too little interest in their demands, a large group of the cult's followers broke into the royal palace, destroying property and violating some of the king's wives. One man even shot at Mensa Bonsu, who barely escaped, thanks to the intervention of his royal guards, whose Sniders killed many of the extremists. As a result of this attack and other palace coup attempts, the embattled king began to use his guards to purge his enemies, and he did so with a terrible vengeance. Now more a warlord than a constitutional monarch, he used his palace guards as he wished, to flout custom, law, and decency. Not only did he have his real or imagined enemies killed, he took pleasure in raping their wives.[13] Like his predecessor, King Kakari, he also indulged in an orgy of debauchery. When drunk, as he often was at this time, he ordered his guards to bring him any beautiful woman who caught his fancy. If her husband complained, the man was killed. In 1882 he began to eye the wives of some of the most powerful men in the kingdom. Ignoring judicial process, he ordered his guards to beat or even kill any who objected, and unless their private armies were stronger than his, he did so with impunity. A British visitor to Kumase in 1882 reported that the situation had become so serious that no one could be certain that "he may not be summoned to appear before the King at any moment, fined for some imaginary offense, a sum he cannot pay, and in the end lose his head."[14]

Later in the year his reign of terror even extended to his closest councillors, some of whom he had executed. So many people in Kumase fled that the city was almost empty. Many left metropolitan Asante for the coast where Snider-wielding palace guards could not reach them. By early March 1883 Mensa Bonsu had alienated every segment of Asante society. The opposition to the king, led by disgruntled young men of good families who saw no future for themselves, was joined by senior councillors who demanded that the king cease his tyranny, especially his rapacious abuse of the husbands and relatives of the women on whom he chose to impose his sexual desires. They also insisted that he no longer order executions without the consent of his chiefs and senior councillors and that he consult them before imposing immense fines on his subjects, as he had been doing. These were reasonable, constitutional demands, but the young men who led the opposition were so angry that some feared they would seize and flog the king. There was every reason to believe that these alienated young men would destroy the monarchy.[15] Only the king's guards prevented his destoolment, and even they finally failed to intercede when coup leaders, led by his brother, General Owusu Koko, seized the king and sent him into exile, where he lived under guard in a small village in miserable poverty.

Though former King Kakari had stayed apart from the political turmoil that had splintered the Asante state for seven long and tumultuous years, he still had powerful friends, and as time passed, many Asante came to remember him fondly for his genial and courteous manner. His adherents began to argue that his years of exile had given him the wisdom he lacked before, and they convinced him to seek the stool. With armed support he mounted a serious challenge to his contender, Kwaku Dua, who eventually invited him and his army to a peace conference in Kumase to discuss the troubled succession. It was a classic trap. When Kakari's six thousand supporters entered the wretched city, Snider fire erupted from all sides. At least two thousand were killed, but Kakari somehow escaped. After wandering alone for two weeks, he was captured and returned to Kumase where, hungry and exhausted, he was imprisoned under heavy guard while Kwaku Dua II was enstooled. A few days after Kwaku Dua's accession to the throne, he ruthlessly but prudently ordered the execution of some three hundred of Kakari's closest relatives, including women and children. Small children were killed by men who held their legs and smashed their skulls against tree trunks.[16] But only forty-four days into his reign, Kwaku Dua II died, apparently poisoned by the general who put him in power. Soon after, former King Kakari was executed. After being strangled with a leather thong, his neck was broken with an elephant's tusk, a traditional way of executing someone of royal birth whose blood could not legally be spilled.[17] The Asante political arena had never been a place for the faint of heart, but it had never been more dangerous than it was now.

The entire kingdom became engulfed in the most horrible civil war the Asante had ever known. States fought states, private armies fought private armies, and what used to be the Asante union burned. There were no safe havens. No large towns survived, and even most small villages were destroyed. Probably half the population fled or was killed. When the fighting finally ended in 1885, after two full years of war, all the formerly tributary states were independent. All that remained of the kingdom was a small area around Kumase, and the city itself was largely abandoned. Elephant grass grew over fifteen feet high in its once immaculate streets, and the palace, rebuilt with bamboo and grass thatch, was a mockery of its former grandeur.

In 1888 a royal faction led by Yaa Akyaa succeeded in putting her son, a fifteen-year-old boy named Agyemon Prempe, on the stool. The challenge before him could hardly have been greater: to reconstruct a kingdom splintered in all directions, most of whose people were either dead or refugees and whose resources had virtually ceased to exist. The national treasury was so depleted that the royal family was reduced to asking the British governor at Cape Castle for a loan of £320 to pay for the enstoolment ceremony. The Colonial Office decided it would be a good investment to lend the money to the "impecunious monarch."[18] However, the British attached so many conditions to the loan that if Prempe had accepted it, he would have yielded his sovereignty to the British crown. Prempe and his advisers refused to sell the kingdom for £320, but they could not restore the dominance of the government in Kumase. In return for their support of the new king, the district chiefs and kings reclaimed much of their lost power.[19]

Partly as a result of the issue of the loan, Prempe's formal enstoolment did not take place until June 1894. But more significant was the matter of whom the new King would rule. If he had been enstooled in 1888, he would have been no more than the king of Kumase district and a very impoverished district at that. Yet thanks to remarkably skillful diplomacy, Prempe's mother and councillors were able to reconcile many of the rebellious states. In fact, conciliatory promises from the new king-in-waiting were so successful in reestablishing the loyalty of the dissident chiefs and kings that by 1893 the Asante kingdom was very largely reunited. Prempe's own qualities had much to do with the successful reunification. Although he was plump and appeared effeminate, he was modest, respectful of his elders, and brave when in danger.[20] He also truly believed in Asante unity, had no personal ambition, never went back on a promise, and possessed what the Asante referred to as "the sweet tongue"—an ability to win people over with his words.[21]

Now that the rule of law had been reestablished, peaceful trade once again began to flourish. This new trade did not concentrate on guns and gunpowder, which were blocked by the British. In 1890 the nearly forty thousand Asante traders who traveled to the coast purchased only 1,312 guns and 2,091 kegs of gunpowder.[22] Asante still controlled major sources of gold, and new trade in cocoa and rubber was flourishing. In 1893 three thousand two hundred pounds of rubber were carried to Cape Coast each day.[23] In 1895 alone, over four million pounds of rubber were exported from the Gold Coast, two thirds of it from Asante.

British "forward policy," as it was known, continued to call for the destruction of the Asante state as an economic power in order to place the increasingly lucrative Gold Coast trade under British control. In support of the goal British administrators at Cape Coast rarely missed an opportunity to characterize the Asante government and its people as unworthy possessors of their empire. In

1892 Governor Griffith wrote of the Asante that "their proper characteristics are deceit, falsehood, treachery. In fact there is hardly a bad quality that they have not got."[24] His successor, Sir Frederick Hodgson, was convinced that the Asante social and political system was nothing but a "blood-thirsty despotism" that must be destroyed at any price. The various missionaries in the Gold Coast agreed, and so did Joseph Chamberlain, new secretary of state for the colonies, who was an outspoken advocate of the use of imperial power in West Africa.

In the past, British foreign policy had given France more or less a free hand in West Africa, concentrating instead on the strategic Nile Valley. Chamberlain, however, was willing to risk war with the French to secure the Gold Coast and the territories to its north. On June 28, 1895, he declared that Asante independence was "an intolerable nuisance." To add to Chamberlain's annoyance, reports began to accumulate that the French, increasingly active in the Ivory Coast just to the west of the Asante, were attempting to establish an alliance with the Asante and that King Prempe was actively negotiating with them. In fact, although he had some preliminary contact with representatives of Almani Samori, the brilliant African rebel against French rule, Prempe was not interested in an alliance with the French. What he wanted was British help in bringing peace and prosperity to his war-weary people. His pleas were communicated to Chamberlain, who dismissed them. The Asante were a "nuisance," and on November 21, 1895, Chamberlain cabled Governor Maxwell that military force would be used to subdue the Asante and bring about their submission to British rule.[25]

This decision to use force was made after Chamberlain's rejection of an extraordinary entreaty for peace from a six-man Asante delegation to the Court of St. James, a delegation led by Prince John Owusu Ansa and including his British-educated brother Albert. The delegation offered the British a large business concession and submission to the British crown. British authorities at Cape Coast, convinced that Ansa posed a danger to their interests, did everything they could to discredit him, even trying to deny him the right to travel to Britain.[26] Chamberlain at first refused to hear from the Ansa delegation on the grounds that the ambassadors were not authorized by Prempe and therefore lacked legal standing.

But Prince Ansa hired a British barrister, who informed Chamberlain that the Asante ambassadors' credentials were authentic and presented their submission that, in addition to offering a huge business concession, King Prempe would accept a British resident in Kumase and faithfully conform to the dictates of the queen or her representatives. They promised that the practice of human sacrifice had been abandoned, as in fact it had been under King Prempe, and asked only for peace and trade.

Chamberlain agreed to consider the matter if the delegation returned at once to Cape Coast; he then traveled to Kumase with British representatives to reach an accord. The Asante sailed back to the Gold Coast, convinced that they had averted war and established a business connection that would benefit both the British and the Asante. But Chamberlain could not overcome his fears that the French were somehow conspiring to control the Asante and through them the Gold Coast. While the Asante envoys were still at sea, he told Governor Maxwell that the planned military expedition to Kumase would go forward. Ironically, Prince Ansa actually arrived at Cape Coast on a ship that was loaded with military supplies for the invasion of Kumase. Maxwell received the Asante diplomats coldly, telling them that a military force would proceed to Kumase but holding out hope of peace. The disillusioned Asante returned to Kumase, where they discovered that their countrymen were well aware of the impending British invasion.

As word spread of the gathering of British military force, the Golden Stool and other valuables were removed from Kumase and hidden. Some factions in Asante wanted to mobilize the army, but Prempe refused, saying, "I am not prepared to fight the British troops in spite I am to be captured by them [*sic*]; . . . I would rather surrender to secure the lives and tranquillity of my people and countrymen."[27] But disturbing the tranquillity of the Asante people was exactly what the British had in mind. When a delegation of Asante diplomats hurried to the coast with promises of payment of all verified debts, Governor Maxwell curtly rebuked them, saying that their promises were empty words and that words alone could not send away the thousands of British soldiers who had been brought to the Gold Coast. Words of peace were not wanted. A British army would march to Kumase.

Command of what was called the Ashantee Expeditionary Force was given to Colonel Sir Francis Scott, who in 1874 had been a young officer in the 42nd Highlanders during Wolseley's march to Kumase. Scott's contempt for Africans was extreme even for his time, and he was as confident of victory as he was eager to fight. He had served in the Gold Coast for some time and in 1893 had led an expeditionary force of four hundred Hausas equipped with a Maxim gun to the north of the Gold Coast to prevent Asante expansion. He was well aware that the Asante could not hope to mobilize more than a few thousand men to oppose him, but several hundred of those men would be armed with Sniders, and a few would have modern French rifles. Properly led, troops with these weapons could be dangerous.

If the Asante chose to fight, they would face a somewhat smaller but much better-armed force than Wolseley had commanded. The West India Regiment of 380 African troops commanded by 20 British officers and 1,000 Hausas led by 30 British officers, as well as perhaps 500 native levies, were joined by the West Yorkshire Regiment of 400 men and 20 officers, as well as a special-service corps of 12 volunteer officers and 254 picked men chosen from some of the most prestigious regiments in the British army, including the Coldstream Guards, Scots Guards, and Grenadier Guards. What is more, Wolseley's radical idea of highly qualified volunteers finally had its day. Each man had to be at least twenty-four years old, have four years of service, be a good rifle shot, and pass a stiff medical examination.[28] Nevertheless, one of these men died of "heat apoplexy" on his first day in the Gold Coast.

Unlike Wolseley's force, Scott's army had no Naval Brigade. He did have various surgeons, engineers, supply and artillery officers, and thousands of carriers, perhaps ten thousand in all. The combat troops would have an even greater advantage in weapons than Wolseley's troops did. The Snider rifle had been replaced by a lighter, faster-firing and longer-range carbine, the Martini-Henry. The cumbersome and unreliable Gatling gun, which had been of little use to Wolseley, had been replaced by another American invention, the Maxim gun, a reliable, rapid-firing machine gun much like those that turned World War I into a slaughterhouse.[29] They also had newly issued 75-mm field pieces, capable of rapidly firing heavy explosive shells for great distances. And, of course, they still had bayonets.

The first troops arrived at Cape Coast in December 1895 on board a far nicer ship than the one Wolseley and his special-service officers so detested. There were few duties, the food was surprisingly good, and the men arranged concerts that mysteriously featured, among other songs, "Swanee River."[30] As it was for Wolseley two decades earlier, health was Scott's constant concern. The senior medical officer posted orders that called for men to eat "immediately" after rising because early morning was the "time of lowest vitality." A cup of soup, cocoa, or coffee was recommended along with bread and butter. Two grains of quinine were to be taken immediately after breakfast. All told, five grains per day were issued on the march. Everyone was ordered to avoid the sun, damp clothing, unboiled water, and any food not supplied by the government. Bowels were to be "open daily," and all men were required to wear a flannel cummerbund at night, apparently to prevent the loss of vital body heat.[31] Hospitals were set up as far into the interior as Wolseley's old camp at Prahsu, and a large hospital ship was anchored off shore. Huge depots of food were established, and as it was in Wolseley's campaign, the emphasis was on meat (once again each man was to receive 1 1/2 pounds of meat each day) and freshly baked bread. Despite all precautions, fever quickly began to take its toll, and victims were rapidly invalided home. One of the first to fall was a robust thirty-one-year-old major named Ferguson, whose fever rose to 110° before he died. He was buried next to Captain Huyshe, who died on Wolseley's campaign.[32]

On Christmas Day two ships arrived carrying the special-service troops and the 2nd Battalion of the West Yorkshire Regiment. The men came ashore much more easily than their unruly mules, which threatened to capsize the small boats, and the white troops immediately began their march inland. Units of the special-service corps, including a company from the same Rifle Brigade that fought in 1874, had no difficulty on the march, but the 2nd West Yorkshire, the Old West Yorks, had a terrible time. This battalion had been stationed in Aden before being ordered to the Gold Coast, and many were ill. They were also said to have consumed far too much beer and done too little marching. On the first day eighty men fell out and had to be carried. It was not until much later in the campaign that the men became reasonably fit.[33] Later that same day Prince Henry of Battenburg, Queen Victoria's son-in-law, came ashore riding a donkey and carrying a small white umbrella as protection against the sun. He was eager to show his enthusiasm for the military actions of his adopted country. With him as an aide-de-camp was His Highness Prince Victor of Schleswig-Holstein. Christmas dinner for the troops included fresh meat, plum pudding, and a bottle of beer. It was declared excellent.[34]

The road that Wolseley's engineers had built two decades earlier was in total disrepair. In many places the troops had to advance in single file, climbing over fallen trees and cutting away vines and underbrush. When clearings were reached, the troops were trained in the tactics Scott thought would be necessary to fight against an unseen enemy in the dense brush. Scott disdained Wolseley's lightweight gray uniforms. This was the last time that British troops wore scarlet tunics on active service, but by the end of the first day's march, the woolen tunics were so soaked with sweat that they turned black and stayed that way throughout the campaign. Somehow Scott had not learned from Wolseley. Before the force entered metropolitan Asante, patrols searched for the Asante army, and spies were paid to provide information about their whereabouts and plans. Though there were several alarms that led the British to take up defensive positions, there was no sign of Asante troops. All the British found were small villages, the formerly prosperous but now ruined towns of Fomena and Amoafo, streams that the engineers had to bridge, and shrines—so-called fetish houses—which the troops destroyed "in a ruthless, unheeding way," despite orders to leave them alone.[35]

As Scott's column approached Kumase, a group of high-ranking Asante envoys, attempting to meet with the colonel to discuss peace, were beaten and robbed by the Hausa soldiers. Officers eventually restored order, returned the Asante envoys' property, and flogged some of the thieves. A newspaper correspondent for the *Daily Telegraph* commented, consistent with the rabidly racist feelings of many Britons on this expedition, "Sambo does not bear flogging well, usually howling piteously."[36] Captain Donald Stewart, Scott's so-called political officer, apologized to the envoys and asked them to assure the king that it was an accident. He also assured them that the British had no intention of deposing King Prempe if he accepted British protection, allowed a resident to be appointed, paid a war indemnity of an unspecified amount, and provided hostages to assure payment of the balance. The Asante were not pleased, but they dutifully returned to Kumase.

On the night of January 16, Scott's army camped just outside Kumase. In a scene reminiscent of Wolseley's expedition, a tremendous thunderstorm kept everyone awake all night. When word came the next morning that Scott's scouts had entered Kumase without opposition, Scott called the correspondents together to hear this fatuous declaration: "I want you correspondents to make a note of it: That it has been entirely owing to the rapidity of my movements there has been no fighting. The celerity of my movements have [*sic*] completely paralyzed Prempe's efforts. Besides, bear in mind, we have come up in far less time than Lord Wolseley took in the last war."[37] One correspondent felt compelled to observe that Wolseley had to fight his way to Kumase.

As a Hausa brass band incongruously played "Home Sweet Home," the British troops marched smartly into the bedraggled city, watched by a small crowd of somber Asante. After posting sentries, Scott met with King Prempe at about 5 P.M.. Prempe greeted him with a wildly discordant medley of drums, horns, and metallic clanging, complete with dancing executioners and dwarfs as well as endless shouted eulogies by pages to the greatness of the Asante monarch. Following an exchange of greetings, Scott told the king that he would meet with him again when Governor Maxwell arrived in a day or so. He also peremptorily told him not to make loud noise at night, to cut the long grass in the streets, and to clean up the "filthy" city. Prempe returned to his palace accompanied by the Ansa brothers, who despite their European clothing joined in some riotous dancing on the way. The British troops put up tents and "slept soundly under cover, convinced there would be no attempt on the part of the miserable natives to disturb their rest," as one member of the expedition scornfully put it.[38]

The next day, as Colonel Scott waited for Governor Maxwell, he was informed that eight people held as captives by King Prempe were pleading to be rescued before they were executed. These people were relatives of King Akrampa, a rival claimant to the throne before Prempe had been enstooled. Most of his followers had already died or been executed, but these eight, including his sister, were still alive, and they begged for their lives. Sir Francis was unwilling to interfere in any way, saying that their rescue might annoy King Prempe, and besides, as a correspondent who was a witness reported, "He was sure the black people did not mind or care much about their fate."[39] Colonel F. J. Kempster of the West Yorkshire Regiment angrily objected, insisting that all human beings cared about their lives. After some vigorous discussion Scott reluctantly agreed to the rescue, and at ten that night British troops drove away the Asante guard and freed the prisoners. Scott would have been surprised by their reaction. "When at last they were made to understand they were set free, their joy and gratitude were unbounded, and they cried and blessed their deliverers again and again."[40]

Two days later at 6 A.M., not an hour King Prempe would ordinarily have chosen to conduct state business, Captain Stewart and an escort of special-service troops waited impatiently for King Prempe. The king, as it turned out, was ready promptly at six, but some members of his large retinue were tardy. When Stewart was told that the king was not yet ready, he testily said that he would give Prempe five more minutes and if he were not ready by then, his troops would enter the palace by force and carry the king to the meeting place. Three minutes later, drums and horns sounded furiously, functionaries of all sorts dashed about, and King Prempe, his mother, and entourage appeared. He was carried in his hammock, where he sat propped up by silk cushions and shaded by a blue velvet umbrella. Led by a detachment of British troops, the Asante were ushered into a large square of more British troops, who were lined up two abreast. The soldiers, with white leather belts and shoulder straps contrasting with once red coats and with bayonets glistening in the sun, were a striking complement to the multicolored silk togas of the Asante court and the formal European clothing of the Ansa brothers. To add a note of even greater incongruity, three scarlet-clad hunchbacked dwarfs danced in front of the king.

Across the square from the umbrella-shaded royal party sat Governor Maxwell, flanked on one side by Colonel Scott and on the other by Colonel Kempster. They sat on folding camp chairs that were perched precariously on top of a dais made of large biscuit boxes. The arrangement was hardly majestic, but elevation over native peoples was always a vital prop of colonial rule, just as it often was with African kings. Wearing a white toga, the light-skinned, plump King Prempe, with what observers found to be intelligent eyes, sat silently holding a kola nut in his mouth. In Asante court tradition the nut symbolized the king's inability to speak an untruth. Not surprisingly, the British found the practice absurd. Major Robert Baden-Powell—who would later found the Boy Scouts and use an Asante scouting sign as the model for the Boy Scout salute—was not impressed. He wrote that the king's "flabby yellow face" glistened with oil and "his somewhat stupid expression [was] rendered more idiotic by his sucking a large nut like a fat cigar."[41] An aristocratic young officer agreed, describing the king as "an oily, well-fed looking brute."[42] Both agreed that he appeared agitated.

Without any diplomatic preamble Governor Maxwell began by accusing the Asante of not maintaining the road to Cape Coast and not abolishing human sacrifice. The first charge was true enough, but the British had not maintained the portion of the road that ran through their colony either, and the abolition of human sacrifice was an utterly bogus issue. It had never been a part of the treaty Wolseley signed at Fomena, it still survived quite openly within the British protectorate, and Prempe had in fact abolished it! What he still practiced was the execution of murderers, something the British preferred to think of as human sacrifice, a nice way to maintain their moral ascendancy. Without any semblance of diplomatic courtesy, Governor Maxwell then told his interpreter to tell the king that he must submit to British rule and pay the remaining forty-eight thousand ounces of the now twenty-two-year-old indemnity of fifty thousand ounces of gold. As these dramatic events were unfolding, soldiers from the Old West Yorks were passing out in the heat, one after the other. In all, thirty-six of them collapsed, joined by one soldier from the special-service corps. They lay unceremoniously in the dust until the ceremony was over.[43]

For some time Prempe sat motionless, apparently struggling with his emotions. No Asante king had ever made a personal submission to another authority. Finally, Prince John Ansa whispered something in his ear, and King Prempe deliberately removed his golden sandals and a golden circlet from his head. Joined by the queen mother, Prempe walked slowly toward the biscuit box dais. Mother and son knelt awkwardly and put their arms around the leather boots of the governor and the two colonels. The Asante onlookers were utterly still as they watched this unprecedented humbling of their monarch. When Prempe regained his seat, he rose again and through John Ansa said, "I now claim the protection of the Queen of England."[44] He added that he had 680 ounces of gold that he was prepared to pay now and would pay the remainder in installments.

Maxwell dismissed the king's offer as "child's play," adding that he could not believe that the king had so little gold. Prempe repeated his offer and Maxwell again demanded more, reminding him that since the treaty of twenty-two years earlier, only two thousand of the fifty thousand-ounce indemnity had been paid. Prempe responded that the Asante government had never been pressed for the money before and that he did not have it now. Maxwell was unyielding. He had already decided that, in order to prevent Prempe from negotiating with the French, he would have to be removed from his stool. Maxwell also believed the widespread rumors that King Prempe had his own fabulously rich gold mine. (In fact, there was such a mine, and when after much difficulty the British found it, southwest of Kumase, in 1900, they were surprised to discover that a rich reef had been dug out for a length of one hundred yards with large, well-timbered galleries built all along the tunnel. How much gold was available to King Prempe in 1895 is, however, not known.) Maxwell next announced that he would take the king, the queen mother, and others of high rank as hostages until the remainder of the indemnity was paid. Prempe again asked to pay in installments: "It is usual for a man, before he takes his meals, to take something to sharpen his appetite. Then, if the Governor takes an instalment, that will sharpen his; he will look the keener after the remainder."[45]

Maxwell was not amused by Prempe's wit. He read the names of the hostages he would take from a list he had drawn up before leaving the coast. He also announced that the two Ansa brothers were under arrest for forgery. The Ansas were immediately handcuffed, while the King was forced to remove all emblems of his sovereignty. The Asante onlookers were stunned and angry, but a large guard of troops with fixed bayonets surrounded the royal party. Led by Major Baden-Powell, as unsympathetic to Africans as anyone could be, two companies of West Yorks smashed the doors of the royal palace and seized more hostages. Once again, the palace was looted, but this time little of value, except to the Asante, was found. As vultures looked on from nearby cottonwood trees, the hostages set out for Cape Coast, carried in hammocks but under heavy guard.

While the despondent royal hostages were being carried away from Kumase, some of Scott's men explored the once vibrant but now almost deserted city. Large parts of Kumase had never been rebuilt after Wolseley burned it, but the royal palace of stone that Wolseley destroyed had been replaced by several huge bamboo huts that to the British resembled barns. Most of Kumase's dwellings and offices were in sad disrepair, but some of the beautifully ornamented, ocher-red-painted structures that impressed earlier visitors still stood. Some British officers actually believed that the ocherous red paint used on the polished clay friezes that decorated these houses was made from the blood of victims of human sacrifice, particularly virgin girls.[46]

Drawn inexorably to the execution area, the British invaders found that it had been in recent use. In addition to skulls and bones displayed on the buttresses of cottonwood trees, decaying bodies were strewn about in the long grass. The stench was as terrible as it had been in 1874, and the vultures as numerous and well fed.[47] The British still did not understand that these victims were considered criminals, not innocent human sacrifices, and that their bodies were exposed in this manner instead of being buried in order further to deter crime.

Many British troops went beyond sightseeing; they ransacked the city, carrying away valuables and smashing and burning what they did not take a fancy to. A British surgeon condemned the burning of old and beautiful houses as sheer vandalism.[48] The royal mausoleum at Bantama, which had escaped destruction by Wolseley, was not spared this time. Many of the valuables buried there had been removed before the British arrived, but the coffins still contained royal skeletons. By Governor Maxwell's order the mausoleum was burned, its religious artifacts smashed, and the nearby sacred trees destroyed by ax, gunpowder, and fire. The blazes lasted all day, as religious shrines were added to the pyres. While Bantama was being desecrated, Fante carriers were busily removing the teeth from bodies in the exhumed grave. They wore them as necklaces.[49]

Scott's expedition marched out of Kumase on January 22 to begin the long, fourteen-day trek back to Cape Coast. The Ansas, under criminal arrest, were made to march the entire distance handcuffed. The royal hostages were carried in hammocks and reasonably well treated, but the queen mother was not impressed. She spat at any white man who ventured close to her. As soon as the hostages reached the coast, small boats took them out to the HMS *Raccoon*, waiting offshore. It was the first time any of the royal family had seen the ocean, and it could not have been a happy day for them. They were imprisoned in the fortress at Elmina, whose people had long been loyal to the Asante kingdom and where European traders had paid rent to Asante kings for over two hundred years. After nearly a year they were taken to Sierra Leone, but so many Asante trekked all the way to Sierra Leone with gifts of gold dust and news of Asante politics that the British moved the royal hostages, their spouses, and children—fifty-six in all—to the totally inaccessible Seychelles Islands, off the coast of East Africa. Prempe would live in exile there until 1924.

The increasingly westernized Fante population at Cape Coast gave a formal dance in honor of Scott's expeditionary force. One officer who attended wrote that he was "astonished" to find the African women dressed in "smart low-necked frocks" and the men "perfectly dressed in evening clothes" except for the fact that all wore red socks. Another officer decided that he would like to dance with one of the African ladies and asked her partner's permission. The man surrendered her reluctantly saying quite sternly: "For dance, yes; for make love, no."[50]

For his bloodless victory Sir Francis Scott was made an honorary major general, and the other officers were promoted at least one grade. No shots had been fired, but the campaign had not been without cost. Despite quinine, over 40 percent of the white officers and men fell ill, some seriously enough to be invalided home before they reached Kumase. Two officers, eight noncommissioned officers, and eight white soldiers died. One of those who died of malaria was Prince Henry of Battenburg; Prince Victor survived his bout with the disease. The African troops suffered almost as badly.[51]

The Ansa brothers were imprisoned without bail until February 12, 1896, when they were tried in the supreme court of the Gold Coast. In May they were acquitted of all charges of forgery. Furious, the government ordered a second trial, this time for embezzlement. It was obvious to everyone that the charges were trumped up to punish the educated Ansas for their many efforts to restore and reunify the Asante kingdom. An editorial in the *Gold Coast Chronicle*, hardly a newspaper sympathetic to the Asante, concluded that "the arraignment of persons before a British Court of Law for alleged offenses committed under circumstances and in a country where the court had no jurisdiction, is a monstrous piece of high-handed despotism for which there is no excuse."[52] Friends of the Ansas in London insisted that they had been maliciously prosecuted, and Chamberlain was forced to defend the role of the Colonial Office in action before Parliament. Neither the question of the Ansas' prosecution nor the more embarrassing question of the legality of the British invasion and the imprisonment of the king was resolved. It was apparent to most that the royal hostages were taken, not as security against payment of the indemnity of fifty thousand ounces of gold, but to prevent the king or his legitimate successor from signing a treaty with the French or Germans.[53] In these heady days of imperial expansion, the niceties of international law were so often waived that wags changed the lyrics of the popular patriotic song "Rule Britannia" from "Britannia rules the waves," to "Britannia waives the rules."

Even in this climate of colonial arrogance, it became increasingly awkward for the Colonial Office to justify the British government's patently illegal takeover of the Asante government. Secretary Chamberlain himself initially had been shocked by Maxwell's unauthorized arrest of King Prempe, but Maxwell was eventually able to bring him around to support the action.[54] To put the best face on his actions, Maxwell asked three Asante to serve in what he called the Council of Administration, which would, as he conceived it, be a puppet government for the British resident. To lead the council he chose Opoku Mensa, the most senior leader left in Kumase and a man totally loyal to King Prempe. Together with the other two well-respected council members, Opoku Mensa was able to subvert many of the resident's plans. The council soon gathered support from districts beyond Kumase, taxed traders for money to support the king at Elmina, and lobbied mightily for his release, even hiring lawyers to draw up petitions on his behalf. As time passed, Opoku Mensa became widely recognized as the representative of the king, ruling in absentia.[55]

It was clear that the Asante government could function quite well even without its king, as a British Colonial Office report sourly noted: "I am afraid the Chiefs are slowly returning to their old ways. . . . There is no doubt that much of their doings are unknown to the Resident."[56] Although his plans were often subverted, the British resident in Kumase was able to force the chiefs to provide men for road building, to build an imposing stone fort for the defense of the residency, and most detestable to the proud Asante, who had never served as carriers, to carry Europeans and their goods. Those who refused were beaten by Hausa soldiers, who often took the law into their own rough hands.

Soon after Prempe's arrest, Maxwell returned to England to assure members of the chambers of commerce in London, Manchester, and Liverpool that "Ashanti is now open to British trade." He urged British traders to become "pushfull" about exploiting economic opportunities in the Gold Coast, which he promised to turn into "one of the brightest jewels in the British Crown." Businessmen were quick to take him up on his invitation. By the end of 1899, twenty-five licenses had been granted to mine gold, exploit timber, and export rubber, all from large parcels of land owned by wealthy Asante or the king. Asante miners had worked every gold-bearing deposit in the country long before European miners arrived, but there was still a great deal of gold to be had, and some of these gold-mining concessions allowed the government and private investors to profit immensely.[57] For example, the Ashanti Goldfields Corporation, Ltd., was given a ninety-nine-year lease not only for mineral rights but for timber and rubber as well. It made its first shipment of gold in 1898. By 1946 it had produced almost six million ounces of gold.[58]

Christian missionaries of the rival Wesleyan and Basel missions who operated nineteen mission schools in the region had done everything in their power to subvert Asante sovereignty for over fifteen years. In addition to spreading lurid tales about Asante despotism and cruelty, especially human sacrifice, they gave intelligence to the British about Asante actions and on several occasions supplied Christian converts to the British as carriers, interpreters, and even soldiers. When Scott invaded, the former captive Reverend Ramseyer supplied hundreds of men to him as carriers. In appreciation for his services, only five days after Prempe was taken into custody, Governor Maxwell invited Ramseyer to open a mission in Kumase. When the missionary arrived, he was exultant: "It is no longer a dream. . . . Kumase is now a Basel missionary station. . . . All Asante lies open before us."[59]

As time passed and British demands for labor and taxes were exceeded only by the missionaries' demands for children to convert to Christianity, Asante bitterness became obvious even to disinterested European visitors.[60] Surreptitiously, the Asante made more and more efforts to acquire modern weapons and ammunition. People still had hope that King Prempe would be restored to his stool, but patience was wearing thin. The British were impatient, too. As Secretary of State Chamberlain later explained in Parliament, the Golden Stool alone gave legitimate supremacy to the ruler of Asante. "Therefore it was of the greatest importance to get hold of this symbol of sovereignty, if we could possibly do it."[61]

The British resident at Kumase, Captain W. B. Davidson-Houston, had no comprehension of the importance of the Golden Stool for the Asante. He and other British government officials thought of it as nothing more than a potent symbol, like the crown or throne of a European king. That the stool embodied the soul and well-being of the Asante people and linked generations of their ancestors in spiritual common cause was simply not grasped. Davidson-Houston made several thinly disguised attempts to find the Golden Stool, but they were as unsuccessful as they were deeply offensive to the Asante. In December 1899, almost four years after Prempe's arrest, a lame Asante boy named Kwame Tua appeared at Government House in Accra, now the seat of British power in the Gold Coast, where he offered to reveal the hiding place of the

Golden Stool. Without bothering much about what the boy's motives might be, the former lieutenant governor, now governor, Sir Frederick Hodgson, immediately dispatched his private secretary, Captain C. H. Armitage, with some Hausa soldiers and carriers in search of the Golden Stool. After marching north for about one hundred miles, the boy slipped away from Armitage and unaccountably told a local chief that the expedition was searching for the Golden Stool. Armitage lamely tried to convince the alarmed chief that the boy was quite mad and quickly marched on, the boy still in tow. Some twenty-five miles north of Kumase, the boy panicked again, refusing to go any farther. Armitage tried both threats and bribery with no success. By now it was widely known that the British were searching for the Golden Stool, and the countryside was thoroughly up in arms. When the chiefs learned that Governor Hodgson would soon visit Kumase, they assumed that he too was in search of the stool. And they were right.

Despite their anger, the Asante people received the governor and his large party with the dignified protocol typical of the royal court. Rose Ramseyer, now ascendant in her new Basel mission station outside Kumase, presented Lady Mary Hodgson with a bouquet, and the children from her mission school sang "God Save the Queen." Later that day bugles sounded to announce his excellency, an honor guard of Hausa soldiers presented arms, and in full-dress uniform, Sir Frederick strode vigorously out of the fort to address an assemblage of Asante chiefs and nobles. The slim, graceful Lady Hodgson sat proudly next to the stocky, bull-necked governor, who spoke while sitting down. After some reassuring words about his pleasure at being in Kumase and some soon-to-be self-evident nonsense about his good knowledge of the people and their customs, the crude, overbearing Hodgson delivered a series of hammerblows to the Asantes' pride, religion, and treasury.

First, he declared, King Prempe would never return. Power would remain forever in the hands of the British. Second, not only would the fifty thousand-ounce war indemnity have to be paid, but interest was accruing. He read out the amounts of interest owed by the various district chiefs and kings. He then launched into this astonishing *casus belli*: "What must I do to the man, whoever he is, who has failed to give to the Queen, who is the paramount power in this country, the stool to which she is entitled? Where is the Golden Stool? Why am I not sitting on the Golden Stool at this moment?" He carried on in this vein, making plain to all Asante that he was a barbarian determined to violate the sanctity of the Golden Stool on which an Asante monarch had only physically sat during the most sacred occasions.[62] When Lady Hodgson wrote her memoirs, she loyally denied that Hodgson had ever mentioned sitting on the stool, but Hodgson's signed transcript of his speech makes it clear that he did, and Asante who were present vividly remember his words.[63] Hodgson's confrontational approach was a calculated one. He firmly believed that only if the Asante knew their king would never return and the Queen of England possessed the Golden Stool would they submit to British rule. But because he had no understanding of the meaning of the Golden Stool for the Asante, his tough talk would start a war.

The Asante audience left without an open display of anger, but there was little hope of averting war now. The loss of land to British mining concessions had already driven many Asante to the point of insurrection. In addition to the loss of land, the Asante were outraged when the British resident ordered chiefs to produce carriers for the European miners. It was bad enough that families had to send their slaves to work for the hated miners, but free Asante were forced to carry supplies as well, something that the Asante found deeply humiliating. The British also forced free men to work as laborers on the roads, and if they refused, they were flogged or their chiefs were fined. The Hausa soldiers who enforced these demands were seen as tyrannical and rapacious agents of a foreign government. Moreover, British efforts to abolish the slave trade, which still flourished, infuriated many others.

Slavery was still vital to the Asante economy, especially to agriculture and the important kola nut trade to the north. These northern people had no other means of paying for kola nuts than slaves, and as several British observers pointed out, by now Asante slavery was such a benign institution that when the British actually freed slaves from their Asante masters, they refused to leave.[64] The French did nothing to discourage slavery in their West African possessions, including the Ivory Coast, which adjoined the Gold Coast to the west, and the Germans encouraged it in Togo to the east;

but the British frequently tried to hold to principle even if social and economic conditions might have called for a more cautious policy. Caution finally won the day. The Colonial Office chose to be pragmatic: "If we make it known that we have entered a crusade against slavery, we will not have any allies and they might all combine against us. So we should move very warily and carefully in this matter. To abolish domestic slavery would mean a social revolution of the greatest character. All in Ashanti who have anything to lose would gravely resist this act."[65]

The Christian missionaries' attack on Asante religion was another factor that led many Asante to consider war. The Asante religion was as meaningful to them as Christianity was to the missionaries, and they saw no reason to embrace alien ideas that would profoundly alter their way of life. The people of Asante had come very close to open rebellion several times during the past two years, and now Hodgson's aggressive declaration that Prempe would "never again" rule in Asante and that he should possess and "sit on" the Golden Stool pushed most of them over the brink.

A few hours after Hodgson's provocative speech, most of the great chiefs and nobles met in secret. After the men had begun to debate the issues, the sixty-year-old queen mother of the kingdom of Edweso stood up. Asante queen mothers were expected to lead in times of great national crisis, and this one, Yaa Asantewaa by name, was a forceful woman with a grievance and a vision. Her son, the king of Edweso, had been one of Prempe's most devoted allies. It was for that reason that he had been arrested and sent into exile along with Prempe. Edweso was so loyal to the monarch that it was there that the Golden Stool was hidden from the British until it had to be moved in December 1899, when the British began to search that area.[66] The queen mother was determined not only to restore her son to his place of authority but to reunite the Asante Empire under King Prempe. She began her impassioned speech by declaring that she would never pay one penny of her portion of the interest on the indemnity that Governor Hodgson had demanded. She then asked the men how they could sit idly while the British humiliated them time and again. "If you, the chiefs of Asante, are going to behave like cowards and not fight, you should exchange your loincloths for my undergarments." She then grabbed a rifle from a startled chief and fired it into the ground. That night, it is said, all the chiefs swore an oath to fight a war of national liberation from the British.[67]

To give their rebellion legitimacy, the Asante ruling council offered the Golden Stool to the closest relative of King Prempe left in Asante, Asibe II, the chief of Kokofu. He humbly agreed to accept the stool and to lead the war effort, but before he could take any action, he was betrayed, and Governor Hodgson had him arrested and detained in the fort. He later—and gallantly—escaped but was again captured. Kept in irons, he was soon after deported. Well advised by British sympathizers, of whom there were many, Hodgson also managed to detain five or six major kings in the fort at Kumase, effectively neutralizing the participation of troops from their districts, but the remaining Asante leaders nevertheless mobilized their men for war.

The war began three days after Hodgson's bellicose speech, when the same boy who led Captain Armitage on a wild-goose chase after the Golden Stool reappeared at the fort in Kumase with a new offer to lead the white men to its hiding place. Ever hopeful and ever naive, Hodgson again sent Captain Armitage, with another British officer, Captain Leggett, and fifty Hausa troops with their many African carriers, to follow the boy in search of the hidden treasure. As the column entered each of two small villages, they found the young men restless and excited, but they were allowed to search the villages without opposition. Leaving Captain Leggett and fifteen Hausas in a village named Bali, Armitage ordered his Hausas to bully and actually whip some of the children in search of information about the stool, but the only product of his brutality was even greater Asante outrage. Armitage then followed the boy through a dense, silent forest for more than three hours before coming to a clearing where they found three small huts. Here, the boy guide assured them, lay the Golden Stool. Picks and shovels dug deeply underneath the floor of each hut until the boy finally admitted that he had made a mistake.

Thoroughly disgusted, Armitage and his men trooped back to Bali, where they discovered Captain Leggett and his men faced off against forty or fifty armed Asante. As perhaps only British officers of that era could do, the youthful-appearing Armitage and the strikingly handsome Leggett calmly sat down to have tea prepared by their thoughtful orderly. The excited Asante looked on in amazement while a folding table (an essential piece of furniture that had been lugged along by sweating carriers) was set with two enameled cups and saucers, a butter tin, condensed milk, and a teapot. While the two sides stared at each other with their fingers on their triggers, the officers sat down on folding chairs. Without warning, the tin of condensed milk flew into the air, followed by the cup and everything else on the table, as Asante slugs flew everywhere, slightly wounding Armitage and Leggett as well as several of the Hausas. The British troops quickly took cover in nearby houses and returned fire. With nightfall such heavy rain fell that the Asante troops could not prime their flintlocks, and the night thus passed quietly.

Early in the morning Armitage and Leggett tried to fight their way back to Kumase. The Asante followed them all day, firing from the thick brush. By late afternoon the column had so many wounded that it could go no farther. Armitage issued ten rounds to Leggett and each of the men still able to march and ordered them to break through to the fort. He divided the rest of his ammunition among the men who remained. It came to three rounds for each man able to fire. Completely out of food and water, the men licked the dew off leaves and waited. Providentially, the Asante did not attack, and Leggett ran into a patrol from the fort that escorted the entire force to safety. The exhausted, thirsty, and wounded men were tended to by the six surgeons in the fort, then fed, and allowed to rest. After having his minor wounds treated and eating breakfast, Armitage slept for days.

So began the ultimate Victorian melodrama: British troops and white women besieged in a fort by "cruel savages," their food running out, hope almost gone, as British troops fought valiantly to reach them in time. It was a script that could have been done for Hollywood. The drama was real enough, but so was the terrible war that had just begun, a war that would see some of the fiercest battles ever fought in West Africa and that, despite conspicuous Asante courage, would result in the loss of Asante independence forever.

✕

8

"We Are Going to Die Today"

As the twentieth century began, the Asante prepared for war—or rebellion as the British always called it. They were surprisingly well organized, considering how unexpectedly the conflict had come. Guided by Opoku Mensa, their political leader, and Kofi Kofia, a vigorous young general, newly mobilized soldiers rapidly assembled outside Kumase where the first battles would have to be fought. Some few of the Asante troops had breech-loading rifles, for the most part older models such as Sniders, but almost all their men were still armed with antiquated flintlock muskets, and they were chronically short of shot and powder. Asante generals were fully aware that the British troops they had chosen to face would not only all be armed with the most modern rifles but also have machine guns, powerful, rapid-firing 75-mm cannon, and seemingly limitless supplies of ammunition.

In searching for a way to neutralize British firepower, Asante military leaders seized on the idea of the stockade, which had apparently been explained to them by Mende travelers who knew of the use of stockades against the British in Sierra Leone in 1898. Despite inexperience with this kind of defensive structure, the Asante accomplished an astonishing engineering feat. There were only a dozen roads or paths that led out of Kumase through the dense jungle barrier that surrounded the city. If these paths were blocked, British reinforcements could not reach Kumase to relieve the British fort, nor could the forces in it hope to escape. In the space of only three weeks, the Asante managed to block all these roads with twenty-one massive log barricades. Using slave labor driven on by armed troops, the Asante cut thousands of huge logs and dragged them into place. Two six-foot-high walls of logs, lashed together with telegraph wire torn down from its route from Kumase to the coast, were filled in with five to six feet of densely packed dirt, stones, and smaller logs. Loopholes were cut to allow firing. Many of these stockades were built in zigzag patterns to allow cross-firing if the British troops were able to press their attacks close to these formidable barriers. These stockades were so monumental that they were impervious to the heaviest artillery fire the British guns could manage. What is more remarkable, these were not narrow structures that merely blocked a path, like the fallen trees that had been used to impede Wolseley's advance. Several stockades were over four hundred yards long, and many others were nearly that extensive. The flanks of these stockades were also fortified and entrenched, so that even if British troops succeeded in cutting their way through the jungle to outflank the stockade, they would still encounter heavy fire from well-protected defenders.

Behind each stockade the Asante leaders built extensive war camps capable of housing many thousands of troops. These camps consisted of a thousand or more well-made huts equipped with bamboo beds, outside sitting areas, and some large structures with reinforced log roofs capable of withstanding anything but a direct hit from a 75-mm shell. The camps included large markets and supply areas well-provided with food and gin, the staple beverage of Asante campaigns. Most of the occupants of the camps were armed men, but there were some women and children, too, and traders came and went with supplies. As was the case in earlier Asante wars, sanitation was poor, but the comforts that these camps provided so amazed British officers when they later examined them that the Europeans wondered aloud why *they* were living in far less comfort.

In addition to the well-built Basel mission station that was now established in Kumase, the British had constructed a prison, a hospital, and large barracks for troops, but the key to their power in the city was the gleaming white fort that commanded the area. Its twelve-foot-high, loopholed stone walls enclosed a fifty-square-yard area that included various multistoried living quarters for residents, large storage rooms, a small hospital, sundry offices, a kitchen, and a well. Large, well-protected circular firing turrets for machine guns and cannon rose above the walls at each of the fort's four corners. The turrets and the living quarters had roofs of red corrugated iron. The only entrance to the fort was a massive iron gate. The fort mounted four cannon and five machine guns that commanded the city, a nearby vegetable garden, and numerous sheds and houses.

While the Asante forces were building their stockades and war camps, Governor Hodgson was frantically telegraphing for reinforcements. The British government was sympathetic to his plight, but the British army was stretched to its limits by the expanding war against the Boers in South Africa and, most recently, by the need to send an expeditionary force to China to help quell the Boxer Rebellion. Even if the War Office had troops to spare, it was not comfortable about asking white soldiers to campaign during the rainy season in the Gold Coast. London had not forgotten that only sixty-eight of the four hundred men of the Royal West York-shire Regiment were fit for duty after Scott's force returned to the coast five years earlier. However, British public opinion, which was already ill-tempered after the many reverses suffered in South Africa, would not tolerate a defeat in the Gold Coast. A victory was badly needed, and African troops led by British officers and noncommissioned officers would have to do the job. As orders came over the telegraph lines, troops began to muster in Accra to march north to Kumase, while others in the Northern Territories made ready to march south. Other troops from Sierra Leone to the west and Nigeria to the east began their march to the coast where ships were waiting to carry them to the Gold Coast.

For the Nigerian troops led by Captain Harold Biss and Captain Charles Melliss (soon to become a major and a recklessly courageous leader), the march included their first, and wildly exciting, ride in a railroad train. These men, who had never before even seen a train, next had their first sight of the sea as they were ferried aboard a modern steamship on their hurried way to Cape Coast.

One of them saw an ice cube for the first time in his life. Fascinated by this strange object, he carefully wrapped it in a cloth and put it in his pack. When he returned with a friend to show off the mysterious object, he found that it had disappeared, and he was convinced that it had been stolen. It took a British officer some time to explain to him what had happened.[1] These African soldiers were not only naive about ice and various aspects of European technology, they were young and inexperienced in the ways of modern warfare. They were so likely to fire wildly, wasting precious ammunition, that British officers chose not to issue them repeating magazine rifles, and many of their officers openly doubted that they would stand against the Asante.[2] Wolseley had used the same concerns to insist on being sent British troops.

The first troops to reach Kumase were 107 Hausas who had marched down from the north, led by an ill-fated captain named Middlemist. Two other officers, named Marshall and Bishop, along with a doctor named Hay (who would prove to be exceptionally brave) accompanied them. They arrived on April 18 without meeting any opposition. The following day, on Hodgson's orders, two columns of troops marched out of the fort to destroy abandoned war camps near Kumase without encountering any hostilities. The Asante leaders were still trying to avoid war. But five days later, when Hodgson repeated the order to punish the Asante, one hundred fifty men led by the recently arrived Captain Marshall marched into a deadly ambush. Four men were killed and fifty-eight wounded, including Marshall, Bishop, and Dr. Hay. The column withdrew to the fort in disorder. All that night the Asante sang and drummed in celebration of their victory. Sleep was impossible in the fort, and Governor Hodgson spent the night sending telegrams requesting more reinforcements. They were the last telegrams to leave Kumase. By morning the line was cut. The construction of the stockades had been completed, and the Asante were ready for war.

The Asante did not intend to starve the British garrison out of the fort. Even though the fort was impregnable to Asante weapons, at ten o'clock on the morning of the next day, the twenty-fifth, the Asante attacked. Despite heavy fire from Hausas deployed outside the fort and from machine guns and artillery in the fort's turrets, the Asante advanced steadily, taking the barracks and other European buildings as well as the Basel mission where they were delighted to find hundreds of bottles of wine. Thousands of African civilians fled toward the fort ahead of the Asante advance, and as some of the British troops withdrew into it, they made a panic-stricken charge to join them inside its walls. Captain Middlemist was so badly crushed against the fort's iron door that he was critically injured, and it was only with the utmost effort that he was pulled inside and the door locked shut. The white missionaries, led by Friedrich Ramseyer and his wife, Rose, were admitted to the fort, but their African students and teachers were forced to remain outside where they huddled together, terrified and utterly disillusioned.[3] There was not enough room inside for all of them, but all the same, it was not an attractive advertisement for the advantages of converting to Christianity. Machine guns and cannon from the fort stopped the Asante long enough to allow a cordon of Hausas to dig trenches and set up a perimeter defense around the refugees, who were now huddled under the protection of the fort's guns. Among these forlorn people were several wives of one of the detained Asante kings. They lived in a green canvas tent and were visited only by their sovereign.

The light from the burning city, the wailing of terrified women and their children, and the triumphant shouts of the Asante troops made the night one that the besieged people in the fort would never forget.[4] This night, as on most that would follow, the forts' occupants were kept awake by the seemingly incessant drumming and shouting coming from the Asante war camps behind their stockades. Well fueled by gin, men in the various camps would shout challenges like these back and forth:

> CAMP A [*to Camp B*]: "We are like the mighty bull that prowls about the forest; what are you?"
> CAMP B [*to Camp A*]: "We also are as strong as that great bull."
> CAMP A: "Are you ready?"
> CAMP B: "Yes, we are."
> CAMP A: "Then man your stockades."[5]

Sounds of cheering men rushing to their positions followed, as one camp after another manned its position. At 5 A.M., when British buglers sounded reveille, the Asante still had enough energy to answer with loud soundings on their elephant-tusk horns.

ASANTE BATTLE ZONE
in 1900

During the afternoon of April 29, the trapped occupants of the fort listened expectantly to the sound of heavy fighting just beyond Kumase. As the light began to fail, they saw a column of troops straggle toward the fort. Led by Captain J. G. O. Aplin, 250 troops from Nigeria had arrived at Cape Coast on the nineteenth. Accompanied by carriers, they immediately began to march north through heavy rain along the same primitive road that Wolseley and Scott had followed. On the twenty-first they met Captain

Davidson-Houston, the British resident at Kumase, who was on his way to the coast to pursue what was referred to as urgent private business. Davidson-Houston told Aplin that there was some unrest at Kumase but assured him that there was nothing to fear—a dubious assessment, considering that only a few months earlier Davidson-Houston had been so concerned about a possible uprising that he forced all the major chiefs to swear an oath of loyalty to the queen. As Aplin continued his difficult trek north, he met non-Asante traders fleeing to the south. These men told a different story. They assured him that there was a great deal to fear—indeed, that there would be war. Aplin's first real evidence of Asante hostility came when his men encountered an injured British employee of the telegraph department who had been waylaid by the Asante. They had used pieces of telegraph wire to beat the soles of his feet bloody before leaving him. Davidson-Houston had assured this man, too, that there was nothing to fear.

Ignoring Davidson-Houston's sanguine appraisal of the situation, Captain Aplin continued to press on as rapidly as he could along the rain-sloshed path, his men fording flooded rivers with great difficulty, making use of the bridges erected by Scott's expedition. On the morning of what he thought would be his last day's march of seventeen miles into Kumase, a sudden glare from unexpected sunlight saved Aplin's life by causing him to tilt his helmet to shade his eyes. As he did, his helmet flew off his head, and he felt pain in his throat. An Asante sniper in a tree had fired a rifle shot that had nicked Aplin before it was deflected through his orderly's calf and then into the ground. It signaled the start of a tremendous fusillade of Asante fire from both sides of the path. Thanks to heavy machine-gun and cannon fire, the Hausa soldiers were eventually able to move forward. After a spirited bayonet charge the Asante troops withdrew into the forest. It was only 2 P.M., but Kumase was still miles away, so Aplin decided to halt to tend to his twenty wounded men, including all six officers. Three men had been killed. As usual it rained that night, and the Asante did not attack.

It was nine the following morning before enough hammocks could be improvised to carry the wounded and Aplin could resume the march. The column crossed the Ordah River without opposition, but three miles from Kumase they once again came under such heavy fire that Aplin later said that if the Asante had not fired high, no one would have survived. Even so, there were many casualties and progress was very slow, until finally the troops saw looming ahead a large, horseshoe-shaped stockade blocking the only path through the jungle. Machine-gun and artillery fire had no effect on it, and a frontal bayonet charge only resulted in heavy casualties. After continual firing their machine gun overheated and jammed, and ammunition for their only cannon was exhausted. Just as a disastrous retreat seemed unavoidable, a small path was found that led through the jungle toward the flank of the stockade. When twenty-five bayonet-wielding Hausas unexpectedly charged around the end of the stockade, the startled Asante defenders fled, leaving the path to Kumase open. Abandoning their dead and their only artillery piece but carrying their wounded as well as they could, Aplin's men dashed for Kumase before the Asante commander could rally his men. The defenders of the fort welcomed the bloody and grimy men, but they were privately horrified to learn that all six officers and 139 of the 250 men were wounded and that the column had lost its food, ammunition, and cannon. Aplin's men had fought splendidly, but they could do nothing to relieve the garrison; and if the siege were a long one, the additional mouths to feed would be a burden.

In addition to the thirty Europeans now in the fort, there were hundreds of Hausa soldiers, many wounded men, and half a dozen Asante chiefs and kings, some of whom were being held against their will. To maintain morale as well as to search for food, the British launched a number of raids, including one at night. All were driven back with losses, even one in which the venerable Chief Kwatchie N'ketia sat calmly on his chair, both arms raised, as Asante bullets flew by. In his left hand he held a gold-hilted sword, while the two forefingers of his right hand were upheld as if in benediction. Since the firing lasted for three hours, the chief's attendants had to hold his arms in place. Food was being rationed ever more tightly, and many of the troops were feeling weak. To keep up their spirits, the fort's garrison played "God Save the Queen" at full volume on their gramophone at night to counter the incessant singing and drumming of the Asante. The spirits of the men in the fort were never high, and they were dampened even more on May 6, when the popular Captain Middlemist died of internal injuries suffered when he was crushed against the fort's gate.

On May 10, some of the ostensibly loyal Asante kings detained in the fort proposed peace talks with the "rebels," as the British insisted on calling the Asante who had taken up arms. Hodgson agreed, and under a flag of truce, talks among the Asante factions began. The British had no reason for optimism. On April 14, before the stockades had been completed, the Asante leaders had presented five peace terms to Hodgson. In addition to demanding the restoration of slavery and the cessation of government demands for forced labor, they insisted that King Prempe be returned from exile and the British, along with all other foreigners, leave. Not surprisingly, these terms were not agreeable to the British. It is also no surprise that, now that the Asante held the upper hand, they did not lessen their demands. Nevertheless, Hodgson allowed the talks to continue because while the truce was in effect, the Asante commanders allowed women to sell food in the Kumase market, to the great relief of the hungry refugees outside the fort as well as the garrison.

On the afternoon of May 15, as the peace talks dragged on, 170 African soldiers and three British officers commanded by Major Morris marched into Kumase past a stockade that was undefended because of the truce. Despite terrific heat each day, rain each night, and several small battles (in one of which Morris had been painfully wounded in the groin) the column had covered 238 miles from the north in only thirteen days. Unlike Aplin's, most of these men were unwounded, and they had with them a fair amount of food and ammunition. Their machine gun and cannon were welcome, too. They also had some ponies, which soon made good eating for the Hausas. Morris knew nothing about a truce, and Hodgson may have known nothing about Morris being on the march, although there were rumors that troops were on the way. Still, the timing of Morris's arrival was suspicious, to say the least, and the Asante were furious. They abruptly canceled the truce and resumed the war.

On May 10, the same day the truce was proposed, forty-one-year-old Colonel James Willcocks, second-in-command of the recently raised West African Frontier Force of northern Nigeria, received orders from London to take command of all the forces preparing to relieve Kumase. Willcocks was only three days away from the exhilarating prospect of launching an attack against a hostile emir in northern Nigeria, but pleased by the chance for his first independent command, he left immediately, pushing himself and his lame pony to their limits in a nightmarish walk and ride toward Lagos where he hoped to board a ship for the Gold Coast. Willcocks suffered acutely from bouts of temporary blindness and from severe gastric pain as a result of food poisoning, and he had badly blistered feet from walking and a sprained knee from a fall, yet he somehow reached Lagos only fourteen days later, a distance of over three hundred miles. Lucky to find a waiting ship, he limped ashore two days later at Cape Coast in a drenching rain. To his dismay he found no staff officers, no troops, no supplies, and no carriers.

During twenty-two years of army service fighting Britain's battles in India and Afghanistan, Willcocks had proven to be a distinguished and aggressive officer who adored action. But he had learned to be prudent, too, and he would not make the mistake of trying to relieve Kumase without adequate force. He was well aware that a premature attack with an inadequate force might inflate Asante morale so much that relief would prove impossible. He resigned himself to wait. Unfortunately, other officers already operating in the Gold Coast outside his command also had orders to relieve Kumase, and they were not at all cautious.

Captain Wynyard Montagu Hall, who had marched to Kumase as an officer with the West Yorks in 1896, had landed at the Cape Coast two days before Willcocks in command of 450 men of the West African Frontier Force from Nigeria. The Fante were so alarmed by the prospect of yet another Asante war that nothing Hall could do would induce them to carry relief supplies to Kumase. Disgusted, he loaded up his soldiers with ammunition and boxes of food and set off through the rain and mud toward Kumase. On the fifteenth of May, he reached the base camp at Prahsu where he found a cable from the colonial secretary in Accra, telling him that the fort's garrison only had food enough to last to the end of the month and urging him to hurry. Hall wasted no time; pausing only long enough to sign a treaty of friendship with the king of

Adansi, he arrived at Fomena on May 20. Fomena was the place where Wolseley had set up his supply base twenty-six years earlier and the principal city of the kingdom of Bekwai, whose King had so far refused to join other Asante states in the war. The king urged Hall to occupy a town named Esumeja, a strategic hamlet on the main road just one day's march from Kumase, and Hall did so on the twenty-second.

The next day he led two hundred of his men toward Kumase, but Queen Mother Yaa Asantewaa's large and formidable army was encamped in his path at Kokofu, the site of one of Wolseley's great battles. Hall's force was stopped in its tracks and was lucky to succeed in retreating before being surrounded. No sooner had Hall returned to Esumeja than the king of Adansi thought better of his pledge of unbounded loyalty and joined in the war against the British, leaving Hall with all he could do to keep the king of Bekwae out of the Asante alliance. Any idea of relieving the fort at Kumase had to be set aside. Hall was barely able to defend his hastily fortified camp at Esumeja.

The next attempt to move toward Kumase was made a few days later, in early June, when Lieutenant Colonel Carter, who had been camped near Hall with 380 men and several machine guns and cannon, tried to join Hall's beleaguered force and together dash to Kumase. Before he could reach Hall, he was ambushed by a large Asante force. Though his men returned fire, the Asante fire was so heavy that all the officers went down, including Carter with a serious wound over his left eye. There was no lack of courage on the British side. A Lieutenant named Edwards was shot down while ramming shells into a cannon with his walking stick. One officer was shot through both wrists but continued to carry ammunition to his men by holding it between his forearms. Another officer went down while firing a machine gun that jammed. All the while Hausas were falling in alarming numbers.

After about two full hours of intense fighting, enough of the vegetation had been cut away that the British could finally see what they were up against. To their amazement they discovered that the Asante troops were firing at them through loopholes in a six-foot-high, six-foot-thick stockade that extended parallel to the road for about a quarter of a mile. It became immediately obvious that the

Asante were completely protected against any fire the British could throw at them. The only unwounded senior officer, a colonel named Wilkinson, could see no hope of victory and tried to organize the battered British force for an orderly retreat. But while he was pondering how to manage this without having it turn into a rout, a Scottish colour sergeant named John Mackenzie, on detached duty from the Seaforth Highlanders, asked permission to lead a bayonet charge against the stockade with his company of Yoruba troops from Nigeria. The colonel reluctantly agreed, and one hundred men with fixed bayonets followed Mackenzie, charging directly at the stockade. Improbable as it may seem, before the Nigerians even reached the stockade, the Asantes abandoned it and ran. For this remarkable feat Mackenzie was awarded the Victoria Cross and was given a commission in the Black Watch.[6] Although the Asante had gone, Wilkinson had too many wounded to continue the advance. He withdrew toward the relative safety of the camp at Prahsu. The first two battles went to the Asante.

When Willcocks was notified that Carter's well-armed force of four hundred men had been driven back with nearly one hundred casualties and that Hall's even larger force was besieged at Esumeja, he telegraphed London, asking for more soldiers, special-service officers, and supplies. While he waited for the troops and supplies to arrive, British forces in the Bekwai district continued to run into difficulties. Captain Wilson and 114 Nigerians were ordered to reinforce the survivors of Colonel Carter's defeat. Wilson was killed in an Asante ambush, while twenty-five soldiers and sixteen carriers were wounded. Led by a British sergeant, the surviving troops fought their way through to Carter's position only to find that he had left the village and his whereabouts were unknown. In great danger of encirclement, the small force somehow survived a thirty-three-mile march through the rain to safety. They left their wounded behind but loyally carried the dead body of Captain Wilson all the way. Six days later a Nigerian soldier crawled into camp. Despite nineteen wounds, some of which were serious, he had covered twenty miles by dragging himself through the jungle at night and hiding from Asante scouts during the day.[7]

While the isolated British columns that had gone up-country before Willcocks assumed effective command did their best to avoid

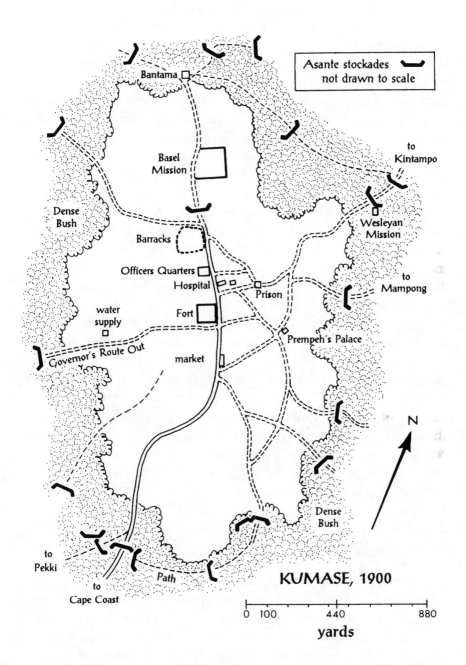

Asante stockades ⌐ not drawn to scale

Bantama

Basel Mission

to Kintampo

Dense Bush

Barracks

Wesleyan Mission

Officers Quarters

to Mampong

Hospital

Prison

Fort

water supply

Prempeh's Palace

Governor's Route Out

market

N

to Pekki

Dense Bush

Path

to Cape Coast

KUMASE, 1900

0   100   440   880

yards

annihilation and to keep the king of Bekwai out of the war, the situation in Kumase was growing desperate. Water was not a problem because the Asante chivalrously allowed parties from the fort, as well as the refugees outside of it, to go to and from a nearby stream without harm (the Asante later said that thirst was not a legitimate weapon of war). But by the end of May, the supply of food had dwindled alarmingly. Major Morris's five ponies had long since been slaughtered, and the last of the four milk cows and all but one sheep in the fort had now been eaten. All birds, cats, snakes, lizards, and rats in Kumase had been eaten as well. The twenty-nine Europeans still in the fort were on a very limited ration of tinned beef and biscuit; the Hausas were on an even more limited diet, and the native carriers received nothing but biscuit. Morris's men boiled their leather belts and sandals for hours to produce a horrid-tasting, pallid broth. They also chewed the softened leather.

Most refugees ate nothing but leaves and grass, and many died in agony after eating poisonous roots.[8] The British tried to maintain a small soup kitchen that gave children a cup of almost clear water, sometimes containing a trace of European table scraps. "Men walking along or sitting on the road outside the fort would suddenly fall forward dead, while others, wasted almost to skeletons, went mad. . . ."[9] Over a thousand refugees, including many carriers, surrendered to the Asante, preferring slavery to starvation. By early June the people outside the fort were dying at a rate of thirty to forty a day, and finding men with the strength to bury them all was not possible. Inside the fort there were endless rumors of relief columns being sighted, of cannon fire being heard, and of European troops in strength at Esumeja. All but the latter proved false. Large rewards were offered to anyone who succeeded in delivering a note (written in French to deceive the Asante) to the commander of the relief force. Several men volunteered, and one actually succeeded. But no word reached the trapped garrison.

By the fifteenth of June, Hodgson, Morris, and the surgeons calculated that their food supplies were so low that they could not delay an escape attempt beyond June 23. Various escape routes were considered but rejected because there were too many stockades to storm and too much hostile territory to pass through. They finally selected a small road through Patasi to Inkwanta. There was only one stockade to pass on this path, and the friendly king of Inkwanta was in the fort with guides. The escape plan called for all but a handful of the fort's occupants to break out with just enough food and ammunition to get them safely to the coast. Enough food would be left with the skeleton garrison to sustain them for about three weeks. Those left behind were Captain Bishop, Lieutenant Ralph, and Doctor Hay (all of whom had been wounded earlier), 109 Hausas with their seventy-year-old Hausa officer Hari Zenua, and twenty-five carriers. Most of these men were sick, wounded, or both. All the other Europeans, including Lady Hodgson and the wives of three Swiss missionaries, would leave along with six hundred relatively healthy Hausas and some eight hundred carriers and followers of the detained chiefs and kings. As many of the civilian refugees as were able to travel were permitted to follow along after the rear guard. It would be a pitifully vulnerable force. With most of the machine guns and cannon left behind in the fort, it would boast only two Maxims, two cannon, and six hundred rifles to protect close to three thousand people.

The carriers were an obvious source of concern. They were so weak that their usual loads of sixty pounds or more were reduced to thirty pounds or less. Nonetheless, the European women and the wounded would also have to be carried from the start, and it was to be expected that there would be many more wounded during the attempted escape. Given the weakness of the carriers, it is remarkable that serious consideration was actually given to protecting the hammocks of the women with an inverted V-shaped cone of corrugated iron. The experiment was only shelved when it was demonstrated that bullets went through the roofing material like tissue paper. It is even more remarkable that Governor Hodgson felt obliged to take all of his personal possessions, including furniture, other household items, and clothing in addition to books and papers. In all, 106 carriers were required to carry them.[10] Aside from Hodgson's decidedly cavalier attitude toward the emaciated carriers, his decision to leave nothing of value in the fort could hardly have made those who were to remain behind feel terribly secure.

The preparations for a breakout could not be hidden, especially when the carriers were moved into the fort for their protection. But to retain as much surprise as possible, no one was told the date of the breakout or the path to be taken except Major Morris and Governor Hodgson. Morris intentionally let word get out that the column would leave by the Cape Coast route. The Asante fell for his deception, moving forces from the northern stockades to reinforce the men stationed along this road by means of a new road encircling Kumase that they had built to allow them to move troops easily.

At 4:30 A.M. on June 23, the escape column began to assemble outside the fort. It took longer to organize than anyone had expected, and instead of leaving at the predawn hour of five, it was nearly 7 and fully light when the rear guard of the column finally moved away. Before leaving, Governor Hodgson told the officers left behind, "Well, you have a supply of food for twenty-three days and are safe for that period, but we are going to die today."[11] One suspects a bit of disingenuousness on Hodgson's part. If he truly believed what he said, it is odd that he would take Lady Hodgson and all of his possessions with him.

The advance guard was led by the young captains Armitage and Leggett. Friends since the fight at Bali, they would be the first to face death. In what Armitage called a "dense, clammy, white mist," the advance guard moved quickly toward the Patasi stockade. Half an hour later they saw the huge barrier, and the Asante behind it saw them, opening fire immediately. With the rest of the column spread out over two miles to the rear, Armitage ordered a bayonet charge, but it was driven back with Leggett shot in the stomach. Armitage then decided to flank the stockade and led twenty men through the jungle, attempting to get around its left side. Seeing movement, his own Hausas promptly fired a volley at Armitage, nearly hitting him. He rushed back, ordered his men to kindly fire elsewhere, and, probably thinking it only wise, took most of them with him into the jungle.

In a deadly game that seems ludicrous only in retrospect, just as Armitage was creeping around the left flank of the stockade, the Asante commander was leading his men around the right, hoping to fire into the British troops from their flank. Armitage and his men got behind the stockade just before the Asante troops left it and poured a volley into their backs, sending them flying in disarray. The short exchange of fire cost four British dead and eleven wounded, including Leggett, who had to be carried back to the main body in great pain. Pushing on toward Patasi as rapidly as they could, the advance guard was ambushed, and Captain Marshall, who had replaced Leggett, received a severe head wound. The captured war camp behind the stockade and the villages along the Patasi path were so well stocked with food that the British officers, who were almost as hungry as the men were, had to pry the famished soldiers and carriers away from the plentiful supply of plantains, bananas, and other food they found. Somehow the column kept moving, although some men stayed behind and were killed by pursuing Asante soldiers.

Asante pursuit of the two-mile-long line of escape was delayed long enough by Captain Bishop's gunners, who sprayed the forests and the ring road with shells, that when significant numbers of Asante troops caught up with the column, they first encountered the civilian refugees who trailed behind it. Caught between the British rear guard and the Asante, some of these pitiable people were able to shove their way past the Hausa soldiers to relative safety, but hundreds of others were caught and killed. Their headless bodies were found later all along the path and in the jungle on each side. As the panic spread, some of the carriers bolted. Among them were the men who were carrying the gray-bearded Reverend Ramseyer and his lame wife. Dumped roughly to the ground, the elderly couple sat serenely on the path, praying and awaiting their fate. It came in the form of the rear guard's commander, Captain Aplin, who ordered other carriers to take them to the relative safety of the main column.[12]

By maintaining continuous fire as it withdrew, Captain Aplin's rear guard managed to keep the Asante from overrunning the rear of the column, while the head of the column continued to keep up a rapid pace. By early afternoon Armitage reached the fortified village of Tereboam where Major Morris hoped to have the entire column spend the night. The small village was loopholed and heavily defended, but when the Hausas of the advance guard saw huge piles of plantains and bananas stacked around the huts in full view, the famished troops wasted no time in driving the defenders out at bayonet point. Then, while waiting for the rest of the column to come in, they gorged themselves so heavily that Armitage was afraid they would be unable to march the next day.

All along the line of march, soldiers, carriers, and refugees darted off into jungle clearings in search of food. Sometimes they found it in lush unharvested fields; sometimes they found death, instead, when groups of Asante soldiers shot them down. By mid-afternoon such heavy rain began to fall that the flintlocks of the Asante became useless, and the entire column safely crowded into Tereboam, which had no more than twenty huts for three thousand people. Although there was little danger of an Asante attack, thanks to the rain, the night was spent in dreadful discomfort. Armitage described what it was like:

> Our loads lay out in utter confusion where they had been dumped down by the carriers, who came staggering in like drunken men. The Governor and Lady Hodgson sat upon boxes waiting for the tent which never came, and finally sought shelter in the wretched hut I had kept for them. The crush was so great that two huts filled with wounded collapsed from the pressure on the walls from without, and the occupants were with difficulty rescued. Fires had been lit everywhere, and from them arose suffocating volumes of smoke, as the damp wood spluttered and cracked. The many trampling feet had churned the ground into a sea of mud over ankle deep. And upon this steaming mass of humanity the torrential rain fell silently, pitilessly, as though determined to extinguish the wretched fires around which squatted shivering groups of natives.[13]

Despite the incessant rain, Asante drums thundered all night, and for all but a handful of people who managed to crowd into a hut, the night was spent standing or sitting in cold mud. Few had any sleep, and there was little food, but by 7 A.M. the wretched column moved out to the south. The rear guard again fought a running battle all day, this time doing more to protect civilian refugees; but many more were killed nonetheless—how many will never be known. That night the column camped in a small village named Moseasu. Major Morris quickly ordered that guards be stationed all around the village to prevent any of the unarmed, starving civilians from crowding into the already packed area. These wretched souls spent the night in the forest, at the mercy of any armed Asante who wanted to take their lives.

Many of the starving carriers had thrown down their loads and staggered into the jungle or had collapsed along the path and died. Even under ordinary circumstances, carriers often collapsed. Always cold and wet during the night, most had dangerous bronchial infections, and their coughing was a constant accompaniment to camp life. They were underfed, cursed at by soldiers, shot at by the Asante, and largely ignored by the officers who recruited them and flogged them when they misbehaved. Now these starving men collapsed by the hundreds. Lady Hodgson wrote about one such man on the march out of Kumase:

> Just as we emerged from the swamp, which, fortunately for us, was not at its worst, a poor carrier, with an ammunition box on his head, fell backwards from exhaustion, gave one gasp, and went to his long home. This was the beginning of many terrible things to happen that day. I shall never forget the sight of this unfortunate man lying on his back in a bed of rushes, his hands still clutching his load which lay up-tilted against his head.[14]

The pursuing Asante troops could not resist the temptation to examine the many supply boxes that now littered the path. Their inexperienced commander, Antoa Mensa, permitted them to loot, believing that his superiors would be pleased by the many valuables he dutifully returned to them. He also appears to have believed that since the British were in a great hurry to leave Kumase, there was little reason to risk heavy losses by exposing his men to their fire. His decision allowed the British to escape against all odds. His superiors rebuked him and fined him heavily.[15]

The second night was more painful to endure than the first. It was still pouring rain and was quite cold. Because so many loads had been lost, there was virtually no food, and nearly three thousand people were forced to spend the night in an area so small that it was only 120 yards in circumference. Governor Hodgson spent the night sitting in a camp chair; Lady Hodgson's devoted carrier managed to find her a camp bed, which enabled her to sleep a little. Armitage was so exhausted that he slept on the floor of one of the huts, all of which had been reserved for Europeans. The next day there was little firing by the Asante, and by early afternoon the column reached the fort of the friendly village of Inkwanta, where they were welcomed by a British flag, much cheering, and ample food. To everyone's surprise and alarm Hodgson promptly passed out, though he soon revived. Not everyone had died, as Hodgson had prophesied, but slim, handsome Captain Leggett and balding Captain Marshall both died of their wounds. No one would ever know how many of the carriers or the hapless civilians that followed the fleeing column had been killed, but their deaths were not important to the overjoyed public in England, where church bells tolled in gratitude. Only two officers and twenty-three soldiers had been killed, with only thirty-seven wounded and thirty-nine missing. That anyone escaped was remarkable; that so many did was amazing. But the British public did not realize that the fighting had just begun.

Not long after Captain Bishop ordered his men to fire the fort's cannon in support of the fleeing column, he watched in disbelief as several score armed Asante walked casually toward the fort, obviously believing that it had been abandoned. Bishop waited until they were well within range before ordering his machine guns to open fire. The approaching Asante quickly scattered, leaving several dead on the ground. After that, the Asante kept their distance, and the terribly weakened garrison settled down to await the relief that Governor Hodgson had solemnly promised would arrive in five days at the latest.[16] Hodgson clearly had no confidence in his prediction, and it is hardly to his credit that he said it. The first day after Hodgson's escape, three men in the fort died. After five days passed, the feeble garrison admittedly lost heart; after ten days Bishop said that even he had given up all hope, although he continued to do what little he could to encourage the garrison.

Bishop's Hausas were so sick and emaciated that he ordered them to sleep on the ramparts next to their loopholes, believing with good reason that if they were to sleep below they would be too weak to climb up to their posts should there be an attack. His soldiers were little more than skeletons covered with running sores. Each soldier received only a cup of linseed meal and a two-inch square of tinned meat as a daily ration. It is no surprise that one or two Hausas died each day. Smallpox also broke out among the starving men, and Dr. Hay had no choice but to have the infected men carried outside the fort where they were left to die. They lay next to some 150 refugees who had been too weak to join the escape column and were slowly starving to death. There began to arise a stench of death so appalling that people in the fort were quite literally nauseated by it. Too weak to dig graves, the fort's Hausas marched out each day to drag the night's victims into one of the abandoned trenches. This action so little alleviated the smell of death that Dr. Hay, himself ill with malaria, and Captain Bishop decided to burn all the huts and bodies around the fort. As they did their horrible work, they found only one living person, a starving woman whose dead child was still held to her flaccid breast. What became of this tragic person is not recorded.

On June 1, Colonel Willcocks was delighted by the arrival of three hundred men of his own West African Frontier Force from Nigeria under the command of Major Charles Melliss, whose sword-wielding exploits at the head of his forces would soon make him famous. Willcocks was so pleased to see "their honest faces" and hear their welcoming salutations that he warmly shook their hands and sat down to listen to their tales of travel across what they called "the big, black sea."[17] On the fifth he led the men (figuratively, that is: his sprained knee was so painful he had to be carried) north on a seventy-one-mile march to the base camp at Prahsu. Despite terrible weather, they arrived there four days later to find the once grand camp now badly neglected and in need of repair. It was here that Willcocks learned that Captain Hall was still pinned down at Esumeja and that Colonel Carter's force of eleven Europeans and 380 Hausas had been defeated near a scenically beautiful place called Dompoase with six killed and seven officers and eighty-six men wounded.

Willcocks immediately sent Melliss with a company of Nigerians to reinforce Carter at the fortified village of Fumasa. Melliss's men had great difficulty crossing flooded rivers, and at one point Melliss had to dive in to save two Nigerian nonswimmers from drowning. He also saved Willcocks's typewriter, which had fallen in as well. (When it dried out, the machine worked surprisingly well.)[18] Once they managed to find a ford over a chest-deep river, Melliss's men marched into an Asante ambush. Never one to be satisfied by exchanging fire with an unseen enemy, Melliss drew his sword and led his men in a wild bayonet charge into the jungle. The Asante fled, but Melliss's boy bugler was killed and thirteen men were wounded, including a British sergeant. Melliss reached Carter without further trouble and delivered the badly needed ammunition his men had carried.

Reinforcements and supplies, now arriving at Cape Coast, began the long trek to Prahsu through torrents of rain that made the road a quagmire. On June 25 a colonel named Burroughs and a battalion of the West African Regiment from Sierra Leone passed through Prahsu on the way to reinforce Hall and hopefully keep the king of Bekwai and his large army on the side of the British. The Bekwai fighting men still wanted to join the Asante rebellion, and their king was only barely able to control them. When Burroughs first arrived at Cape Coast, he did not make a favorable impression. One of Willcocks's staff officers described him as "an extraordinary little colonel called Burroughs who has gout and can't wear a boot and has never been on [active] service in his life. . . ." The same officer reported of Burroughs's officers, "They also brought all their mess plate and many cases of champagne, all of which our transport officer left behind at Cape Coast by mistake."[19]

To reach Hall, Burroughs had to drive the Asante out of Dompoase, the village where Carter had been so badly defeated. Arriving at nightfall in a pouring rain, Burroughs's men caught the Asante troops with wet powder and easily drove them away, destroying their stockade and burning the village. Burroughs was able to join Hall without further opposition. Thanks to this victory, Willcocks on July 1 decided to move his newly arrived forces north of the Pra River. The next day he received what appeared to be authentic news of the governor's escape, and on the fourth a telegraph message confirming the breakout came from the governor himself at Cape Coast. The telegram also reported that the fort could not be held beyond July 15. Willcocks promptly sent a telegram to the colonial secretary promising to relieve the fort by the fifteenth, and he moved north with all the force he had.

Burroughs's orders were to tie down Queen Mother Yaa Asantewaa's large army of Kokofu by consolidating Hall's troops with his own at Esumeja; but the "gouty little colonel" had ideas of his own. Though Hall warned him that Yaa Asantewaa's army held a strong position behind stockades, Burroughs, puffed up by his easy victory at Dompoase, decided to drive through Kokofu and relieve

Kumase himself. The day before Willcock's men marched north toward Kumase, Burroughs's West African Regiment led the attack, with Hall's men relegated to duties as a rear guard. After maneuvering his men through relatively open terrain on a broad front, Burroughs ordered them to advance. Protected by their stockades, the Asante troops poured tremendous fire from Dane guns and a considerable number of Sniders into Burroughs's men, who began to go down. Burroughs himself was painfully wounded and his second-in-command killed. When Asante troops began to work their way around his flanks, the wounded colonel ordered a retreat. A panicky staff officer ran back to Hall, telling him that the attack was hopeless and that Hall had been ordered to use his machine guns and 75-mm cannon to cover the retreat. He also apologized for the ignominy of it all but made it plain that there was no alternative.[20]

Hall's rapid fire slowed the Asante soldiers who had come out from behind their stockades in pursuit, and after a hard fight the British force was able to withdraw to its fortified position at Esumeja. Happy to escape at all, Burroughs quickly decamped for the safety of Bekwai with his regiment and some eighty wounded men, leaving Hall to defend Esumeja. Hall's men had barely taken up their former positions around the town when the queen mother's troops launched an impetuous attack. They were shot down in large numbers but came on again and again against rifles and machine guns being fired by Hall's men, who were protected by trenches and log barriers. Despite their losses, the Asante refused to break off the battle, and for the first time they continued to fire against Hall's men well into the night before finally withdrawing to their stockades.

Willcocks was in Kwissa when he learned of Burroughs's defeat on the morning of July 8. Furious that Burroughs had disobeyed his orders and disturbed by his defeat, he marched to Bekwai, arriving the next day. Even though Burroughs was wounded, Willcocks did not hesitate to berate him for making the attack and, once having made it, for not ordering a bayonet charge, which Willcocks was sure would have succeeded. Burroughs defended his actions, and Willcocks let the matter drop. He had to get his own force ready to continue the march on Kumase, and Yaa Asantewaa's army at Kokofu stood across his path.

Willcocks would make the march with one thousand troops—seven hundred of his own men from the West African Frontier Force, two hundred men from the West African Regiment, fifty Sierra Leone Frontier Police, and fifty gunners to handle his six cannon and six machine guns. He also had about three thousand supply carriers, one thousand five hundred of whom had come all the way from East Africa by ship. The day after Willcocks arrived in Bekwai, a starving, exhausted Hausa soldier from the fort at Kumase crawled into Hall's camp at Esumeja on his hands and knees. He took a crumpled, sweat-soaked piece of paper out of his loincloth. It read: "From O.C. [officer in command] Kumassi to O.C. troops Esumeja. His Excellency and main troops left for the coast seventeen days ago; relief most urgently wanted here. Remaining small garrison diminishing: disease, etc. Reduced rations for only a few days more." It was signed by Captain F. E. Bishop. The messenger was carried to Bekwai in a hammock where Willcocks promoted him to sergeant on the spot and gave him some money. Willcocks later regretted that he had not recommended the unnamed man for a Victoria Cross.[21]

Always concerned about the threat that Yaa Asantewaa's army at Kokofu posed to him, the king of Bekwai urged Willcocks to attack her before moving on to Kumase. Willcocks agreed to do so; he even asked the king to send word to the Asante troops at Kokofu that Willcocks would attack them the next day. As soon as this threat was received, two thousand Asante troops left their stockades around Kumase, seventeen miles to the north, to reinforce Kokofu. On July 11, four hundred of Willcocks's men moved out toward the Asante position, laboriously widening the road as they went as if in preparation for a larger force to follow. After several hours they withdrew. Willcocks explained to the king of Bekwai that this maneuver was simply a reconnaissance for the real attack, which would come soon enough. In fact, Willcocks only wanted to tie down the Asante troops at Kokofu. He had no intention of repeating Burroughs's attack against them.

The twelfth of July was spent making preparations for a do-or-die dash to Kumase. To make the one thousand man fighting force more mobile, only one thousand seven hundred carriers would be taken, but these men would have to carry large amounts of ammunition in addition to the food and hospital supplies the starving garrison was waiting for. After a long day of checking weapons and packing loads, the carriers tried to sleep on the muddy ground as a steady drizzle fell. At the extraordinary hour of 2 A.M., Willcocks called for the king of Bekwai and explained that he would not attack Kokofu after all but would move directly on Kumase. The king angrily accused Willcocks of deceiving him, something the colonel freely owned up to, saying that in war a commander had to deceive even friends, an admission that the old king accepted with surprising good humor, especially considering the hour. Willcocks also meant to deceive the Asante, who did not know that a European gold miner named Behne, one of fifty who were working at nearby mines, had offered to lead Willcocks to Kumase on a little used path that bypassed Kokofu. By taking this path through the Bekwai village of Pekki, the column would not encounter any stockades until they were just outside Kumase.[22]

British-paid spies were sent to Kokofu to spread the word that the delayed British attack would begin on the morning of the thirteenth. Early that morning Willcocks sent a force toward Kokofu as a feint while the main body began its march through the jungle toward Pekki. The path was only barely passable at best, and the bare feet of the advance guard soon turned it into a quagmire for the rest of the troops and carriers. Several neck-deep rivers also had to be forded. Exhausted, the advance guard did not cover the fifteen miles to Pekki until after dark, and the rear guard was not settled in until 2 A.M. While his men were trickling in, Willcocks conferred with the chief of Pekki, who told him that a large force of Asante held the religious center of Treda, only two miles away across the Bekwae frontier into Kumase district.

As Willcocks was digesting the information that these men had many modern rifles, two terrified Asante prisoners were brought to him. Expecting to be killed, the men were clearly amazed when Willcocks told them they were free to return to Treda, where they should tell their commander that the British would camp the next day at Pekki, but if the Asante persisted in their rebellion, Willcocks would attack them the following day. Waiting until eight the following morning, to give the appearance of being true to his word and also to give his men a chance for some rest, Willcocks attacked Treda without warning, taking the Asante by surprise and driving them away after little resistance. Pausing only to burn the Asante village, including its temple, Willcocks's men rapidly pressed on. In one small village they found a Hausa who had been captured when Hodgson's column escaped from the fort. He was very hungry but had not been mistreated. In another village Willcocks himself found a two-year-old child all alone in a hut, shrieking in terror. He left some bread and a cup of tinned milk for the child, and the column again pressed on. Some days later, when Willcocks's troops passed through the village again, the child was found dead in exactly the same place, the food untouched.[23]

That night was spent in the village of Ekwanta, five miles south of Kumase. Three rounds were fired from a 75-mm cannon in the hope that they would be heard in the fort, but they were not. At daybreak on the fifteenth, Willcocks's last day to relieve the fort, the advance guard under Major Melliss set off for the fort. Soon after, the Asante fired on the long column from its left flank, and the Asante commander, who survived to be questioned after the war, then ordered an attack on the carriers, hoping to create panic and disrupt the march. He very nearly succeeded, but the rear guard's machine guns finally drove the Asante back after the loss of many loads that the carriers dropped. During this action the rest of the column continued its march. Before Willcocks realized it, a gap a mile long had opened up between the main body and the rear guard fighting to save the carriers. At just this point in the battle, Asante reinforcements from Kokofu were hurrying north parallel to Willcocks's column. Unaware that the huge gap in the British column existed, they attacked the rear guard and were driven off. Had they moved into the gap, Willcocks later wrote, they would have caused "much trouble, if no worse."[24] In fact, they might well have stopped the advance.

At 4:15 P.M. the advance guard reached the stockade that blocked the Pekki road. It was small, nothing like the huge stockades that had given the British such problems earlier, but the men who were behind it and hidden around it in the forest opened fire with everything they had. Willcocks called the roar "the best moment of my life" because it meant that he was engaged in the last great battle that would, he was sure, lead to the relief of the fort.

The British gunners were ordered to fire as rapidly as possible at the stockade in order to keep the Asante busy while the infantry formed up on each side of the road along a front of about six hundred yards. Still uncertain whether his African soldiers would obey his order to charge, Willcocks hesitated, then ordered his massed buglers to sound cease-fire. His troops obeyed, and as their fire ceased, so did that of the Asante. After a moment of eerie silence, Willcocks ordered his buglers to sound the charge, and his troops instantly obeyed. Led by sword-waving British officers, Melliss in front as usual, they rushed forward with bayonets fixed. The charge was so infectious that all of Willcocks's staff officers joined in, leaving the colonel alone with an African sergeant. Turning to this French-speaking man, Willcocks asked in all seriousness where his staff was. "Voila, c'est moi," was the answer.[25]

As Willcocks had expected, only a few Asante stood against the bayonet charge. Asante officers tried to rally their men, but the flight could not be halted, and those Asante officers who fought back quickly fell to swords and bayonets. After Willcocks paused to examine the shattered Asante bodies that lay behind the stockade, he wrote that "it was impossible not to admire the gallantry of these savages, who could stand up against the modern guns and rifles"[26] Willcocks also understood that without bayonets of their own and unable to reload their cumbersome Dane guns in time to defend themselves, the Asante soldiers, so brave in withstanding artillery and machine-gun fire, would have to yield to a bayonet charge. Captain Harold Biss was shocked by what he called the "very gruesome sight" of the dead Asante behind the stockade. "A shell from one of the guns had penetrated and done terrible execution, bespattering the timbers with blood and shreds of human flesh. Its defenders themselves presented a loathsome spectacle. A pile of mangled forms, some still breathing, lay in confusion, many having fallen across one another, some disembowelled, another with the whole face blown off—all variously mutilated. Limbs had been carried yards away into the bush beyond, and the ground was slippery with blood."[27]

With dark coming on, Willcocks hurried his troops toward Kumase, but his men were so exhausted by their march and the excitement of the charge that he called a brief halt. One of his officers lay down in a pool of mud and water and instantly fell asleep. When Willcocks woke him a few minutes later to continue the advance, the man commented, "I don't see much difference between this and other beds in Ashanti."[28] On the march again, they passed burned-out houses, litter of all sorts, and headless bodies, but everyone's mind was on the fort. When it finally came into sight, the British flag was still flying, and at the sound of a bugle from the fort playing "general salute," everyone began to run through the long grass, often stumbling over unburied bodies but cheering at the top of their lungs.

The garrison of the fort had known that relief was close at hand since 4:15, when they had heard the heavy firing close to Kumase. Captain Bishop opened fire with a machine gun to let the rescuers know the garrison was still alive, but no one with Willcocks heard it over the sounds of battle. The three Europeans in the fort then searched anxiously with their field glasses for the first sign of rescue. It came at 6 P.M., only shortly before dark. Incredibly, the first thing they saw was, not a conquering army, but Major Melliss's fox terrier, who had somehow survived the entire campaign with the troops and was now dashing toward the fort. In those singular times it was so commonplace for British officers to take their dogs into battle with them that no one thought to record the terrier's name. Not far behind the fox terrier came dozens of running British officers, their faces filthy under their white helmets, and many African soldiers wearing fezzes. When they heard the forts's two buglers playing welcome, they ran even faster, cheering even louder.

Bishop and his feeble men tottered out of the fort, "cheering to the best of our ability."[29] Bishop ordered his emaciated Hausas to stand at attention, and these gallant men somehow managed to do so with great dignity, even as the rescuers threw their helmets in the air and gave three cheers for the queen. Willcocks, who had run ahead despite his bad knee, was so overcome with emotion that he could scarcely speak. He thought the Hausas seemed to be near death and the Europeans were gaunt and sallow-faced, but other British officers, while agreeing that the Hausas were terribly thin and covered with open sores, thought that the Europeans looked quite fit, in marked contrast to their own appearance, which one of

Willcocks's staff officers likened to "scarecrows."[30] They were indeed ragged soldiers, their boots falling apart, their uniforms in tatters. But before the men lay down for the first decent sleep they had had for three days, Captain Bishop opened his last bottle of champagne and shared it with his rescuers. Later, British cannon fired starshells, like giant fireworks, high above Kumase.

✗

9

"An Inaudible Murmur of Admiration"

THAT NIGHT PASSED QUIETLY, AND EARLY MORNING PATROLS REported no Asante activity near the fort. The stench of decaying human flesh was overwhelming in the still morning air, and while four hundred men began to tear down the stockade they had attacked yesterday, the rest of Willcocks's men hurriedly attempted to bury the bodies that lay in the long grass around the fort. But there were so many hundreds of dead that the idea of burial had to be abandoned. Tearing down the nearby huts, the men set huge fires and cremated the bodies. The job of tossing the decomposing bodies onto these pyres was given to the African troops, but everyone was assailed all that night by the unbearable smell of burning flesh. An officer found some fragrant roses in bloom at the Ramseyers' abandoned mission station, but their sweet scent seemed to make the stench of burning flesh even more terrible. Despite their exhaustion, few of Willcocks's men were able to sleep that night.

The following morning, July 17, the air was fresh, and there was still no sign of Asante forces. The fort's new garrison would consist of 150 African troops, some British sergeants, a doctor, and three officers including the commander, Captain Eden. Willcocks left them enough food for almost two months plus large stores of ammunition and other supplies, but he gave himself barely enough food to sustain his column on the return march to the relative safety of Bekwai. In addition to the fort's old garrison, many of whom would have to be carried, he had over thirty wounded of his own to tend to. Willcocks could not afford to delay his return march to Bekwai, so that morning, without ceremony, he wished Captain Eden and the others well and marched away, fervently hoping that his vulnerable force would not be attacked. Soon after Willcocks's column moved off, a large group of Asante troops left their stockades and casually walked toward the fort, obviously believing that it had been abandoned. Captain Eden waited for them to near the fort before cutting down many of them with machine-gun fire. Remarkably, this was the second time the Asante had made this grim mistake. Willcocks's men heard the firing and picked up the pace of their march. They need not have worried; the Asante commanders were too dispirited and divided to organize an attack.

There were many reasons why Asante morale was low. The successful relief of the fort's garrison had shown once again that British weapons and tactics were difficult to overcome. Also, the lack of overall leadership was increasingly a problem. Opoku Mensa was a political leader, not a military man, and he had none of the Asante king's cachet as commander in chief. Yaa Asantewaa was a vital force, but her powers were largely symbolic. Kofi Kofia was a regional commander from the Atchuma district to the north of Kumase, and he soon left the capital to rejoin his own people. Most difficult of all to overcome, the Asante were trapped by their defensive role. They had built nearly impregnable stockades complete with comfortable war camps (as the French were to build the Maginot Line some thirty years later), and it was difficult to motivate them to take offensive action. Finally, because the war camps were in such close proximity to one another, when a stockade's garrison was defeated—as happened at Kumase—other garrisons shared their sense of demoralization.

Without their king and without an overall military commander, Asante forces were more like the private armies of rebellious warlords than the unified national army that had opposed Wolseley. Queen Mother Yaa Asantewaa was an inspirational voice, but even she could not bring the various leaders into common cause. For the most part, each leader's troops remained in war camps in their own district, ready to defend themselves against a British attack should one come but unwilling to unite in a large force to attack either the British troops or their long and temptingly vulnerable supply lines. And when a district army like the one in Kumase suffered defeat, the survivors' memories of British machine-gun and cannon fire followed by a bayonet charge were long and painful. Although the Asante troops in their war camps around Kumase had not given up—they would fight again when attacked—they had seen too much of British firepower to think of an attack against Willcocks just then. The greatest danger to the British column as it marched away from Kumase was posed by an occasional booby trap on the path, like the one that almost killed Captain Hall. As Hall bent down to remove a wooden "idol" that had been placed in the middle of the path, two African sergeants quickly pulled him back. As Hall watched, they carefully disconnected the figure from a cord that led to the trigger of a loaded Dane gun buried in the ground. It would have blown him to pieces.

By the nineteenth Willcocks's column was safely camped in Bekwai, much to the relief of the old king, who had lived in dread of an attack by the Asante army at Kokofu. Willcocks was relieved, too. His troops and carriers were exhausted, and all had coughs, sore throats, and fever. They needed a rest, and Willcocks ordered no new operations for some days. After sending the wounded and the worst of the sick to the coast, he began to plan the next stage of his campaign—the destruction of several large Asante armies that were still prepared to oppose British rule and the punishment of those villagers who continued to support the insurrection. To achieve success in what promised to be an arduous campaign during the rainy season, he needed more troops and carriers. These men arrived in frustratingly small numbers, partly due to Governor Hodgson's infuriating refusal to use any of the now healthy and mostly idle Hausa soldiers that had escaped from the fort with him to guard the road from Cape Coast to Bekwai. Hodgson's widespread local reputation as a selfish boor was confirmed once again. Willcocks had to use his own troops to guard the road. He also had to suffer in silence as accusations flew that he could have relieved the fort much earlier if he had only chosen to do so. It was said and written that his dramatic arrival on the last possible day was a crass attempt at self-aggrandizement. (No less a figure than Lady Hodgson made this claim, doing nothing to improve relations between Willcocks and the governor.) These accusations were unfair. Willcocks had faced enormous difficulties, and if he had not been lucky enough to find an undefended path, he probably would not have made it to Kumase by the fifteenth. With no staff and few troops when he arrived, he had made it to Kumase in fifty days during the height of the rainy season. It took Wolseley 120 days during the dry season to do the same thing.

Willcocks's plan for the defeat and punishment of the rebels called for British officers to recruit large numbers of untrained and undisciplined Africans, officially referred to as "levies." Some of these men would be armed with old muskets, but they were not expected to serve in combat. Unofficially called "locusts," they would straggle along behind Willcocks's troops, burning Asante villages and destroying their crops. Given the opportunity, they would also murder, rape, and with the knowledge of British officers, enslave any Asante women and children they were able to capture. Colonel A. F. Montanaro wrote approvingly of this policy of allowing traditional enemies of the Asante to enslave their women and children, noting that it was especially "galling" to them.[1] (One wonders what the British public would have thought of this practice had word of it leaked out. Unlike Wolseley, Willcocks was fortunate to have no newspaper correspondents with him to spread the news of unsavory forms of warfare; hence, there was no public furor.) To distinguish the locusts from Asante, they were made to wear a red-and-white-cloth sash draped over the right shoulder and tied under the left armpit. As Willcocks candidly put it, the job of these men was to make themselves "as unpleasant as possible," and they did so with a vengeance.[2]

While Willcocks was recruiting his locusts to wage a war of terror and waiting for more troops to arrive, several senior officers recently arrived from England made themselves thoroughly unpopular by trying to impose parade-ground discipline on the sick and battle-weary troops and junior officers. The veterans' annoyance about this unnecessary drilling and button polishing was temporarily suspended by the seemingly miraculous arrival in camp of a Hausa soldier who had marched out of the fort with Hodgson. Left behind after being wounded, the man had hidden in the bush for six weeks, slowly crawling south by night. He survived, although just barely, by eating roots. It had taken the poor man all that time to cover just eleven miles.

Willcocks's first target would be Kokofu, the stronghold that had twice before beaten off British attacks. Close to eight hundred men with five artillery pieces would be led by a newly arrived officer, Lieutenant Colonel Morland. Morland knew nothing about forest warfare and was quite ill with fever to boot, but Willcocks believed that every senior officer should be given the opportunity to command. Fortunately for Morland, he had the good sense to consult Captain Hall, whose men at Esumeja had been faced off against nearby Kokofu for months. Hall recommended that Morland's troops make a long halt at Esumeja to convince the Asante scouts—who watched all military movements from treetop perches—that the force was meant only as a reinforcement or replacement for Hall's men. Arriving at Esumeja in mid-morning, Morland's men stacked their weapons and appeared to make themselves comfortable. Hall's men began to pack their gear as if they were being relieved. At midday the Asante sentries returned to their war camp for a meal, convinced that there was no immediate threat. As they did so, the British troops, led by Melliss, moved unseen toward the main stockade. When they reached it still unseen, bugles sounded attack, and Melliss clambered over the unmanned stockade followed by his company.

The Asante army leapt up from its meal almost as one man, and seeing only a small force advancing, the troops formed up to charge, just as several hundred soldiers hurtled over the stockade, firing as they came. At the sight of so many swords and bayonets, most of the Asante fled in disorder, leaving many of their weapons behind. One of the Asante turned to fight and was clubbed over the head with a rifle butt. Several were bayoneted in the back as they ran, and Captain Biss recalled seeing one man turn a complete somersault when he was shot through the back as he tried to escape.[3] Once again, Major Melliss killed several Asante with his sword.

In addition to two hundred Dane guns and large amounts of powder, the British troops found several British rifles and carbines, fourteen kegs of gunpowder, dumdum bullets, and some .303-caliber ammunition, intended for modern British rifles, that had been cleverly wrapped with tow to make it fit the older, larger, .470-caliber Martini-Henry rifles that some of the Asante had. There were also hundreds of large wooden bowls filled with steaming hot food, and many of the Hausas began to help themselves. While the camp was being searched, some of the triumphant Hausas danced ecstatically to the beat of captured Asante war drums. One man put on an Asante war-dance costume that looked like a straw kilt with a straw cock's comb headdress. He led the others in the dance as they pirouetted, waved their carbines overhead, and slashed at the air with their bayonets. They worked themselves into such a frenzy that the British officers finally had to intervene to prevent them from injuring themselves.[4]

There were five separate war camps at Kokofu, each capable of housing at least three thousand men. From the amount of unconsumed food left behind, it appeared that the camps had been fully manned. While the troops systematically looted the huts before burning them, Captain Biss inspected the stockade. It was three hundred yards long, six feet high, and six feet thick with entrenchments on each flank. Behind the stockade there were numerous small grass-roofed huts to protect the Asante troops manning it from the sun and rain. The Asante had also hidden kegs of gunpowder in the roofs of the huts so that anyone setting fire to them would be killed, and in fact, when the British did set fire to them, several men and one officer were injured. Sharpened stakes planted in the ground protected the center portion of the stockade. The British officers were surprised to discover that there was an inviting gap near the center of stockade, but any man who had attempted to run through it would have fallen into a deep pit and impaled himself on sharpened stakes in the pit's bottom.[5]

After burning the camp and destroying the stockade, Morland's men gleefully marched back through Esumeja to Bekwae carrying incredible amounts of booty. When they arrived, they were delighted to find the entire garrison standing at attention under torchlight to honor them. Willcocks was so elated by their victory that he ordered a sizable issue of "medical comforts"—rum, champagne, and whiskey—and spent hours listening to accounts of this unbelievably easy victory over the previously impregnable Kokofu. Morland's men had captured one Asante prisoner, a well-built young man in apparently fine health. However, when his hands were bound that night to prevent him from escaping, he fell dead. Fear of the torture he had expected was apparently too much for him.

A few days later a force half the size of Morland's was sent to find and destroy the Adansi army that was thought to be located to the east of Dompoase. Thanks to the cooperation of a prisoner who agreed to show them the way in return for his life, the column knew where the Asante war camp was, but after a march of several days through largely open and beautifully scenic terrain, it nevertheless walked into an ambush, and its commander, Major Beddoes, was wounded. Captain Greer continued to lead the British forces forward until heavy fire from hills on both flanks stopped them. Only a well-led bayonet counterattack drove the Asante back. After two hours of heavy fighting, the British force tried to advance to destroy the war camp they knew lay ahead. But the Asante troops from Adansi district formed into lines and, urged on by a priest dressed in leopard skin, charged at the British troops, yelling and firing their Dane guns and rifles from the hip as they ran forward.

Greer was amazed by the audacity of the Asante attack because it came across open ground into the teeth of British artillery, machine-gun, and massed rifle fire. Despite the deadly British fire, some of the Asante troops came to within ten yards of the British line before they were shot down. As more and more men were killed at close range, the Asante slowly withdrew until another British bayonet charge, led by sword-waving officers including Captain Hall, finally forced them to run. Greer ordered his artillery to shell the war camp as the Asante retreated through it, and these explosive shells devastated the retreating Asante, tearing men to pieces. Greer's men counted three hundred dead Asante, including the leopard-skin priest; blood stains indicated that other bodies had been carried away.

This was yet another striking victory. With a force of only four hundred men, the British had routed an Asante force that numbered over three thousand. Led by Opoku Mensa, the surrogate king, the Asante had fought gallantly beyond anything that rational men could have expected, but as usual, once they began to run they did not stop. The camp was burned, and Greer returned to Bekwai with only one dead and forty wounded. One of the invalids was Hall, who had collapsed from exhaustion after running into the war camp, brandishing his sword at the fleeing Asante.[6]

After the unexpected victories at Kokofu and Dompoase, the southern portion of Asante was relatively quiet; so early in August, after learning that he had been both promoted and knighted, Willcocks decided to clear away the forces defending stockades at Kumase. He had received reports that the Asante might attempt to capture the fort, and while that prospect did not worry the colonel, he wanted to break Asante power around Kumase and move his headquarters there. He sent close to one thousand men, three cannon, several machine guns, and thousands of carriers to Kumase under the command of the same Colonel Burroughs of whom so little had been expected when he first arrived and who had annoyed Willcocks when he retreated from Kokofu. Willcocks was a forgiving commander, and this time Burroughs would repay his kindness. On the march Burroughs's column was joined by Major Melliss and his Nigerians. The Asante sniped at the long column as it meandered through the jungle, sometimes panicking the carriers, but little damage was done. The Asante had cut paths parallel to the main path taken by Burroughs's men, and every few hundred yards they had cut the brush away to allow them to fire into the unarmed carriers. Once the British began to spray machine-gun fire into the jungle on each side of the path, this practice ended. Burroughs's men reached the fort without a serious fight and found the garrison well and delighted to have visitors to enliven their boring confinement.

The next morning two armed columns left the fort to begin the job of stockade smashing around Kumase. The Asante had made no attempt to consolidate their forces. They still remained in their war camps behind the same large stockades. Melliss led the first column toward the stockade at Bantama, where they came under rapid fire from loopholes in the stockade and nearby trees. There was also heavy fire from both flanks. The British answered with volleys of rifle fire, machine guns, and cannon, but the Asante fire only grew heavier. Every officer in the leading company was hit, and so were many of the soldiers. With more men falling all the time and his cannon fire having no effect, Melliss tried to outflank the stockade, but the brush was so thick around the position that Melliss's three companies of Nigerians could not cut their way through it. A machine gun eventually killed the Asante who were firing from the trees, but shells from the 75-mm cannon did little damage to the heavy stockade.

Although a frontal charge seemed suicidal, Melliss nevertheless ordered his badly wounded teenaged bugler to sound charge, and despite blood in his eyes, the boy not only sounded the call but joined the charge himself. Melliss led his men directly into the teeth of the Asante fire. Barely ahead of his men, Melliss climbed over the wall, but this time many of the Asante stood to fight. After a few minutes of hand-to-hand fighting, bayonets and swords were again too much for the Asante, who began to run. Once again Melliss killed a man, this time by running him down and driving his sword through his back. Many others fell to bayonets. After destroying that stockade and another undefended one nearby, Melliss returned his column to the fort. Many of his men—including a British sergeant, Captain Biss, as well as Melliss himself—had been wounded. The bugler survived his wounds to receive a medal.

That same morning a column of troops from the Central African Regiment, joined by fifty veteran Sikhs and a company of the West African Regiment, encountered heavy fire from the Kintampo stockade near the Wesleyan mission. The stockade was over three hundred yards long and so well defended on its flanks that it took two hours for the British troops finally to outflank it and rout the defenders. The war camp was burned and the stockade destroyed, but not without cost. The British commander, Major Cobbe, was badly wounded, as was his colour sergeant. One Sikh was killed and seventeen wounded, seven of them seriously. Another twenty-six African soldiers were also wounded. Burroughs had a right to be proud of these attacks, but they were far more costly than he had expected. Willcocks had expected the Asante opposition to be so weak that he ordered Burroughs's men to carry only three hundred rounds per man. The two long battles had used up most of that, but several important and heavily defended stockades remained. The most important of these blocked the direct road from

Kumase to Kokofu. Anticipating correctly that this would be the next British target, the Asante reinforced it.

Burroughs was already concerned about his losses, and he knew that a conventional attack on this stockade would cost him many more casualties. He also needed to conserve ammunition in case he was attacked on the march back to Kokofu. Anyone who had seen the "gouty little colonel" when he first arrived in the Gold Coast would have been amazed at what he ordered done next. Audaciously deciding to test the willingness of the Asante troops to stand up to a bayonet attack at night, he sent a company out in daylight to scout their position. Based on the information obtained, Burroughs decided to attack at around nine that same night. He would take only five hundred men, plus some two thousand unarmed carriers to help with the stockade's destruction. No shots would be fired; the men would rely entirely on bayonets and swords. After the colonel's orders were explained, all the men had a meal, Biss and Melliss sharing a pint bottle of champagne with their dinner on the very good grounds that they might not live to have another.[7]

They moved out after dinner as planned under a clear, moonlit sky. As the troops approached the stockade, officers whispered orders that were passed quietly back down the column: "No smoking, no talking, no noise, no firing, bayonet only, follow me."[8] Everything possible had been done to silence the men's equipment, and it appeared that everything was now ready for a stealthy approach to the stockade. But as the tense soldiers crept silently toward the stockade, the Mende carriers from Sierra Leone burst forth into a wild crescendo of song meant to encourage the troops to victory. Horrified, the troops froze, expecting an answering volley from the Asante, while the British officers rushed back to whack the Mende carriers with the flats of their swords. Eventually, but by no means easily, the officers succeeded in quieting them. Hoping to cover up the racket, the fort bugler played "last post" as if it were just another ordinary night.

The troops crept closer to the stockade, hoping against all reason for a complete surprise until, in what sounded like a thunderclap, two sentry signal guns exploded with seemingly deafening roars. Immediately, a volley came out of the stockade's loopholes, and a British lieutenant fell mortally wounded. The African troops were stunned and began to waver, but as the young officer lay dying, he waved his sword, indicating the charge, and all the British officers shouted the word "charge." Everyone went forward, scaling the stockade with an ease they later could not understand. The Asante troops were caught so unaware that they rushed out of their huts in the war camp just in time to be impaled by a bayonet or sword. One officer was so tired by his exertions with his sword that he had to put it down and disobey orders by firing away with his pistol. Captain Biss recalled that only exhaustion on the part of the British officers and men allowed most of the Asante to escape.[9] As the war camp was being set fire and the stockade pulled down, a child was found and taken back to the fort. Remarkably, the entire force was back in bed by 11 P.M.

The next day, after leaving reinforcements behind in the fort, Burroughs marched his men back toward Bekwai, picking up on the way a young Asante woman who reported that the night attack had so distressed Yaa Asantewaa that she had called various commanders together to discuss this new tactic. While the Asante were considering their options, the British wounded were being conveyed to the coast, and those who remained in Bekwai were delighting in listening to news of the world, which the newly strung telegraph brought them. For a week the troops at Bekwai enjoyed a badly needed rest, and the officers had time to shave with hot water, drink cocoa and tea (which, unfortunately, often contained a dead fly or two), and read mail from home.

No one needed rest more than Willcocks, who suffered from a severe sore throat, a badly abscessed ear, a sprained knee that refused to improve, and bouts of nausea and diarrhea. His chief surgeon strongly advised him to return to England, but he refused, saying that he could not honorably leave until the Asante war had ended. He also believed that the climate at Kumase was much healthier and that once his headquarters was moved there, he would improve. This was a forlorn hope because neither Willcocks nor his surgeon understood malaria. Although both British and Italian pioneers in tropical medicine had shown several years earlier that malaria was transmitted by anopheles mosquitos, British officers on this campaign continued to believe that fever, as they still called it, was a product of the vile vapors of swamp land. They recommended five grains of quinine per day as a preventive dose and ten if fever actually struck. Whiskey, too, was still thought to be helpful, but not until evening.

During this period of rest, several Asante prisoners were brought in charged with murder, mutilation, or both. Willcocks convened a military court, but because he was concerned that these men might have behaved in ways that were permitted by their own laws, he asked the king of Bekwai to join the court, an offer the elderly monarch gladly accepted. Before the trial began, Willcocks gave the king's interpreter a copy of the charges against the two men so that the king could prepare for the trial. Willcocks was surprised when, half an hour later, the interpreter "returned, beaming with smiles, and said, 'I am glad to inform you that the King has already found both prisoners entirely guilty.' Considering that he had never seen either of them, nor heard a single word of evidence, I came to the conclusion that future prisoners under trial would stand a rather better chance without the presence of one of their own Chiefs on the tribunal."[10]

About this time, Lieutenant Colonel R. A. Brake, a highly decorated officer, arrived in Bekwai with a battalion of the Central African Regiment, a well-disciplined unit fresh from fighting in Somaliland (now Somalia). Brake's troops quickly proved that their reputation was well earned by carrying out several successful small-scale attacks. In one raid, in the direction of Queen Mother Yaa Asantewaa's headquarters at Edweso, his men surprised a force of Asante, killing their leader and driving them out of their war camp, where they found a remarkable collection of valuables including £100 in bank notes, bags of gold dust, books, parts of machine guns, and sundry flags, chairs, and umbrellas.

Before Willcocks was ready to move his headquarters to the now partially pacified city of Kumase, he sent two columns to the east to despoil the area around the large lake called Bosumtwi that covered at least forty square miles. Its many fish were the property of the Asante king, and under ordinary circumstances fresh deliveries were made to Kumase every day.[11] The only hostility the British troops encountered was produced by a lone Asante man, who decided to fight a one-man war. Sitting astride a large log in the lake and paddling with his hands until he was more or less in range of the incredulous British forces on the shore, he somehow managed to fire his Dane gun without knocking himself off his perch. Having made his point, he unhurriedly turned his awkward conveyance around and paddled away. The British officers who witnessed his attack were amused and impressed by what one of them referred to as a "most absurd mixture of dignity and comedy."[12] There was no other Asante resistance, but the British troops caught immense numbers of fish, violating all the royal proscriptions against fishing as they did so, and burned many of the fertile fields in the area before marching back again, the unruly locusts who followed them happily destroying everything in sight and capturing unwary women and children.

Toward the end of August, Willcocks decided to move toward Kumase in two powerful columns, leaving only a token force at Bekwai to pacify its still-skittish king. With one thousand infantry and four guns Willcocks marched north through Pekki, reaching Kumase on August 30 with no serious opposition. At the same time, Colonel Brake, with over seven hundred infantry and two guns, moved northeast to attack Edweso, where Yaa Asantewaa's army was said to be camped. He was to be supported by a large force of untrained African soldiers moving toward Edweso from the east, led by Captain Benson of the Shropshire Light Infantry, with a handful of British officers and noncommissioned officers. Benson's orders were to block the retreat of Asante forces, not to attack them with his ill-disciplined, nearly mutinous mob of men. For some reason Benson advanced anyway, was attacked, and saw his men flee in wild disorder while the Asante pursued and killed many of them. Benson and his British officers fought their way to safety, but shamed by his failure, suffering from malaria, and aware that he had disobeyed orders, he shot himself to death the next day.

On the morning of August 31, Brake attacked the Asante stockade at Edweso, where he met with tremendous fire, much of it from captured British rifles. In by-now-standard fashion he sent troops into the brush to flank the stockades and wheeled up artillery to blast away at it. For the first time these cannon, commanded by a lieutenant named Halfpenny, fired eighteen-pound shells called "double common" (the usual shell weighed twelve pounds), which blew great chunks out of the log-and-dirt barrier. These quick-firing cannon blasted away at the stockade for two interminable hours, killing and maiming hundreds of defenders, but other Asante resolutely maintained a heavy fire until the British finally fought around their flank through log barriers, rifle pits, and brush entanglements and made a bayonet charge that successfully ended the battle. Colonel Brake was wounded in the chest, another officer was killed, and two more wounded. Thirty-four soldiers were hit, many severely. The dead Asante had been so terribly mangled by shell fire that one British officer described the sight of them as "sickening".[13] Yaa Asantewaa was said to have been in the thick of the battle, but hers was not one of the many bodies, including those of prominent commanders, that were identified. If the sixty-year-old queen mother was present at this battle, it was only because she lived in Edweso. She wore a leather belt and a sword to symbolize her defiance of the British, but despite her size (five-foot ten and about two hundred pounds) neither she nor any other Asante woman was known actually to have fought in battle.

Within days the British forces were consolidated in Kumase, which quickly became a major camp and supply depot, thanks to the efforts of some eight thousand carriers, the best of whom were two thousand experienced men shipped in from Zanzibar and Mombasa in East Africa. In addition to tons of rice and tinned meat, even luxuries such as butter, jam, milk, various sauces, and wine were now becoming plentiful. Whiskey and sparkling water began to replace the earlier staple for officers, a concoction known as "a doctor," made from rum, tinned milk, and water stirred together. A bakery was opened, officers began to invite each other to impromptu dinners, and on the seventh of September, the telegraph line to Kumase was reopened. Officers were now able to discuss the latest news from Reuters over an evening whiskey. The African troops, carriers, and locusts soon enjoyed a thriving market filled with local food products. They also sang, danced, drank palm wine, and enjoyed the women who came to the market with their wares. The only troops accused of raping women, however, were some from Sierra Leone.

The best evidence that Kumase was no longer besieged was the daily occurrence of a cricket game on the parade ground in front of the fort. British officers used hand-carved cricket bats to smack homemade India rubber balls far into the outfield where long grass concealed various parts of dead human beings that disconcerted the fielders when they stepped on them. Some of the African soldiers had seen cricket played by their officers before, but the carriers and Asante market women watched in fascinated bafflement. There were also endless card games. Despite continuing bouts of malaria and dysentery, Kumase was beginning to resemble a peacetime garrison.

The war was over in the town of Kumase, but the district outside Kumase was still defiant, and so was much of northern metropolitan Asante. Willcocks soon sent various columns of troops followed by the inevitable carriers and locusts to crisscross Kumase district, burning villages and chopping down anything that still grew in the fields. Some Asante began to surrender, and those not charged with being war leaders or murderers of British subjects were sent back to their villages with a pass indicating their surrender and told to fly a white flag. Some war leaders were captured and hanged, and it was becoming clear that most Asante had lost their enthusiasm for war. Late in September even Queen Mother Yaa Asantewaa sent envoys to Kumase to discuss peace terms, but some of the locusts intercepted them, insulting them so profoundly in the process that they left in a rage without ever meeting with British authorities.[14]

To encourage more surrenders, on September 15 Willcocks invited every Asante who could be persuaded to come to Kumase to witness a display of British military might. As a large crowd of Asante looked on, a trio of 75-mm cannon fired double-common shells into a stout stockade, tearing it to bits. It may have been this demonstration that convinced Asante commanders to abandon their stockades for the duration of the war. Willcocks also paraded 1,750 infantry and nine 75-mm artillery pieces in another display of British power that was said to have impressed many of the Asante who looked on. Some important chiefs began to inquire about peace terms, but even though it was obvious to everyone that the remaining Asante armies could not defend themselves against a British attack, the area north of Kumase nevertheless remained defiant.

Determined to end all resistance, Willcocks decided to send two columns north. The first of these marched over two hundred miles without encountering any serious fighting, but it did accept the surrender of a king and eleven important chiefs. Many villages and crops were also destroyed, weapons were captured, and the area thoroughly terrorized. The second column was led by a veteran commander, Lieutenant Colonel Arthur F. Montanaro of the Royal Artillery. It was Montanaro who first devised the use of the double-common shells to cope with stockades, and now, fittingly, he would be the first to lead troops in a battle that would take place in the open. He led 950 infantry, two cannon, many carriers, and about one thousand locusts north to attack the still defiant Kofi Kofia and his army of several thousand men. Some dozen miles north of Kumase at a village named Dinassi, Montanaro's advance guard, once again led by the indestructible Major Charles Melliss, learned that there were indeed Asante still willing to contest British power. Returning fire with everything his troops had, Montanaro was surprised to see that instead of firing from behind a stockade, the Asante troops were fanning out on both flanks, attempting to envelop his column. Recognizing this as the classic Asante tactic from the Wolseley war, Montanaro ordered the favorite response of the British—another bayonet charge. For a few minutes the fighting was hand to hand, and one British officer was killed, but Melliss, though slightly wounded again, killed two more men with his saber. The Asante force, which was not very large, then withdrew in reasonably good order, leaving thirty-four dead bodies behind but taking many others with them.

These men were an advance guard of Kofi Kofia's army, but he would choose another place for his showdown with the British. Montanaro marched on to the town of Ofinsu where five major chiefs surrendered along with 320 muskets and other war supplies. Montanaro returned to Kumase on September 26. Willcocks had planned to send Montanaro back into the field to punish Atchuma villages to the northwest, an expedition that the Asante quickly learned about, but before troops could march, some scouts returned with a challenge from Kofi Kofia. He wanted the British commander to know that he had gathered five thousand men and he invited the British to fight him in the open. With a well-calculated sneer he added that he was certain the British would not dare to do so.[15] Sensing a chance to end the war by answering this challenge, Willcocks mustered every able-bodied man in Kumase—one thousand two hundred infantry with five cannon—and on September 29, followed by thousands of carriers, he marched out to accept Kofi Kofia's invitation to battle. Montanaro was with the force but, bad leg and all, Willcocks would command. Near nightfall they met an Asante patrol that withdrew, and Willcocks's column settled down to spend the night in the open under a drenching rain. After a dinner of tinned beef, rain-sodden biscuits, and a dose of quinine washed down with whiskey and rainwater, the officers tried to sleep under banana leaves but with no success. The sun warmed the sleepless men as they marched forward at daybreak on the following day, the thirtieth. It was Sunday, to the Asante a dangerous day when they would try to avoid warfare, but so far a lucky day for the British, who had won several major battles on their Sabbath. By 8 A.M. the advance guard under Montanaro ran into Asante fire, beginning what the veteran Captain Harold Biss called "one of the fiercest encounters ever fought in West African warfare."[16]

Montanaro found his advance guard under heavy fire from captured British rifles as well as Dane guns in the hands of a long line of Asante lying in a shallow ditch with open ground in front of them. Without waiting for Melliss, who was behind him with three hundred men, Montanaro positioned a machine gun on his flank to cover the advance and sent his four companies forward in a flanking maneuver. When he thought he saw signs of wavering on the part of the Asante, he immediately ordered a charge. Four hundred men with fixed bayonets ran forward toward the Asante line. For the first time in such a major battle, the Asante did not quaver at the sight of bayonets. Instead, they delivered such a steady fire that if they had not fired high, the British line would have been shot to pieces. Even though few were hit by the lead whistling over their heads, Montanaro's men slowed, then hit the ground. Unable to urge his men forward, Montanaro sent word to Melliss to come up. By now the Asante held an eight hundred-yard-long front with wings drawn back to prevent flank attacks. The pinned-down British forces were still firing, but like most infantry the world over, once they had been forced to take cover, it was difficult to get them going again. The remarkable Melliss ordered his three hundred men to charge over them, and though they did so with great verve, they too were soon forced to take cover to avoid the hailstorm of lead that the Asante fired at them. In perfect order the Asante then withdrew a short distance to a crest, which gave them an even stronger position.

No Asante army had stood so resolutely against a British bayonet charge before, and these men had now done so twice. Nevertheless, they had been continuously exposed to machine-gun and cannon fire along their extended line and were taking many casualties. After the second charge Willcocks arrived at the front with his staff and a unit of Sikhs under Captain Godfrey. These bearded veterans with their tall turbans were such champions of the bayonet charge that Willcocks thought they might be able to inspire the seven hundred pinned-down African soldiers to follow them. Willcocks ordered the heaviest fire possible all along the front while Godfrey extended the Sikhs into a line, preparing for the charge. Unable to resist the lure of battle, Willcocks's staff officers again left him alone as they ran to join the Sikhs. Major Melliss had seen the Sikhs' maneuver, and before Godfrey could give the order to charge, with the inspirational help of massed bugles and drums, he was somehow able to drive his men to their feet. His Africans charged before the Sikhs did, closely followed by the English officers just ahead of the now-sprinting Sikhs.

As this frontal charge was bearing down on the Asante line, two African companies turned the Asante left flank. At this point of danger in all previous battles, the Asante had broken and run, almost every man for himself. But these men of Kofi Kofia's army were different—they stood and fought, sometimes with their bare hands. As Melliss was slashing at Asante soldiers with his saber, he found himself in single combat with a man who shot at him at point-blank range but missed. Melliss wounded the man with his sword but was immediately thereafter shot through the foot, leaving it paralyzed. The wounded Asante flung himself on Melliss, and the two men wrestled each other to the ground. Just as the Asante appeared to be getting free to unsheath his knife, Captain Godfrey rushed up and shot the man in the head.

The bayonets of the British troops slowly prevailed but not without cost. Fully half of the Sikhs were wounded, many seriously. But the Asante left flank now caved in just as more British troops, behind heavy cannon fire, burst into the Asante rear. Only then did these Asante soldiers run from battle, leaving their wounded and many rifles behind. Sixty-two Asante dead were counted in the hand-to-hand fight alone, with hundreds of other bodies found elsewhere. Willcocks came upon seventeen men lying dead together in a pile who "were literally riddled" with machine-gun bullets. In another pile he saw seven or eight men jumbled together in death. He wrote that they were "splendid-looking fellows, far superior in physique to any I had seen before."[17] So much blood had been shed in the grass that officers' legs were stained red to the knee. Many hundreds of Asante wounded were acknowledged, but no one who participated in the battle reported their fate.

A British column pursued Kofi Kofia's fleeing Atchumas, finding guns, baggage, and a few wounded men alongside the road. They met an old woman who assured a British officer that the Asante were moving far too fast to be caught. She was right. Even though they were carrying many wounded, the Asante outdistanced their British pursuers. On the long march back to Kumase, the British column encountered an elaborate log fort built into several trees that commanded the road. Montanaro tried to destroy it with eighteen-pound shells, but after a dozen shots it was still undamaged. Willcocks was relieved that it had not been defended.[18] The force returned to Kumase on October 3, trailed by the locusts, who carried large numbers of Asante heads slung from long poles. How they came by these trophies is not recorded.

With no large body of hostile troops still at large, Willcocks gave his men some time to rest and refit. Melliss was among the first to be placed in a hammock for the long trip to the coast and evacuation to England, where his foot required surgery. He would receive the Victoria Cross for his actions, the first man to do so from newly crowned King Edward VII, the eldest son of Queen Victoria. When Melliss left Kumase, the entire garrison enthusiastically turned out to honor him. Melliss recovered fully from his wounds, but three years later he was badly mauled by a lion while campaigning in Somaliland. Once again he recovered.

Of the British officers who began the campaign, all were either dead or invalided home as a result of disease or wounds except for Hall and Willcocks. Hall somehow never contracted malaria, and although he refused to take quinine, neither did Willcocks. Of course, malaria was just about the only malady Willcocks did not suffer from. The Sikhs who had not been wounded were quite healthy, but the African troops were in poor condition. Due to the rain and cold nights, most had bronchial infections, and the continual marching through mud left their always bare feet badly cut and their legs ulcerated. Dysentery was a continuing problem for them, too, and smallpox outbreaks were common as well. Their uniforms, like those of the long-serving officers, were torn and faded. They looked terrible and felt even worse, but their discipline was always excellent. Carriers and locusts were flogged and sometimes given long prison sentences, but the fighting troops seldom required punishment.

The fleeing Asante troops had taken refuge in the northwestern corner of Asante where Willcocks feared they would once again come together under either Kofi Kofia, who survived the last battle, or Kobina Cherri, a leader notorious for mutilating his enemies, some seventy-six of whom he was alleged to have killed. He was a favorite of Yaa Asantewaa, who was still free and quite defiant. On the first of November, long after many in the Colonial Office believed the war had ended, Willcocks sent Major Montanaro with seven hundred men, five machine guns, and several 75-mm cannon northwest toward Berekum to find and punish the remaining hostile Asante. They were to rendezvous with another, only slightly smaller, force on the way. With over one thousand two hundred infantry, two thousand five hundred carriers, and numerous locusts this was a major expedition. On November six they received an insolent message from Kobina Cherri that he would fight. As Montanaro pressed forward, his troops mistook some of their locusts for the enemy and opened fire, killing six. Their faded and dirty shoulder sashes could not be seen at a distance. The families of the six men were compensated for their deaths, but the rest of their fellow tribesmen left the column and returned to Kumase, refusing to participate any longer in the campaign.[19] Soon after these men left, a tremendous storm struck, nearly blinding everyone with lightning and knocking down huge trees, one of which barely missed killing Montanaro and his staff.

Despite these misfortunes, Montanaro continued his march northwest to confront Kobina Cherri. Several Asante kings and war leaders surrendered, including the man who had commanded the stockade at Bantama. Through an interpreter he told Montanaro that his men had been determined to defend their position at all costs, but when a white man with a sword charged straight at them all by himself, they were so unnerved by what they took to be a madman that they fled.[20] The lone man was Melliss, and he may have owed his survival to Asante law, which forbade the killing of madmen. Another Asante commander who surrendered complained that it was unfair of the British to use swords and bayonets when the Asante had neither.

The British continued the march through open grasslands, where at first they enjoyed the sun but soon wilted in the heat. It became increasingly apparent that Kobina Cherri had been unable to raise an army. There was no resistance, but the British listened to stories of the terror Kobina Cherri had rained on the rubber traders in the area. It was said that some seventy-six men who either could not or would not pay the amounts of money he demanded were tortured to death. On the thirteenth the column arrived in Berekum, whose king had remained loyal to the British throughout the war. He was delighted to see so many British troops. The next day they began the return march, and thanks to information provided by a girl whose father had been killed by Kobina Cherri, a small British force captured the fugitive. Montanaro described him as defiant and insolent but could not help admiring his courage.[21] On the twenty fourth the troops returned to Kumase with thirty-one kings and chiefs as prisoners, nine hundred guns, and five thousand pounds of rubber. They also laid waste much of the countryside along their route.

In a monument to timely justice, Kobina Cherri was tried by military tribunal the next day, charged with murdering over fifty British subjects. It was testified that after torturing these people, he cut off their hands and drove them into the forest to die. He was found guilty, and Willcocks, who headed the tribunal, sentenced him to be hanged the following morning. Later that night Kobina Cherri asked to see Willcocks. When the colonel went to the guardroom to see the handcuffed prisoner, he was told that if he pardoned the Asante war leader, Kobina Cherri would reveal the hiding place of a large sum of gold and the Golden Stool. Willcocks urged him to do both as a last good deed but said that the death sentence was final. An unknown number of Asante had already been hanged, and some had been tied to trees and executed by firing squad.[22]

Early the next morning the prisoner again sent for Willcocks and asked if there were any possibility of a pardon. Told no, he then offered to reveal the name of the man who actually committed the murders, a close friend of his as it turned out. These negotiations, which were not inappropriate for a high-ranking Asante, did nothing to diminish his dignity. Indeed, when Kobina Cherri was marched to the gallows, he did so with imposing courage, pausing only to spit at two African traders whose testimony had helped to convict him. Once he mounted the bamboo scaffold, he stood as erect as any soldier and glared defiance.[23] When he fell to his death, "an involuntary murmur of admiration arose."[24]

Colonel Willcocks left Kumase on December 3, passing down a two-mile-long avenue of troops and Asante chiefs, who fired their Dane guns exuberantly. The war was over, and authority would now be exercised by a British resident, Captain Donald Stewart (the son of a field marshal), who had campaigned with the troops during the latter stages of the hostilities and served as Colonel Scott's political officer in 1896. No significant number of armed Asante were still hostile to British rule; but even though an amnesty for all but those accused of murder had been in effect since October, a substantial number of people who had played prominent roles in the war were still at large. Stewart let it be known that unless these people surrendered, he would use his remaining 1,225 troops under Colonel Burroughs and twenty-three other British officers to devastate even more of the Asante countryside. In no time several hundred Asante, including many women, surrounded a forested area and seized two wanted men. Within two weeks all of the prominent leaders had surrendered. One of the last to do so was Yaa Asantewaa. Most of these last leaders to surrender were deported to Sierra Leone, but the queen mother was sent to the Seychelles to join her son and King Prempe in exile.

A sad footnote to the campaign was written by the men of the West African Regiment from Sierra Leone. Like the other African soldiers under British command, they had fought bravely and well throughout the long and savage war. However, when they were told that they would remain in Asante indefinitely, they rebelled, insisting that they had been promised that they would return home as soon as the fighting ended. All the old British officers whom they had known and trusted had been killed or invalided home and their replacements knew nothing about any past promises. Taking matters into their own hands, the frustrated men seized an ample supply of food and ammunition and marched off to Cape Coast in perfect order under their own Sierra Leone sergeant. Unwilling to start a blood bath, Colonel Burroughs let them go. When they arrived at Cape Coast, the new governor attempted to reason with the men, explaining the seriousness of mutiny, but they refused to listen and set off on the thousand-mile walk back to Sierra Leone. Pursued by Hausas and fired at by a gunboat, some were killed and a few were captured, including the man most responsible for organizing the mutiny. He was found guilty and shot. The great majority disappeared into the jungle and were not seen again. Perhaps they were able to return to their homes. If they did, the British government did not attempt to track them down.

British losses since the beginning of the war in April were comparatively slight. Only 16 officers had been killed, but 52 had been wounded, and another 54 had to be sent home in hospital ships. Of the various African and Sikh troops only 113 had been killed in action, although another 102 died from disease, and 41 were missing and presumed dead. Nearly 700 had been wounded, and almost 5,000 had to be admitted to hospital at one time or another.[25] Although only 1 carrier was officially considered to have been killed in action, it is likely that at least 500 were killed and an equal number probably died of disease, because of the 15,000 carriers who served, over 5,000 had been admitted to hospitals. It was also reported that 50 locusts had been killed, although the actual number must have been larger.[26]

Many of the surviving British officers went on to distinguished careers. Willcocks became a major general and commanded the Indian Corps in France in 1914. Surprisingly, given his reckless courage, Melliss lived to be a Lieutenant General. Several others reached general rank or became colonial governors. Hodgson became the governor of Barbados and British Guiana, Montanaro became the governor of Sierra Leone, and after World War I Willcocks served as the governor of Bermuda, a plum post for an aging hero. Some, of course, died in later wars. Godfrey was killed in Somaliland while saving the life of another officer, as he had earlier saved Melliss. Sergeant Mackenzie, who won a VC, was killed in World War I, where he served as a major in the Black Watch. Hall eventually lost his sight from a wound he later suffered in Nigeria. A medal was issued to all who served in the war, and England feted its returning heroes.

How many Asante died in the war can never be known, but shells, bullets, and bayonets must have slain several thousand; many others must have died of their wounds, and still others of disease. Opoku Mensa, who as much as anyone had led the Asante resistance, died in captivity in the fort at Kumase, apparently from natural causes. While Willcocks was receiving a gold Sword of Honor from the city of London, the Asante kingdom was in ruins, its golden swords of diplomacy of no further use. Villages had been burned, fields devastated, and its leaders dead or in exile. Except for the limited powers of local chiefs, all authority now rested with the British. They divided the former area of metropolitan Asante into four districts, each with its own British-appointed commissioner. The traditional districts such as Kumase, Mampon, and Dwaben ceased to have political significance.

In 1903 the railroad that Wolseley had hoped for was actually opened, when a track was completed that connected Kumase to the coast at Sekondi, west of Elmina. The ravaged city of Kumase received new life, rapidly becoming a trading and administrative center. Government offices were built, and men were once again making a profit from rubber, timber, gold, and especially cocoa.

The economic recovery was so rapid and the political climate so tranquil that when the chiefs petitioned for King Prempe's return in 1910, the British governor gave it some consideration before rejecting it, and he pointedly did not repeat Hodgson's declaration that Prempe would never return.

Peace and prosperity continued until 1921 when once again the fate of the Golden Stool threatened to lead to armed conflict. The British-led Gold Coast government had undertaken an extensive program of road building, and one of the proposed roads was to pass directly over the still-secret hiding place of the Golden Stool. By the time that word of this was passed to the handful of men who knew where the hiding place was, the laborers were on the verge of digging up the sacred area. By inventing a story about dangerous supernatural forces in the area, the laborers were induced to flee, and the roadwork was delayed long enough to permit the Golden Stool to be removed. But the damage had been done. The Asante remembered Hodgson's heavy-handed attempts to find the stool, and they assumed that the road-building activity was simply another ruse by the government to seize the it. Rumors spread all over Asante, and preparations were made for war.

However, before the stool had been reburied, one of the men entrusted with its protection secretly removed some of the gold from it. Just before hostilities seemed ready to break out, an Asante woman recognized the golden ornaments from the stool as they were being offered for sale. Thanks to the research of a government anthropologist, R. S. Rattray, the British now understood the significance of the Golden Stool and took immediate steps to arrest fourteen Asante men accused of desecrating it. They also allowed the accused to be tried by the Kumase council of chiefs. Six of the accused were sentenced to death, and seven were given life prison terms. Although all these sentences were commuted by the British, usually to exile, the Asante were favorably impressed by the trial and by British assurances that the Golden Stool would forever remain in Asante hands.

Shortly after the trial the principal spokesman for the chiefs of Kumase referred to the stool and its meaning for the Asante with the same sentiments that had led to the uprising of 1900: "The Golden Stool is very great. It contains the soul of the nation. We honor it so much that if it had been tampered with by anyone from outside we would have risen in arms, and it would not have mattered to us if we all perished the same day."[27]

In November 1924, only three years after the peaceful resolution of this crisis, King Prempe was allowed to return to Kumase. He and his relatives had been well treated in the Seychelles, where they were paid a monthly allowance, adequately housed, treated with respect, and allowed the freedom of the island. Some of the king's children married Seychelles islanders. British education was also made available, and so was Christianity. King Prempe eventually became an enthusiastic convert but was unsure which denomination to declare as his own until he asked a British official which church the British monarch belonged to. He then quickly declared that he too would join the Church of England, and he became a devout Anglican who attended church every Sunday and preached Christian values.

Prempe was not above having a drink, or even several, but he was not given to any of the excesses of many of his royal ancestors.[28] He enjoyed lively conversation and was skilled at many games, including bridge, and while sailing from the Seychelles to Accra on his return home, he defeated everyone who played against him at checkers.[29] Much had changed in the twenty-eight years since his humiliating and illegal arrest. British officials met him with appropriate ceremony when he left the ship, and a special train took him to Kumase, where he was met by a huge throng of Asante wearing white clothes, their faces painted with white stripes as a sign of joy. When he stepped off the train, there were loud cheers, and many people wept with joy. He was dressed in a European suit, and despite the heat, he wore a wool overcoat. As they greeted him, he smiled and lifted his black-felt homburg to them. He then stepped into a waiting automobile, which took him to a house that had been prepared for him.

Prempe was recognized only as the king of Kumase by the British although he was clearly king of Asante to his people. He certainly comported himself as if he were king, and his political activities became meddlesome enough at times that Governor Maxwell was convinced he was planning to usurp British power.[30] The shrewd Prempe always stopped short of sedition, however, and lived a rewarding seven years until his death in 1931. In 1935 he was succeeded by the son of his eldest sister, who like Prempe I was light-skinned and a Christian. Nana Osei Agyeman Prempeh II was installed by the British as the king of Asante, and the Asante state was reborn as a confederacy. For the first time since 1896, the Golden Stool was displayed in public. Every Asante present honored it by standing.[31]

10

"For the Ashes of Their Fathers and the Temples of Their Gods"

IN REFLECTING ON A CENTURY OF ARMED CONFLICT BETWEEN THE Asante and the British, nothing stands out more dramatically than the lost possibilities for peace. Despite the militancy of many members of the dominant inner council, the only Asante king who actually sought war with the British was Osai Yaw, whose campaign resulted in a politically embarrassing defeat near Dodowa. With this one exception, from the beginning of the nineteenth century to its bloody end, Asante government actively pursued peaceful relations with the British. They did not do so because they were unwilling to use war as an instrument of policy—they initiated war with several African opponents at various times throughout the century, including the peaceful era generated by Maclean—but because they well understood that only peace with Britain could ensure that their trading lifeline to the coast would not be broken. They found the peace they sought during Maclean's era; but before Maclean's time and after his death, British policy was to circumvent the Asante or to destroy their power, not to make them friendly trading partners.

British reasons for rejecting a peaceful alliance with the Asante were not confined to economic self-interest, although that was an important consideration especially during the latter part of the century. The implacable hostility of the Fante to their Asante overlords spawned such vivid claims about Asante cruelty, rapacity, untrustworthiness, and lust for war that British officials seemed to be blinded to a more balanced view. Their reliance on Fante interpreters did nothing to achieve this balance. The British were also appalled by Asante executions, which they believed were human sacrifice, not a form of criminal justice, and which they were led to believe were far more frequent and cruel than similar practices engaged in by other societies in the Gold Coast. Despite abundant evidence that Asante kings were constitutional monarchs with whom binding treaties could honorably be negotiated, they persisted in thinking of them as bloodthirsty and untrustworthy autocrats. And even after a century of contact with the Asante, the British failed to comprehend Asante values, their veneration of their ancestors, their ideas of an afterlife, their pride and honor, their loyalties and obligations, and least of all, the central significance of the Golden Stool. These factors and others played a part in bringing about conflict, but at bottom neither the British traders early in the century nor the British government officers who came later had any desire to share power on the Gold Coast with the Asante. The Asante were seen as dangerous adversaries, and it only remained for changing circumstances to dictate when British military power would be called into play.

The power of the two adversaries changed profoundly over the century. When King Osei Bonsu's army swept down on the Fante at Cape Coast in 1806, the Asante Empire was still at the pinnacle of its political and military power. Its wealth was great, and not only was its army superior to any of its African enemies, it could have held its own against anything short of a large-scale European expeditionary force. The Asante army of the early nineteenth century had no cannon, but its flintlocks were nearly as efficient as the smooth-bore muskets carried by European soldiers. Given this relative parity in weapons, the huge size of the Asante army, along with the hostile forest terrain, the hot, rainy weather, and the ravages of disease, would have made it impossible for anything less than a major European military force to have marched to Kumase, won a battle, and returned to the coast with more than a small fraction of its men still able to fight. With the British army stretched to its limits in wars against the French and Americans, there was no realistic possibility that the British government would have dispatched such a large force to West Africa. The Asante Empire could not begin to match the technological marvels of Great Britain, but early in the nineteenth century the Asante were supreme in their own domain.

Sir Charles MacCarthy's disastrous campaign against them in 1824 suggests that the balance of power had changed little even then, although his campaign was hardly a true test of either Asante or British strength. As the years passed, however, Asante political control over its empire gradually eroded, and by the time Sir Garnet Wolseley led his expeditionary force to Kumase, the political power of Greater Asante had been weakened in many ways, and the disparity in the means for making war had grown extreme. Wolseley's men had modern breech-loading rifles, Gatling guns that fired five hundred rounds a minute, and much-improved artillery. The Asante troops still relied on their antique flintlock, smooth-barrel muskets. By the end of the century, when Colonel Willcocks was called upon to quell an Asante rebellion with his even more modern rifles, machine guns, and artillery, Greater Asante was largely depopulated, its sense of political community was in disarray, and its weapons, except for a small number of British rifles, were the same as those used in 1806. Willcocks did not have white British troops as Wolseley did, but his African soldiers were well disciplined, and their weapons were as devastating as any then available in the world. At the close of the nineteenth century, the British Empire was still a great world power while the Asante Empire had ceased to exist.

In view of the British superiority in weaponry, it is truly extraordinary that Wolseley's force came so close to being defeated in 1874 and that Willcocks's superbly armed men took so long to overcome Asante resistance in 1900. The dense rain forest was an obvious Asante ally, as were malaria, other diseases, and rains, all of which adversely affected the British; but even in 1874, when the Asante army had been devastated by the long and disastrous campaign of 1873, it was still a formidable force. Its discipline was unique among African armies and, in fact, very few preindustrial armies anywhere were able to inculcate such discipline. Officers gave orders and they were obeyed. Troops marched with precision and maneuvered precisely, their muskets held at exactly the same slope, and they fired volleys on their officers' orders. By comparison the vaunted Zulu armies were ill disciplined. They fought with great courage but so regularly violated orders that they often defeated themselves.

The Asante accomplishment in forging a strictly disciplined army is the more remarkable because most of its common soldiers were slaves, many of whom had only recently been captured. We have no first-person accounts to tell us how these men, who were ordinarily gold miners or laborers, were so successfully made into part-time soldiers. We know that officers carried whips and used them and that deadly force was sometimes used as well. We know that newly captured slaves who did not yet have a stake in Asante life were not allowed to use firearms. They were required to carry supplies under close guard.[1] We know, too, that class distinctions set officers well above commoners and slaves. Recall the words of the captured prince (see chapter 7) who complained bitterly that he had been held with a "mere" captain, and the latter with a lowly warrior. But we also know that slaves could be unruly and sometimes rebellious, so much so that the government continually worried about outbreaks of violence. Yet when these men were on campaign, they were somehow made to obey their officers, and they fought superbly. We can only marvel at the organizational genius that made this possible.

Though discipline was crucial to its success, the greatest military asset of the Asante army was the courage of its men. The Asante troops unfailingly impressed British officers with their courage, or pluck, as they usually called it. Most of these white officers were themselves such conspicuously brave men that it took a great deal to impress them, but Asante valor impressed them in battle after battle. To be sure, the British sometimes scorned the Asante for running when charged with bayonet and sword, but they were simply in awe of the Asante willingness to stand and die against rifle bullets, machine guns, and modern artillery. When they examined the terrible wounds the Asante dead and wounded suffered and realized that these men had stood their ground for hours while men next to them were being shot to pieces or blown apart, they were even more impressed. Lord Moran, who served in both world wars and was in addition Churchill's doctor, observed that courage is finite and expendable.[2] All troops have a breaking point, but the Asante were willing to stand against deadly fire for far longer than the British had thought possible. It is worth recalling that the experienced and undeniably valiant soldiers of the Black Watch and the Rifle Brigade wavered under Asante fire in 1874 and they were not under well-aimed fire, much less a devastating cannonade of high-explosive rockets or shells. And while it is true that the West African soldiers who fought for Willcocks in 1900 were unexpectedly brave and resolute, they were also not under machine gun or artillery fire, nor were they asked to stand with empty rifles against a bayonet charge.

Why did the Asante fight so bravely for so long? As nearly as we can tell from this distance in time and culture, they did so for many of the same reasons that British officers did—personal honor, unit pride, social recognition, the hope of reward, and the fear of being branded a coward. Peer pressure was also an important factor (Thomas Fuller aptly wrote in 1732, "Many would be cowards if they had enough courage.") Asante military units were drawn from the same locality. Men knew one another, and even slaves were members of families; their future well-being, like that of freemen, depended in no small measure on their conduct in battle. Every Asante boy was raised in a warrior culture that called for great deeds in battle like those of his ancestors, his kinsmen, and his peers.[3] Every young Asante man, especially those of prominent families, also knew that success in warfare was the royal road to honor, wealth, and power. Victorious officers received formal honors, great wealth, and the king's personal recognition. Ordinary soldiers were honored and rewarded, too. An Asante general who won a particularly significant victory could become immensely rich, as Adu Bofo did just before Amankwatia's abortive invasion of the coast in 1873. Adu Bofo received more wealth in land, gold, slaves, and villages than Wolseley did for his victory the following year, and Wolseley was more than handsomely rewarded.

But bravery was not inspired solely by the expectation of wealth and glory; there were terrible punishments for a defeat, especially when it was thought to have been caused by cowardice. Every senior commander took a public oath in the presence of the king swearing that he and his men would die before they would retreat in the face of the enemy. Many junior commanders repeated the same oath before their general. These oaths were treated with deadly seriousness. Many Asante commanders were known to have killed themselves when the fortunes of war turned against them, and those few commanders who were accused of cowardice yet did not kill themselves were, depending on their rank and social connections, either executed or publicly humiliated and stripped of wealth and social standing. Soldiers from all parts of the Asante Empire were bound by the same covenant, and they joined with their officers in the daunting task of assuring that the many slaves in the army would fight as bravely as the native Asante did. The details of how they accomplished this are not known beyond the documented facts that Asante prevented them from retreating by the use of sword and whip and that slaves sometimes benefited from the spoils of war as well as the honors that came to brave and victorious men.

To see Asante bravery in perspective, it is important to keep in mind that they were only part-time soldiers. Each Asante man over the age of eighteen was required to own his own musket and other weapons, but years could go by before a man might be called to serve in a military campaign. British soldiers were full-time warriors, who spent every day of their military service, which could last for many years, learning to follow orders without question and to believe that their regiment was the most magnificent fighting machine on earth. Led by officers and noncommissioned officers for whom bravery in battle was everything, it is little wonder that British soldiers fought so courageously. Like the Asante, the Zulus were only part-time soldiers, but they too belonged to regiments, each with its own name, great traditions, distinctive shields and uniforms, and a determination to outdo all other regiments in battle. The Asante had no equivalent experience. Unlike the Zulus, Asante soldiers did not come together on a regular basis to dance or practice military tactics. They did not even wear uniforms or carry shields that distinguished one unit from another. The Asante were farmers, traders, and craftsmen who, like European militiamen, only occasionally went to war, but when they did, they displayed great discipline and fought with uncommon valor.

What may be most important of all is the role that women played in encouraging bravery. Any able-bodied Asante, free or slave, who failed to answer his chief's call to war was subjected to the most vicious verbal and physical assaults by the women of the village. The life of such a man would scarcely be worth living, and if he had a wife or wives, these women would freely join in the public humiliation heaped upon him. On the other hand, men who staunchly went off to war had their virtue extolled by their women, many of whom marched at least part of the way into battle with them, singing praise songs, carrying their gear, and cooking their food. A common soldier might not gain by going to war, indeed he might be maimed or killed, but Asante women saw to it that he could not gain by avoiding his duty. Why women took so active a role in promoting bravery in military service is not well documented, but far more so than in most African societies, women and men among the Asante had relative equality and a similar stake in all affairs of the state. As a result of their adherence to a cultural system of reckoning both descent and inheritance through the female line, women played a central role in Asante affairs, including, through the office of the queen mother, the decision to go to war. It is obvious that a woman could stand to gain if her husband, son, brother, or close kinsman achieved wealth, honor, or power, but well beyond this profit motive Asante women were taught to believe in the greatness in the Asante union and the need for war to maintain and enlarge it. Doubtless, much suffering came to these women when their men died in battle or their homes and fields were destroyed by invading armies, but the willingness of Asante women to support warfare was as consistent over the century as it was essential to the success of Asante armies.

Defeated Asante armies, such as those at Dodowa in 1826 and Abrakrampa in 1873, were capable of conducting such skillful fighting retreats that they earned the admiration of British officers; yet Asante soldiers, particularly in 1900 and to a lesser extent in 1874, sometimes broke ranks and ran, although usually only after they were charged by sword-waving British officers leading soldiers with fixed bayonets. It must be understood, however, that few troops anywhere were known to stand resolutely against bayonets during the nineteenth century. European armies often charged their enemies with bayonets, but with the major exception of the Russians and Japanese, who often fought to the death with bayonets in Manchuria during their 1904/05 war, it was uncommon indeed for these weapons actually to be used—the defenders usually fled long before the attackers' bayonets could be brought into play. In fact, a British surgeon who served in the Peninsular War between the British and the French, both great proponents of bayonet charges, concluded that no regiment on either side ever stood against bayonets in that long and bloody war.[4] The Asante were in very good company when they fled from a long line of bayonet-wielding enemies. It should also be recalled that sometimes they did stand and fight against bayonets even though their weapons put them at a deadly disadvantage.

It is also true that once Asante soldiers began to turn tail and run, they seldom re-formed to fight a rearguard action. Precipitous retreat was known to all armies, although it was extremely rare for British troops, who usually fought from a square formation, to run. But compared to the Zulus, for example, no doubt the most celebrated warriors in Africa, the Asante ran under some semblance of control. When the Zulus ran away, there was no stopping them, as they freely and good-naturedly admitted. Asante soldiers could be brought under control by their officers and turned about to fight again. And sometimes, as we have seen, they fought hand to hand before they were willing to retreat.

In view of the Asante fear of bayonets, it is puzzling that they made no apparent attempts to provide themselves with weapons to defend against them. As mentioned earlier, their Dane guns took so long to reload that unless the troops were lined up in at least three lines to fire in sequence, they were defenseless against bayonets. And during the nineteenth century wars against the British, the only times they were thus deployed, the battles were fought in the jungle, and there was no bayonet charge. Their six-foot-long muskets were too long and heavy to be used effectively as clubs; apparently, such a use was rarely even attempted, though the British sometimes used their lighter rifles and carbines in this way. Nevertheless, the Asante did not attempt to make or purchase bayonets of their own. It would not have been difficult for Asante blacksmiths to manufacture bayonets, and a bayonet on the end of a six-foot-long Asante musket would have been more than a match for one on the end of a four-foot-long British rifle. Perhaps the problem was that a bayonet would have to be permanently fixed to the barrel, making the musket more difficult to load and use in the thick brush.

Whatever the reason for their failure to use bayonets, it is also odd that the Asante did not use swords to defend against them. An Asante sword was an inferior weapon against a bayonet—or a steel saber for that matter—but it was better than no weapon at all. When in 1900, the Asante fought the British hand to hand, they used neither swords nor (except rarely) even the knives they carried to behead their victims.[5] At the beginning of the century, the Asante threw spears with great accuracy, but they soon after abandoned them, leaving the musket as their only weapon.

Much was made by the British of Asante reluctance to fight at night. It is true that many African armies would not fight at night because of fear of the evil spirits thought to attack men in the darkness; the Asante to some extent shared this dread. Other armies, such as the Zulu, chose not to fight at night because military honors could only be won if a man's heroism were witnessed by others; the Asante shared this view as well. But the reality is that the Asante army did sometimes—though seldom—fight at night. When the army approached Dodowa in 1826, its commander urged a night attack led by torch-carrying scouts. King Osei Yaw chose, in general, to attack in daylight so that the pageantry and invincibility of his army could be seen by his enemies. Earlier at Cape Coast, however, Osei Yaw had planned to attack the fort at night, shielded by the diversionary tactic of burning the houses of the surrounding town. Asante troops fought several battles at night during civil wars that followed the Wolseley invasion, and after Captain Hall had been driven back from Kokofu to Esumeja in 1900, the Asante continued their futile but furious attack throughout the night. Other night fighting was aborted because torrents of rain during these battles fell more heavily at night than during the day, making it impossible for the Asante to prime their flintlocks.

Night fighting has become an issue because the reluctance of the

Asante to attack at night deprived them of a possible tactical advantage. The Asante often drummed and sang for much of the night, keeping the British awake; but if they had used the night to attack British camps—particularly when Wolseley was marching on Kumase—they could have slowed their advance significantly. As it was, Wolseley only beat the rains by a day or two. Without the threat of night attack, the British did nothing to fortify their camps and seldom took the precaution of posting sentries. What is more, night attacks against the unprotected carriers could have created panic and conceivably disrupted Wolseley's campaign altogether.

Another reason why Asante bravery and discipline did not produce more victories was the relative inflexibility of their tactics. For at least one hundred years before the Asante army ever collided with the British, they had enjoyed success against their enemies by using their classic enveloping formation, which sent large numbers of men around each flank of the enemy to, if all went well, surround and destroy them. Used against African opponents, most of whom conceded defeat if threatened by envelopment, their traditional tactics were usually successful. When an African opponent's flanks were threatened, they withdrew, and when their rear was attacked, they broke and scattered.[6] The Asante themselves always marched into battle supported by a large rear guard that faced to the rear to beat off any attack that might come from that direction. This tactic succeeded against MacCarthy but failed against Wolseley, who simply charged straight ahead in his large square formation, confident that his strong rear guard could hold off the expected Asante attack.

Had Asamoa Nkwanta, the Asante commander in 1874, agreed to mass his troops in front of the British, as had been proposed, instead of dispersing most of them around the flanks of Wolseley's formation, he would have had a far better chance of stopping the British advance, which as it was, broke through only after hours of heavy fighting against a thin screen of Asante soldiers. The British tactic of advancing despite threats to their flanks and rear surprised the Asante. Asante tactics rarely surprised the British, but occasionally there were signs of innovation. Osei Bonsu's troops were preparing to blow up the fort at Cape Coast when a peace treaty was agreed upon, and later, scaling leaders were used in a failed attempt to take the fort at Elmina. The proposed night attack at the battle south of Dodowa would probably have succeeded had it been attempted, and some of the Asante ambush strategies were novel.

The most original innovation was the widespread use of stockades in 1900. The idea of stockades was not original to the Asante, but their use of these defensive structures was an effective response to the British use of machine guns and powerful artillery. In fact, the construction of so many large stockades surrounded by flanking fortifications and supported by well-built war camps was a considerable achievement for people who had to use rude axes to cut down huge trees before shaping them into logs. Slaves were used for most of the heavy labor, but the design of the stockades, as well as the transport and supply system developed to support the troops sheltered behind them, was ingenious and quite effective until British flanking tactics and even heavier artillery eventually turned stockades into death traps. In a final tactical innovation the Asante commander Kofi Kofia had his men fight on the defensive by lying down in the open in an inverted crescent to protect their flanks. The Asante commanders were not as flexible as the British were in devising better ways to defeat their opponents, but they were far more creative about warfare than the Zulus, who in 1879 fought seven major battles against the British and used the same enveloping tactics in all seven.

A major tactical failure on the part of the Asante was their inability to disrupt British supply lines. In all the British campaigns against the Asante, survival as a fighting force depended on the regular provision of supplies from the coast. Thousands of men, women, and children carried food, ammunition, and medical supplies on their heads along narrow roads that were often little better than paths, and they were rarely guarded by more than a handful of armed men. Small groups of Asante soldiers could easily have moved unseen through the dense forest to positions from which they could have fired devastating volleys at short range into these easy targets. They did attack these supply columns on a few occasions and always with some success, but if they had done so more often and with greater force, carriers would have refused to work without large escorts of troops, and the British never had enough soldiers available to them to guard their long supply lines and still conduct offensive operations. Such a tactic could have slowed British operations to a standstill, and the need for larger numbers of troops to defend miles of jungle paths might have made operations against the Asante more costly than the British government would have thought tolerable. The British were well aware that their campaigns were terribly vulnerable to disruption by such attacks, and they were as surprised as they were grateful that the Asante largely left their supply lines alone. Guerrilla warfare also could have tipped the scales toward the Asante, but Asante armies had always fought in large formations and continued to do so throughout the century, despite the fact that their enemies had sometimes been quite effective in using guerrilla warfare tactics against them.[7]

That the British officers who led African troops against the Asante in 1900 showed considerable tactical initiative, just as Wolseley had done in 1874, should not be taken to mean that the British army always showed greater flexibility than the Asante did. In South Africa in 1900, British battalions again and again marched shoulder to shoulder against Boer machine gun and artillery fire only to be slaughtered by an enemy they never even saw. Almost one hundred years earlier, at the Battle of New Orleans, British battalions that marched slowly toward the American breastworks were shot down so easily and in such numbers that the American riflemen actually wept as they pulled their triggers.[8] The appalling losses of World War I were due in no small measure to British tactical rigidity.

It is quite obvious that as the nineteenth century progressed, the Asante inferiority in weaponry put them at a decisive disadvantage, but of equal if not greater significance in the outcome of most battles against the British was the astonishing inability of the Asante to shoot straight. In most battles the Asante soldiers were armed only with Dane guns, whose limited range gave the British a tremendous advantage, but even so, in battles like the crucial ones in Wolseley's march to Kumase, Asante fire was so heavy that it stripped the bark from the trees above head height, and leaves from overhead showered down on British troops who were for the most part unscathed. In 1900 almost all Asante fire, except for that at short range, went over the heads of the British troops, and in this war the Asante had enough captured British rifles that even reasonably accurate fire would have inflicted heavy losses. Sometimes, as in the war's last great battle, the sheer volume of Asante rifle fire was so heavy that the British troops refused to advance even though almost all of the bullets were passing well over their heads. The Asante were hardly unique in their inability to aim Western firearms accurately. Loaded as heavily as they were and fired from the hip, Dane guns were wildly inaccurate, and men unfamiliar with sights on modern rifles or with their tendency to fire high due to recoil were likely to fire over their enemy's heads unless carefully drilled to fire low, as British troops were. This pattern of firing high allowed European armies to defeat many African armies, including the Zulus, whose rifle fire in 1879 was, if anything, even more inaccurate than that of the Asante.

The wars between the Asante and the British were not chivalrous, but neither were they as brutal as might have been expected. British officers were often kind to Asante civilians and military prisoners, and their troops were under orders not to loot, rape, or brutalize in Asante villages. With a few exceptions they behaved well. However, Kumase was burned, the palace was destroyed, royal tombs were desecrated, and in 1900—by which time civilization might have been expected to set higher standards of military conduct—a campaign of terror against civilians was carried out that included the enslavement of Asante women and children. Even so, British officers often attempted, sometimes successfully, to save Asante wounded or prisoners from torture and death at the hands of their merciless African allies, who also regularly slashed and mutilated Asante corpses so savagely that British officers were sickened.

For their part the Asante beheaded wounded supply carriers and Hausas but did not generally mutilate dead bodies or torture prisoners, although there is no reason to believe that they would never have done so had there more often been victories in battle. When they did win, as against Sir Charles MacCarthy in 1824, they exercised remarkable restraint. They took two officers and two British soldiers captive. One officer was killed because he could not keep up with his captors, but the other was treated reasonably well and later released in good health. The two soldiers were both well treated, as were the European prisoners held in Kumase by King Kofi Kakari.

The Asante fought with undeniable valor, discipline, and skill, and on the whole they followed their rules of war without excessive cruelty. Colonel Willcocks wrote that he felt he had been in a fair fight against them. He added that they were such fine soldiers the British army in West Africa should attempt to recruit them. Until 1917 the loyalty of the Asante was so much in doubt that they were not permitted to join the British-led Gold Coast Regiment, which was, not coincidentally, headquartered in Kumase and seen by most Asante as the enemy. The pressing need for more manpower eventually led the British to attempt to recruit Asante, but few volunteered and most of those soon deserted.[9] Even greater efforts to recruit Asante into the British army were made in World War II, but the Asante did not flock to the colors of Britain this time either. They remained loyal, but they were not interested in soldiering. Though the Asante were much the largest ethnic group in the region, they provided fewer than 10 percent of the entire Gold Coast military establishment during the war, and by the time of independence, only 5 percent of Ghana's army was Asante.[10] Asante militarism did not revive during the struggle for independence that led to the birth of Ghana in 1967 or during the turbulent years that followed. Although the Asante formed their own national liberation movement in 1954 to demand self-rule in what would soon become the independent state of Ghana, their leaders and their king prevented armed Asante from using military means to alter the electoral process.[11]

If it is true, as it appears to be, that the Asante would have taken up arms to defend the Golden Stool in 1921, it seems equally true that once the stool's safety and sanctity were ensured, they saw no further need for war. In earlier times they had figuratively fought "for the ashes of their fathers and the temples of their gods," as Victorian poet Thomas Macaulay once wrote of British warriors. With impressive finality the Asante put aside their great warrior tradition to become prosperous farmers, traders, businessmen, artists, engineers, lawyers, educators, and doctors—not soldiers. Abruptly, without declarations or fanfare, they were through with war.

Notes

Chapter 1. A Cause Worth Dying For

1. Davidson (1966:42–43).
2. Fynn (1971a).
3. Rattray (1929).
4. Bowdich (1819; rev. ed. 1966:122).
5. Posnansky (1987).
6. T. 70/31. Governor John Hippisley, Cape Coast castle, 13 July 1766.
7. Wilks (1975:20).
8. Reindorf (1966:130–31); Wilks (1975).
9. Bender (1978:137).
10. Muffett (1978:280).
11. Peires (1989).
12. Muriuki (1975:155).
13. Ibid.
14. Iliffe (1979:93).
15. Bridgeman (1981).
16. Edgerton (1989).
17. Stratton (1964).
18. Hubert (1938).
19. Wilks (1975); Hagen (1971).

Chapter 2. The Empire of Gold

1. Ramseyer and Kühne (1975); Morris (1970).
2. Fynn (1971b:135).
3. Yarak (1990).
4. Davidson (1966:19).
5. Anquandah (1982).
6. Davidson (1966).
7. Wilks (1975:692–693). Estimates like these are necessarily imprecise because the exact weight and purity of the gold was not known.
8. Gros (1884:197).
9. Bowdich (1866; original 1819). For a discussion of his accuracy, see Busia (1951).
10. James indiscreetly revealed to Dr. Tedlie that he was jealous of Governor Smith and intended to divert Asante trade to his own fort of Accra. James was also unable to cope with Asante negotiators. When James was confronted by King Osei Bonsu about British interests, he was so taken off guard and unable to explain the purpose of his mission that young Bowdich had to step in to save the day. Thereafter, Bowdich was the de facto head of the mission, and James returned to Accra in disgrace.
11. Bowdich (1966:23–24).
12. Ibid., 31.
13. Ibid., 34.
14. Hutton (1821).
15. Ibid., 216.
16. Schildkrout (1987:86).
17. Bowdich (1966:115).
18. Freeman (1843).
19. Huydecoper (1962:26).
20. Bowdich (1966:76).
21. Hutton (1821:208).
22. Ellis (1893:292).
23. Freeman (1843:147).
24. Huydecoper (1962:25).
25. Tufuo and Donkor (1969:47–48).
26. Rattray (1929).
27. Freeman (1843:132).

28. Wilks (1975).
29. Freeman (1898:135).
30. Freeman (1843:132).
31. Bowdich (1966).
32. Bowdich (1966:32).
33. Lewin (1978).
34. Schildkrout (1987:107).
35. Wilks (1975:130).
36. Tufuo and Donkor (1969:70).
37. Bowdich (1966:278).
38. Hutton (1821).
39. Aidoo (1975:142).
40. Huydecoper (1962:24).
41. Freeman (1843:128).
42. Ramseyer and Kühne (1875:164).
43. Bowdich (1966:421).
44. Claridge (1915).
45. Bowdich (1966:123–124).
46. Robertson (1819).
47. Dupuis (1966:140).
48. Lewin (1978).
49. Bowdich (1966:421).
50. Rattray (1929:91).
51. Aidoo (1975:106).
52. Rattray (1916:118).
53. Tufuo and Donkor (1969:26).
54. Bowdich (1966:295).
55. Wilks (1975:695).
56. Ibid.
57. Bowdich (1966).
58. McLeod (1981); Wilks (1975).
59. Tufuo and Donkor (1969:77–84).
60. Adjaye (1984).
61. Ibid., 68.
62. McLeod (1981); Lewin (1974:I, 186).
63. Bowdich (1966:320).
64. Arhin (1987:56).
65. Fynn (1971a:7); Arhin (1987).

66. Wilks (1975).
67. McLeod (1981:72).
68. Dummett (1987).
69. Anquandah (1982).
70. Fynn (1971a:78); Dummett (1987:223); Herskovits (1962:173–174).
71. Yarak (1990).
72. McLeod (1981:15).
73. Fortes (1950).
74. Bowdich (1966:302).
75. Busia (1951:7).
76. Busia (1951:27).
77. McLeod (1981).
78. Ramseyer and Kühne (1875:167).
79. Rattray (1929:360).

Chapter 3. *"A Bravery Not to Be Exceeded"*

1. T. 70/26. Committee of Merchants, London, to John Hippisley, Cape Coast castle, 3 September 1766.
2. Claridge (1915:I, 245).
3. Ibid., 248.
4. T. 70/35; H.D. 431 Accounts and Papers [1817] vi, 401.
5. Cruikshank (1853:I, 79–80).
6. Dupuis (1966:263).
7. Claridge (1915:I, 254).
8. C.O. 267/144.
9. Claridge (1915).
10. Bowdich (1966:317); Wilks (1975:676).
11. Hagen (1971).
12. Aidoo (1975:I, 73).
13. Rattray (1929:123); for an outline of Asante army organization, see Miles (1968) and Arhin (1980).
14. Fuller (1921:14).
15. Rattray (1929:122).
16. Kea (1971:213).
17. Bowdich (1966:36).
18. Ibid., 37.

19. Ibid., 298.
20. Rattray (1929:103).
21. Bowdich (1966:300–301).
22. Wilks (1975:226).
23. Rattray (1929:126).
24. Bowdich (1966:300).
25. Wilks (1975:222).
26. Huydecoper (1962:47).
27. Hutchinson (1966:419).
28. Dupuis (1966:213).
29. Wilks (1975).
30. Arhin (1983).
31. Ramseyer and Kühne (1875:52); Jones (1993).
32. Reade (1874:50).
33. Ramseyer and Kühne (1875).
34. Rattray (1929:124).
35. Ibid., 157.
36. Wilks (1975:38).
37. Ramseyer and Kühne (1875:33).
38. Ricketts (1831:85).
39. Tufuo and Donkor (1969:94).
40. Ibid.
41. Huydecoper (1962).
42. Ibid., 4.
43. Ibid., 8.
44. Bowdich (1966:289).
45. Ramseyer and Kühne (1875:136).
46. Ffoulkes (1945).
47. Kea (1971:200).
48. Yarak (1990:220).
49. Kwamena-Poh (1973:28–29).
50. Lewis and Foy (1971).
51. Ffoulkes (1945:78).

Chapter 4. "The Bush Is Stronger Than the Cannon"

1. Bowdich (1966:124).
2. Ibid., 146–147.

3. Claridge (1915:I, 302).

4. Dupuis (1966:xxxvii).

5. Claridge (1915:I, 305).

6. Dupuis (1966:xxxv).

7. Wilks (1975:485).

8. Claridge (1915:I, 338).

9. Ricketts (1831:54).

10. Ibid., 105.

11. Ibid., 84.

12. Ibid., 150–152.

13. Wilks (1975).

14. Claridge (1915:I, 362).

15. Ibid., 362.

16. Wilks (1975:486).

17. Ibid., 373.

18. Cruikshank (1853:I).

19. Ibid., 160.

20. Ellis (1893:178).

21. Ricketts (1831:120).

22. Wilks (1975:439).

23. Ricketts (1831:121).

24. Claridge (1915:I, 389).

25. Ricketts (1831:123).

26. C.O. 267/74: Campbell to Bannerman, 12 November 1826.

27. Owusu-Ansah (1987).

28. Wilks (1975:185).

29. Ricketts (1831:146).

30. Ibid.

31. Metcalfe (1962:vi).

32. Cruikshank (1853:I, 196).

33. Cruikshank (1853:I).

34. Buckley (1979).

35. Yarak (1990:132).

36. Van Dantzig (1965).

37. McLeod (1987:187).

38. Freeman (1843:139).

39. Curtin (1969:336–337).

40. Wilks (1975:222).

41. Ibid.
42. Claridge (1915:I, 529).
43. Ibid.
44. Ward (1958); Aidoo (1975:I, 194).
45. Wilks (1975:494–496).
46. Ramseyer and Kühne (1875:309).
47. Aidoo (1975:I, 287).
48. Ibid., 218.
49. Ward (1958); Wilks (1975).
50. Saffell (1965:96).
51. Maier (1987).
52. Steiner (1901:22).
53. Ramseyer and Kühne (1875:86).
54. Ibid.
55. Ramseyer and Kühne (1875:136–138).
56. Fuller (1921).
57. Saffell (1965).
58. Ramseyer and Kühne (1875:187).
59. Ibid.
60. C.O. 96/98, J. Craig Loggie to Harley, 22 April 1873.
61. Boyle (1874).
62. Ramseyer and Kühne (1875:239).
63. Brackenbury (1874).

Chapter 5. *"Does It Not Make One's Heart Ache?"*

1. Butler (1876:52).
2. Maxwell (1985:18).
3. Stanley (1874).
4. As early as 1889 American scientists had shown that insects could transmit diseases, and in 1894 British pioneer in tropical medicine, Sir Patrick Manson concluded that the mosquito was the vector for malaria, but it was not until 1889 that two Italian scientists actually demonstrated in the laboratory that malaria was transmitted by anopheles mosquitos.
5. Maxwell (1985).
6. Maurice (1874:274).
7. Wolseley (1903).

8. Brackenbury (1874:I, 340); Cabinet minute, 21 November 1873, 44641/223.
9. Maurice (1874:155).
10. Brackenbury (1874:I, 117).
11. Henty (1874).
12. Brackenbury (1874:I, 141).
13. Claridge (1915:II, 40).
14. Arthur (1922:10).
15. Wolseley (1903:288).
16. Brackenbury (1874:I, 275).
17. Ibid., 258.
18. Henty (1874:111).
19. Reade (1874:178).
20. Wolseley (1903:279).
21. Wood (1874:258).
22. Brackenbury (1874:II, 202).
23. Ibid., 204.
24. Ibid., 212.
25. Boyle (1874:119–120).
26. Reade (1874:229–230).
27. Brackenbury (1874:I, 271).
28. Maurice (1874:140).
29. Lehmann (1964:177).
30. Reade (1974).
31. Ibid., 268.
32. Maxwell (1985:42).
33. Brackenbury (1874:I, 366).
34. Ibid., 323.
35. Ibid., 327.
36. Reade (1874:275).
37. Boyle (1874:252).
38. Lehmann (1964:186).
39. Henty (1874:297).
40. Maurice (1874:232).
41. Stanley (1874:138).
42. Wolseley (1903).
43. Stanley (1874:138).
44. Boyle (1874:266).

45. Henty (1874:303); Stanley (1874:133).
46. Ramseyer and Kühne (1875:175).
47. Ibid.
48. Ramseyer and Kühne (1875:200–211).
49. Boahen (1965:3).
50. Maurice (1874:268) citing Kühne; Reade (1874:285) also attributed this information to the newly released prisoner Kühne.
51. Ramseyer and Kühne (1875:247).
52. Maier (1987).
53. Ramseyer and Kühne (1875:250).
54. Ibid., 256.
55. Ibid., 252.
56. Ibid., 260.
57. Ibid., 114.
58. Ibid., 270.
59. Claridge (1915:III) citing the French prisoner, Bonnat.
60. Ramseyer and Kühne (1875:250, 271).
61. Dooner (1874:45).
62. Boyle (1874).
63. Ellis (1893:128).
64. Ramseyer and Kühne (1875:124).
65. Fuller (1921).
66. Ramseyer and Kühne (1875:278).
67. Ibid., 279.
68. Ibid.
69. Ibid., 281.
70. Ibid.
71. Ibid., 284.

Chapter 6. "The Most Horrible War"

1. Wolseley (1903).
2. Brackenbury (1874:II, 153).
3. Ibid., 152.
4. Wolseley (1903:335).
5. Aidoo (1975:I, 281).
6. Ibid., 234.
7. Reade (1874:122).

8. Wolseley (1903:337).
9. Brackenbury (1874:II, 143).
10. Wood (1874:263).
11. Maxwell (1985:64).
12. Stanley (1874:165).
13. Brackenbury (1874:II, 165).
14. Reade (1874:338).
15. Brackenbury (1874:II, 164).
16. Claridge (1915:II, 121).
17. Brackenbury (1874:II, 165).
18. Wood (1874:277).
19. Wolseley (1903).
20. Ibid., 343.
21. Ibid., 344.
22. Henty (1874:237).
23. Reade (1874:339).
24. Wolseley (1903:350).
25. Aidoo (1975:I, 274).
26. Brackenbury (1874:II, 182).
27. Aidoo (1975:I, 286–88).
28. Wood (1874:283).
29. Ibid., 284.
30. Brackenbury (1874:II, 205).
31. Wood (1874:279).
32. Brackenbury (1874:II, 213).
33. Ibid., 219.
34. Lehmann (1964:195).
35. Stanley (1874:203).
36. Brackenbury (1874:II, 217).
37. Ibid., 224.
38. Stanley (1874:227).
39. Dooner (1874:60).
40. Brackenbury (1874:II, 231).
41. Ibid., 232.
42. Maurice (1874:355).
43. Brackenbury (1874:II, 236).
44. Boyle (1874:350).
45. Ibid., 363–364.

46. Reade (1874:370).
47. Butler (1876:298).
48. Ibid., 254.
49. Lehmann (1964:184).
50. Maurice (1874:378).
51. Kimble (1963:271).
52. Lehmann (1964:205).
53. Ibid.
54. Wolseley (1903:370).

Chapter 7. "Britannia Waives the Rules"

1. Aidoo (1975:I, 289).
2. Ibid.; Fuller (1921:145–146).
3. Stanley (1874:18).
4. *African Times* 10, no. 148, 30 October 1873.
5. Ramseyer and Kühne (1875:52–53).
6. Aidoo (1975:I, 316).
7. Ibid., 42.
8. Ibid., 343.
9. Ibid.
10. C.O. 96/139: minute, E. A. (Ashley) 6 June 1882; minute by K. (Kimberly), 28 July 1882.
11. Freeman (1898:368–369).
12. Aidoo (1975:II, 383).
13. Ibid., 424.
14. C.O. 879/19, 128: Lonsdale's report of his mission of 1882.
15. Wilks (1975:554).
16. Aidoo (1975:II, 492).
17. Ibid., 494.
18. Ibid., 562.
19. McCaskie (1984).
20. Lewin (1978:114).
21. Aidoo (1975:II, 612).
22. Ibid., 595.
23. Ibid.
24. C.O. 96/224: Griffith to King Kwabena Asante of Atebubu, 29 June 1892; end. 4 in secret, Griffith to Knutsford, 4 July 1892.

25. Wilks (1975:654–655).
26. Ibid., 642.
27. Aidoo (1975:II, 618).
28. McInnes and Fraser (1987:48).
29. It is an oddity that all of the machine guns used by the British army until 1915, including the Lewis gun of World War I fame, were invented by Americans (Ffoulkes 1945:91).
30. Burleigh (1896:394).
31. Ibid., 395.
32. Ibid., 445.
33. Ibid., 432.
34. Ibid., 490.
35. Ibid., 493.
36. Ibid., 500.
37. Ibid., 505.
38. Ibid., 542.
39. Ibid., 543.
40. Ibid., 544.
41. Baden-Powell (1896:117).
42. McInnes and Fraser (1987:60).
43. Ibid., 65.
44. Claridge (1915:II, 413).
45. Burleigh (1896:522).
46. Ibid.
47. Musgrave (1896:166).
48. Freeman (1898:123).
49. Burleigh (1896:540–541).
49. McInnes and Fraser (1987:66).
50. Ibid., 73.
51. Burleigh (1896:551).
52. *Gold Coast Chronicle*, 30 June 1896, 3.
53. Wilks (1975:661).
54. Tordoff (1965:69).
55. Aidoo (1975:II, 642 ff).
56. *Gold Coast Chronicle*, May 1897, 3–4.
57. Aidoo (1975:II, 662).
58. Wilks (1975).
59. Aidoo (1975:II, 663).

60. Freeman (1898).

61. *Parliamentary Debates*, House of Commons, Committee of Supply, 18 March 1901.

62. The assertion that the Golden Stool was never sat on comes from a single informant of Rattray. Other informants have said that kings did sit on it during special ceremonies but never routinely. Kimble (1963:321).

63. Aidoo (1975:II).

64. Ibid., 661.

65. Lewin (1978:189).

66. Aidoo (1975:II, 668).

67. Ibid., 669.

Chapter 8. "We Are Going to Die Today"

1. Willcocks (1904:278).

2. Ibid., 243.

3. Steiner (1901).

4. Armitage (1901:33).

5. Biss (1901:196).

6. Claridge (1915:II, 515–517).

7. Biss (1901:137).

8. Myatt (1966:91).

9. Claridge (1915:II, 494).

10. Myatt (1966:85).

11. Myatt (1966:86).

12. Steiner (1901:177).

13. Armitage and Montanaro (1901:102).

14. Hodgson (1901:203).

15. Aidoo (1975:II).

16. Claridge (1915:II, 507).

17. Willcocks (1904:278).

18. Ibid., 295–296.

19. Myatt (1966:99).

20. Hall (1939).

21. Willcocks (1904:318).

22. Ibid.

23. Ibid., 333.

24. Ibid., 336.
25. Ibid., 339.
26. Ibid., 341.
27. Biss (1901:189–90).
28. Willcocks (1904:342).
29. Fuller (1921:208).
30. Myatt (1966:127).

Chapter 9. "An Inaudible Murmur of Admiration"

1. Armitage and Montanaro (1901:156).
2. Willcocks (1904:372).
3. Biss (1901:223).
4. Ibid.
5. Ibid., 225; Hall (1939:297).
6. Hall (1939:307).
7. Biss (1901:254).
8. Ibid., 255.
9. Ibid., 259.
10. Willcocks (1904:369).
11. Rattray (1929).
12. Biss (1901:267).
13. Armitage and Montanaro (1901:178).
14. Myatt (1966:157).
15. Willcocks (1904:395).
16. Biss (1901:299–300).
17. Willcocks (1904:402).
18. Ibid., 404.
19. Claridge (1915:II, 563).
20. Armitage and Montanaro (1901:206).
21. Ibid., 210.
22. Biss (1901:289).
23. Willcocks (1904:416).
24. Claridge (1915:II, 565).
25. Ibid., 566.
26. Biss (1901:314).
27. Ward (1958:343).
28. Boahen (1987:155).

29. Tordoff (1965:185).
30. Ibid., 237.
31. Ibid., 344.

Chapter 10. "For the Ashes of Their Fathers and the Temples of Their Gods"

1. Rattray (1929:124).
2. Moran (1950).
3. Busia (1951).
4. Barnett (1970:245).
5. Lewin (1978).
6. Ward (1958:267).
7. Maier (1987).
8. Brooks (1961).
9. Thomas (1975).
10. Lefever (1970:41).
11. Allman (1993).

Bibliography

Adjaye, J. 1984. *Diplomacy and Diplomats in Nineteenth Century Asante*. Landham, Md.: University Press of America.

Agbodeka, F. 1971. *African Politics and British Policy in the Gold Coast 1868–1900*. London: Northwestern University Press.

Aidoo, A. A. 1975. *Political Crisis and Social Change in the Asante Kingdom, 1867–1901*. 2 vols. Ann Arbor: University Microfilms.

———. 1977. Order and Conflict in the Asante Empire: A Study in Interest Group Relations. *African Studies Review* 20:1–36.

Allman, J. M. 1993. *The Quills of the Porcupine: Asante Nationalism in an Emergent Ghana*. Madison: University of Wisconsin Press

Anquandah, J. 1982. *Rediscovering Ghana's Past*. Accra: Sedco.

Arhin, K. 1967. The Structure of Greater Asante (1700–1824). *Journal of African History* 8:65–86.

———. 1980. Asante Military Institutions. *Journal of African Studies* 7:22–31.

———. 1983. The Political and Military Roles of Akan Women. In C. Oppong, ed., *Female and Male in West Africa*. London: George Allen & Unwin; 91–98.

———. 1987. Savanna Contributions to the Asante Political Economy. In E. Schildkrout, ed., *The Golden Stool: Studies of the Asante Center and Periphery*. Washington, D.C.: Anthropological Papers of the American Museum of Natural History: 51–59.

Armitage, C. H., and A. F. Montanaro. 1901. *The Ashanti Campaign of 1900*. London: Sands.

Arthur, G. 1922. *The Letters of Lord and Lady Wolseley*. London: Heinemann,

Baden-Powell, R. S. S. 1896. *The Downfall of Prempeh: A Diary of Life with the Native Levy in Ashanti 1895–96*. 2d ed. London: Methuen.

Barnett, C. 1970. *Britain and Her Army, 1509–1970: A Military, Political and Social Survey*. London: Allen Lane The Penguin Press.

Beecham, J. 1841. *Ashantee and the Gold Coast*. London: John Mason.

Bender, G. J. 1978. *Angola Under the Portuguese: The Myth and the Reality*. Berkeley: University of California Press.

Biss, H. C. J. 1901. *The Relief of Kumasi*. London: Methuen.

Boahen, A. A. 1965. Asante-Dahomey Contacts. *Ghana Notes and Queries* 7:1–3.

———. 1987. A Nation in Exile: The Asante on the Seychelles Islands, 1900–1924. In E. Schildkrout, ed., *The Golden Stool: Studies of the Asante Center and Periphery*. New York: American Museum of Natural History; 146–160.

Bowdich, T. E. 1866. *Mission from Cape Coast Castle to Ashantee*, London: John Murray.

Bowles, T. G. 1874. The Ashantee War Unnecessary and Unjust. *Fraser's Magazine* IX, 49;124–134.

Boyle, F. 1874. *Through Fanteeland to Coomassie: A Diary of the Ashantee Expedition*. London: Chapman and Hall.

Brackenbury, H. 1874. *The Ashanti War*. 2 vols. Edinburgh and London: Blackwood.

Braimah, J. A. 1970 *The Ashanti and the Gonja at War*. Accra: Ghana Publishing.

Bridgeman, J. M. 1981. *The Revolt of the Hereros*. Berkeley: University of California Press.

Brooks, C. B. 1961. *The Siege of New Orleans*. Seattle: University of Washington Press.

Buckley, R. N. 1979. *Slaves in Red Coats: The British West India Regiments, 1795–1815*. New Haven: Yale University Press.

Burleigh, B. 1896. *Two Campaigns: Madagascar and Ashantee*. London: T. Fisher Unwin.

Busia, K. A. 1951. *The Position of the Chief in the Modern Political System of Ashanti*. London: Oxford University Press.

Butler, W. F. 1876. *Akim-Foo: The History of a Failure*. London: Sampson Low, Marsden, Searle and Rivington.

Claridge, W. W. 1915. *A History of the Gold Coast and Ashanti*. 2 vols. London: John Murray.

Cornford, L. C., and F. N. Walker 1915. *The Great Deeds of the Black Watch*. London: J. M. Dent.

Crowder, M., ed. 1971. *West African Resistance: The Military Response to Colonial Occupation*. London: Hutchinson Library for Africa.

Cruickshank, B. 1853. *Eighteen Years on the Gold Coast of Africa*. 2 vols. London: Frank Cass.

Curtin, P. D. 1969. *The Atlantic Slave Trade, A Census*. Madison: University of Wisconsin Press.

Daaku, K. Y. 1966. "Pre-Ashanti States." *Ghana Notes and Queries*, 9, 10–13.

Davidson, B. 1966. *The African Genius. An Introduction to African Cultural and Social History*. Boston: Little, Brown.

Dooner, W. T. 1874. *Jottings en route to Coomassie*. London: published anonymously.

Dummett, R. E. 1987. Precolonial Gold Mining in Wassa: Innovation, Specialization, Linkages to the Economy and the State. In E. Schildkrout, ed., *The Golden Stool: Studies of the Asante Center and Periphery*. New York: American Museum of Natural History; 209–224.

Dupuis, J. 1966. *Journal of Resistance in Ashantee*. London: Frank Cass. Orig. ed. 1824.

Edgerton, R. B. 1988. *Like Lions They Fought: The Zulu War and the Last Black Empire in Africa*. New York: Free Press.

———. 1989. *Mau Mau: An African Crucible*. New York: Free Press.

Ellis, A. B. 1893. *A History of the Gold Coast of West Africa*. London: Negro Universities Press.

Fage, J. D. 1969. Slavery and the Slave Trade in the Context of West African History. *Journal of African History* 3:393–404.

Ffoulkes, C. J. 1945. *Arms & Armament: An Historical Survey of the Weapons of the British Army . . . with a foreword by Field Marshal Sir Claud W. Jacob*. London: G. G. Harrap.

Fortes, M. 1950. Kinship and Marriage among the Ashanti. In A. R. Radcliffe-Brown and D. Forde, eds., *African Systems of Kinship and Marriage*. London: Oxford University Press; 252–284.

Freeman, R. A. 1898. *Travels and Life in Ashanti and Jaman*. Westminster: Archibald Constable.

Freeman, T. B. 1843. *Journal of Two Visits to the Kingdom of Ashanti*. London: John Mason.

Fuller, F. C. 1921. *A Vanished Dynasty: Ashanti*. London: John Murray.

Fyfe, C. 1972. *Africanus Horton, 1835–1883: West African Scientist and Patriot*. New York: Oxford University Press.

Fynn, J. K. 1966. The Rise of Ashanti. *Ghana Notes and Queries* 9:24–30.

———. (1971a) *Asante and Its Neighbors 1700–1807*. Evanston: Northwestern University Press.

———. (1971b) Ghana-Asante (Ashanti). In M. Crowder, ed., *West African Resistance: The Military Response to Colonial Occupation*. London: Hutchinson: 19–52.

Gordon, C. A. 1874. *Life on the Gold Coast*. London: Baillière, Tindell and Cox.

Gros, J. 1884. *Voyages, aventures et captivité de J. Bonnat chez les Achantis*. Paris: Librarie Plon.

Hagen, G. P. 1971. Ashanti Bureaucracy: A Study of the Growth of Centralized Administration in Ashanti from the Time of Osei Tutu to the Time of Osei Tutu Kwamina Esibe Bonsu. *Transactions of the Historical Society of Ghana* 12:43–62.

Hall, W. M. 1939. *The Great Drama of Kumasi*. London: Putnam.

Henty, G. A. 1874. *The March to Coomassie*. London: Tinsley Brothers.

Herskovits, M. J. 1962. *The Human Factor in Changing Africa*. New York: Knopf.

Hodgson, Lady. 1901. *The Siege of Kumassi*. London: C. Arthur Pearson.

Hubert, C. 1938. *Le Colonel Domine*. Paris: Berger-Leurault.

Hutchinson, W. 1966. *Mr. Hutchinson's Diary*. In T. E. Bowdich, 1966 *Mission from Cape Coast Castle to Ashantee*. London: John Murray: 419.

Hutton, W. 1821. *A Voyage to Africa*. London: Longman, Hurst, Rees, Orme, and Brown.

Huydecoper, W. 1962. *Huydecoper's Diary, Journey from Elmina to Kumasi, 28th April 1816–18th May 1817*. Translated by G. Irvine. Legon. Original journal in General State Archives, The Hague, KvG 349.

Iliffe, J. 1979. *A Modern History of Tanganyika*. Cambridge: Cambridge University Press.

Jones, A. 1993. "My Arse for Okou": A Wartime Ritual of Women on the Nineteenth Century Gold Coast. *Cahiers d'Etudes Africaines* 132:545–566.

Kea, R. A. 1971. Firearms and Warfare on the Gold Coast and Slave Coasts from the Sixteenth to the Nineteenth Centuries. *Journal of African History* 12:185–213.

Kimble, D. 1963. *A Political History of Ghana: The Rise of Gold Coast Nationalism, 1850–1928*. Oxford: Oxford University Press.

Klein, A. N. 1981. The Two Asantes: Competing Interpretations of "Slavery" in Akan-Asante Culture and Society. In P. E. Lovejoy, ed., *The Ideology of Slavery in Africa*. London: Sage.

Kwamena-Poh, M. A. 1973. *Government and Politics in the Akuapem State, 1730–1850*. London: Longman.

Lefever, E. W. 1970. *Spear and Scepter: Army, Police, and Politics in Tropical Africa*. Washington, D. C.: Brookings Institute.

Lehmann, J. H. 1964. *All Sir Garnet: A Life of Field Marshal Lord Wolseley*. London: Jonathan Cape.

Lewin, T. J. 1974. The Structure of Political Conflict in Asante, 1875–1900. Ph.D. dissertation, Northwestern University, Evanston, Il.

———. 1978. *Asante before the British: The Prempeh years, 1875–1900*. Lawrence: University of Kansas Press.

Lewis, R., and Y. Foy. 1971. *The British in Africa*. London: Weidenfeld and Nicolson.

Lloyd, A. 1964. *The Drums of Kumase: The Story of the Ashanti Wars*. London: Longmans.

Maier, D. J. E. 1987. Asante War Aims in the 1869 Invasion of Ewe. In E. Schildkrout, ed., *The Golden Stool: Studies of the Asante Center and Periphery*. New York. American Museum of Natural History; 232–244.

Maurice, J. F. 1874. *The Ashantee War*. London: Henry S. King.

Maxwell, L. 1985. *The Asante Ring: Sir Garnet Wolseley's Campaigns, 1870–1882*. London: Leo Cooper.

Maxwell, W. 1896. The Results of the Ashanti Expedition, 1895–96, *Journal of the Manchester Geographical Society*, XII: 1–3, 37–54.

Mazrui, A., ed. 1977. *The Warrior Tradition in Modern Africa.* Leiden: E. J. Brill.

McCaskie, T. C. 1984. Ahyiamu—'A Place of Meeting': An essay on Process and Event in the History of the Asante State. *Journal of African History* 25:169–188.

McInnes, I., and M. Fraser. 1987. *Ashanti 1895–96.* Chippenham: Picton.

McLeod, M. D. 1981. *The Asante.* London: British Museum.

———. 1987. Gifts and Attitudes. In E. Schildkrout, ed., *The Golden Stool: Studies of the Asante Center and Periphery.* New York: American Museum of Natural History: 184–91.

Metcalfe, G. E. 1962. *Maclean of the Gold Coast.* London: Oxford University Press.

Miles, J. 1968. *Ashanti Military Organization and Techniques: The War of 1873–74.* Long Essay Requirement, M.A., SOAS, London.

Moran, Lord 1950. *The Anatomy of Courage.* 2nd ed. London: Constable.

Morris, R. B., ed. 1970. *Encyclopedia of American History.* New York: Harper and Row.

Muffett, D. J. M. 1978. The Nigeria-Sokoto Caliphate. In M. Crowder, ed., *West African Resistance: The Military Response to Colonial Occupation.* London: Hutchinson Library for Africa: 268–299.

Muriuki, G. 1974. *A History of the Kikuyu.* Nairobi: Oxford University Press.

Musgrave, G. C. 1896. *To Kumassi with Scott: A Description of a Journey from Liverpool to Kumassi with the Ashanti Expedition, 1895–96.* London: Wightman.

Myatt, F. 1966. *The Golden Stool: An Account of the Ashanti War of 1900.* London: Kimber.

Oliver, R. 1991. *The African Experience.* London: Weidenfeld and Nicolson.

Owusu-Ansah, D. 1987. Power or Prestige? Muslims in nineteenth-Century Kumase. In E. Schildkrout, ed., *The Golden Stool: Studies of the Asante Center and Periphery.* New York: American Museum of Natural History: 80–92.

Peires, J. B. 1989. *The Dead Will Arise: Nongquwuse and the Great Xhosa Cattle-Killing Movement of 1856–7.* London: James Curry.

Posnansky, M. 1987. Prelude to Akan Civilization. In E. Schildkrout, ed., *The Golden Stool: Studies of the Asante Center and Periphery.* New York: American Museum of Natural History: 14–22.

Ramseyer, F. A. and J. Kühne. 1875. *Four Years in Ashantee*. New York: Robert Carter.

Rattray, R. S. 1916. *Ashanti Proverbs: The Primitive Ethics of a Savage People*. Oxford: Clarendon Press.

————. 1923. *Ashanti*. Oxford: Clarendon Press.

————. 1929. *Ashanti Law and Constitution*. Oxford: Clarendon Press.

Reade, W. 1874. *The Story of the Ashantee Campaign*. London: Smith, Elder.

Reindorf, C. C. 1966. *History of the Gold Coast and Asante*. 2d ed. Accra: Ghana Universities Press. Orig. ed. 1895.

Ricketts, H. J. 1831. *Narrative of the Ashantee War*. London: Simpkin and Marshall, Egerton and Ridgway.

Robertson, G. A. 1819. *Notes on Africa*. London: Sherwood, Needy and Jones.

Saffell, J. E. 1965. *The Asante War of 1873–74*. Ann Arbor, Mich. University Microfilms.

Schildkrout, E., ed. 1987. *The Golden Stool: Studies of the Asante Center and Periphery*. Washington, D.C.: American Museum of Natural History.

Stanley, H. M. 1874. *Coomassie and Magdala: The Story of Two British Campaigns in Africa*. New York: Harper.

Steiner, P. 1901. *Dark and Stormy Days at Kumassi, 1900; or, Missionary Experience in Ashanti According to the Diary of Rev. Fritz Ramseyer*, London: S.W. Partridge.

Stratton, A. 1964. *The Great Red Island*. New York: Scribners.

Tenkorang, S. 1968. The importance of firearms in the struggle between Ashanti and the coastal states. *Transactions of the Historical Society of Ghana* 9:1–16.

Thomas, R. 1975. Military Recruitment in the Gold Coast during the First World War. *Cahiers d'Etudes Africaines* 15:57–84.

Tordoff, W. 1965. *Ashanti under the Prempehs, 1888–1935*. London: Oxford University Press.

Tufuo, J. W., and C. E. Donkor 1969. *Ashantis of Ghana: People with a Soul*. Accra: Anowuo Educational Publications.

Van Dantzig, A. 1965. The Dutch Military Recruitment Agency in Kumasi. *Ghana Notes and Queries* 8:21–24.

Ward, W. E. F. 1958. *A History of Ghana*. 2d ed., rev. London: Allen and Unwin.

Wilks, I. 1975. *Asante in the Nineteenth Century: The Structure and Evolution of a Political Order*. New York: Cambridge University Press.

———. 1992. On Mentally Mapping Greater Asante: A Study of Time and Motion. *Journal of African History* 33:175–190.

Willcocks, J. 1904. *From Kabul to Kumassi: Twenty-Four Years of Soldiering and Sport*. London: John Murray.

Wolseley, G. 1903. *The Story of a Soldier's Life*. 2 vols. Westminster: Archibald Constable.

Wood, E. 1874. *The Ashanti Expedition of 1873–4*. London: Methuen.

Yarak, L. W. 1987. Kwasi Boakye and Kwame Poku: Dutch-Educated Asante "Princes." In E. Schildkrout, ed., *The Golden Stool: Studies of the Asante Center and Periphery*. New York. American Museum of Natural History; 1–331.

———. 1990. *Asante and the Dutch, 1744–1873*. New York: Oxford University Press.

Index

Printed in the United States
By Bookmasters